Business Process Management Cases Vol. 3

Jan vom Brocke • Jan Mendling
Michael Rosemann

Editors

Business Process Management Cases Vol. 3

Implementation in Practice

 Springer

Editors
Jan vom Brocke
European Research Center for Information
Systems (ERCIS)
University of Münster
Münster, Germany

Jan Mendling
Humboldt-Universität zu Berlin
Berlin, Germany

Michael Rosemann
Queensland University of
Technology (QUT)
Brisbane, QLD, Australia

ISBN 978-3-031-80792-3   ISBN 978-3-031-80793-0   (eBook)
https://doi.org/10.1007/978-3-031-80793-0

This Springer imprint is published by the registered company Springer Nature Switzerland AG
The registered company address is: Gewerbestrasse 11, 6330 Cham, Switzerland

If disposing of this product, please recycle the paper.

Preface

Welcome to the third volume of the very successful Business Process Management Cases Collection. We are excited and overwhelmed by the uptake of the BPM Cases, which are used today around the world by BPM professionals and educators to showcase and study Business Process Management. The BPM Cases Volume 3 adds 16 new cases to the existing 53 cases from Volumes 1 and 2, bringing the case collection to a total of 69 cases from many well-known organizations across industries, sizes, and the world.

Business Process Management (BPM) is at a pivotal moment as new opportunities and demands emerge. On the one hand, artificial intelligence and process mining facilitate entirely new process design and analysis options. On the other hand, organizations are facing new demands and need to ensure that their business processes are also sustainable, responsible, and explainable. In light of this fast moving context, insights into the actual practice of BPM have become indispensable points of reference.

Our BPM Cases Collection is dedicated to providing a contemporary and comprehensive, industry-agnostic insight into the realities of BPM. In particular we focus on the lessons that only authentic, case-based insights can provide. As a result, the experiences documented cover both the positive impact of deploying BPM and the lessons learned from failed attempts.

The focus of Volume 3 is on the return on BPM, its operationalization in light of constraints (e.g., data inaccuracies), scaling BPM across an organization and how to blend BPM into unique cultural settings. The cases show among others how to apply process mining to generate business value and how data-led BPM ensures evidence-based ways to manage processes.

We keep the successful unified structure of each case, which makes it easy to access each case:

- Introduction—What is the story of the case? The authors give a brief narrative of the entire story to grasp your interest in the case. This part includes a summary of the key figures of the case company.

- Situation faced—What was the initial problem or the opportunity at hand? What situation led to the actions taken? The authors specify the context of the case as to needs, constraints, incidents, objectives, and beyond.
- Action taken—What has been done? What measures have been taken, e.g., regarding process redesign or process innovation? Which methods and approaches have been used? The authors share a factual passage of the course of events.
- Results achieved—What effects could be observed resulting from the actions taken? This could be changes in performance measures as well as qualitative feedback from employees, customers, or other stakeholders. Here, the authors also discuss how far expected results materialized and how far expectations were met, or not.
- Lessons learned—Reflecting on the overall case, what can others learn from it? The authors derive around five lessons learned, which are grounded in the case and which have the potential to impact the planning and acting of BPM professionals beyond this case.

As a prelude to these cases, we introduce four key challenges of making BPM a reality: Economize (the return on BPM), Operationalize (the feasibility of BPM), Democratize (the scale of BPM), and Culturalize (the adoption of BPM). The cases are grouped into these four major themes.

- The Return on BPM: These cases show how to leverage innovative technology, specifically data-driven approaches to deliver strategy and generate value in organizations.
- The Feasibility of BPM: These cases unpack the challenges and practices of implementing BPM, including technical as well as organizational aspects in various application domains.
- The Scale of BPM: These cases demonstrate how to grow and leverage BPM on an enterprise level, including transformational and governance-related challenges and strategies.
- The Adoption of BPM: Finally, the cases in this theme exemplify how organizations succeeded in making BPM a daily practice, specifically by incorporating BPM into the organizational DNA.

We would like to thank the following people and institutions for their continuous support with the compilation of this book.

- First, we thank our research teams in Münster, Berlin, and Brisbane, as well as Liechtenstein, Vienna, and Maynooth, for the continuing inspiration they bring to our work.
- Second, we thank the organizers of the International Conference on Business Process Management as well as the International Conference on Process Mining for their ongoing support. We have had the pleasure to organize industry-related sessions at these conferences, which provided us with the opportunity to identify and discuss many of the cases presented in the BPM Cases collection.

- Third, we thank our colleagues and friends who served on the editorial board of this book and who have dedicated much time and effort in multiple rounds of reviews to further develop the cases presented in this book, namely, Saimir Bala, Jörg Becker, Jonas Bokstaller, Johannes De Smedt, Benoît Depaire, Claudio Di Ciccio, Dirk Fahland, Maria Fay, Kathrin Figl, Gregor Kipping, Henrik Leopold, Sonia Lippe, Frederik Milani, Markus Otto, Ralf Plattfaut, Stefan Schönig, Peter Trkman, Merih Seran Uysal, Amy Van Looy, and Bastian Wurm.
- Fourth, we wish to express our gratitude toward AIBA—the Liechtenstein Agency for International Educational Affairs, supporting our work through the ERASMUS+ projects "Reference Module Design for Explorative Business Process Management" (grant agreement No. 2018-1-LI01-KA203-000114), "BPM and Organizational Theory: An Integrated Reference Curriculum Design" (grant agreement No. 2019-1-LI01-KA203-000169), and "Developing Process Mining Capabilities at the Enterprise Level" (grant agreement No. 2021-1-LI01-KA220-HED-000027575).
- Finally, we are very grateful for the continuing support of the Einstein Foundation Berlin, the Hilti Family Foundation Liechtenstein, and the Dr. Theo and Friedl Schöller-Foundation for their ongoing support of our Process Science work.

We very much hope you will find these cases inspirational, educational, and enjoyable to read and would be thrilled to hear from you at some point.

Münster, Germany   Jan vom Brocke
Berlin, Germany   Jan Mendling
Brisbane, QLD, Australia   Michael Rosemann
September 2024

Contents

Part I
Introduction

The Four Challenges of Making Business Process Management a Reality

Michael Rosemann, Jan vom Brocke, and Jan Mendling

Our collective understanding of Business Process Management has substantially matured since Michael Hammer, James Champy and Thomas Davenport initiated the global uptake of BPM three decades ago (Hammer & Champy, 1993; Davenport, 1993). Nowadays, we have advanced and validated frameworks such as process life cycle models, maturity models, modelling standards (e.g., BPMN 2.0), proven improvement approaches (e.g., lean management, six sigma), robust governance frameworks and detailed templates for role descriptions. Similarly, solutions for the modelling, analysis, execution or mining of business processes are available and the related literacy has grown rapidly among the world's community of BPM professionals.

However, despite this advancement of methodologies, techniques and embedded artefacts as well as the available capability in the market, individual BPM initiatives are characterized by their own unique challenges, adoption models and objectives to be achieved. In particular, the transition from textbook BPM to successful BPM realities in the idiosyncratic context of an organization is characterized by the following four challenges:

1. *Economize*: The financially and time-constraint environment of an organization and competing management approaches require a sound narrative regarding the

M. Rosemann
Queensland University of Technology (QUT), Brisbane, Australia
e-mail: m.rosemann@qut.edu.au

J. vom Brocke (✉)
European Research Center for Information Systems (ERCIS), University of Münster, Münster, Germany
e-mail: jan.vom.brocke@uni-muenster.de

J. Mendling
Humboldt-Universität zu Berlin, Berlin, Germany
e-mail: jan.mendling@hu-berlin.de

individual *return on BPM*. However, more often than not our body of BPM knowledge is focused on the BPM capability itself (e.g., comprehensive process documentation, establishment of a BPM centre of excellence, conduct of process mining) rather than on the assessment *whether* the related investment in BPM itself is worthwhile. BPM research has investigated into the application of investment accounting to calculate business cases in BPM and developed measures such as the 'Return on Process Transformation' (vom Brocke & Sonnenberg, 2015). In practice, additional considerations, especially no-monetary ones, are important, including strategic alignment, customer/employee satisfaction, compliance, carbon footprints or corporate responsibility. This makes the calculation of the return on BPM a task that is as much needed as it is challenging.

2. *Operationalize:* Whereas an academic contribution to BPM can rest on assumptions and idealizations (e.g., complete event logs), BPM realities are full of noise, lack information and contain previously unknown challenges. This is the challenge of the *feasibility of BPM*. Therefore, organizations have to spend substantial time and effort on preparing for a BPM initiative (e.g., convincing relevant stakeholders, data cleansing) and to develop the most appropriate BPM operating model. Such activities are essential and difficult but often have not attracted the same academic attention like intellectually more attractive topics.

3. *Democratize*: The textbook process life cycle is compelling in its simplicity. The real-world scale of BPM, however, is daunting in its complexity. What seems straightforward for the management of one process becomes a completely different challenge when 100 s if not 1000 s of processes need to be managed and BPM is democratized across an organization. BPM-in-the-large (Houy et al., 2010), i.e., the *scale of BPM*, has so far only attracted limited attention in the academic world of BPM and is without any doubt an area where the practical experiences exceed the theoretical or empirical body of knowledge.

4. *Culturalize*: As much as BPM approaches highlight the technological, methodological or quantitative dimensions of BPM, the actual *adoption of BPM* is a cultural challenge (Schmiedel et al., 2015; Indihar Štemberger et al., 2018). Tailoring standard BPM to the cultural nuances of a firm remains a tricky endeavour. Not done well, it is one of the most significant risks of a BPM initiative. This includes finding the right balance between directive top-down and engaging bottom-up approaches, translating BPM terms into more acceptable local language or socializing BPM/process literacy and ultimately a BPM appetite across the organization.

These four challenges, and most likely others not discussed here, are significant roadblocks in the conversion of 'textbook BPM' into organizational BPM realities. Therefore, and now for the third time, we aim with this book featuring BPM case studies to close an important gap by providing important knowledge for all those BPM professionals who want to initiate, grow, mature or further intensify their process-related activities. In particular, we aim to provide 'page time' to the fascinating world of authentic and insightful BPM experiences across the globe and various industry sectors. Cases, in which the questions are more nuanced than what we witness in BPM education and research, in which the demands are multidimensional, fast paced and pragmatism need to trump perfection.

In the following, we provide a brief overview for how the cases in this book map to the four challenges outlined above.

1   Economize: The Return on BPM

Organizations deploy BPM for various economic drivers and for very specific outcomes. This is also true in the case of the Belgian *Acerta Consult*, an HR service provider with 1600 staff members and 25 offices, who uses process mining to derive employee journey maps and deeper insights into internal mobility. Simon De Vos and his co-authors emphasize that this is an ambitious objective as career journeys are longitudinal HR data with comparatively few data points (De Vos et al., 2024). The data-driven results of this initiative help Acerta to better understand the real complexity of employee career paths and to proactively build HR programs aiming towards improved talent attraction and retention.

The economic impact, and not the widely discussed technical details of process mining, is the focus of the chapter by Marieke de Ruijter (2024). Using the anonymized example of a financial service provider with more than 20,000 employees, the author presents the compelling reduction in costs-to-model achieved via a well-defined process mining centre of excellence. The chapter elaborates on the design decisions, performance measures, critical success factors and the process mining-related revisions required to establish process life cycle models. The results achieved, up to 60% reduction in process analysis work and even up to 95% less involvement of domain experts, are truly impressive.

Whereas these previous two cases rely on an internal return on BPM, it is often only the customer's response to a redesigned process that constitutes the economic success of a BPM initiative. An example for such a project is the case shared by Christoph Stoiber and Stefan Schönig who report on the substantial renewal of the distribution process of a large Scandinavian producer of chemicals (Stoiber & Schönig, 2024). Here, IoT solutions are used to respond to customer-centric process design objectives leading to a 'smart vending cabinet'. The use of process patterns and end user training are highlighted as being critical for the process performance and acceptance.

2   Operationalize: The Feasibility of BPM

Process mining is typically discussed in terms of its value proposition and outcomes, less often in terms of the requirements with regard to its input. Using the case of the *Dutch Employee Insurance Agency*, Bart Hompes and Marcus Dees unpack the so-called event log mutability problem which results from the fact that event logs are discreet sets of data with often incomplete event data (Hompes & Dees, 2024). The two authors discuss alternative mitigation strategies and how the case organization utilizes these with the outcome to arrive at truly trustworthy event logs.

Business processes tend to span multiple areas of an organization and as such leave a data trail in various related databases. This is the challenge of the Dutch logistics company *Vanderlande*. Joost van Montfort and his co-authors explain how conventional process mining needs to be expanded to deal with multi-layered systems and multi-object business processes (van Montfort et al., 2024). Exploratory use cases informed highly innovative visualization and advanced root cause analytics. Most of all, the project results enable the development of an AI-augment process management solution—a 'thinking assistant'.

Another operational data challenge in the context of process mining is the repurposing of process-related data in existing databases. Tobias Brockhoff et al. describe how the German *Penn Textile Solutions* explores the potential of process mining for its manufacturing and quality control process (Brockhoff et al., 2024). The case illustrates how process performance variations can be explained and root causes of issues can be identified (e.g., a bottleneck). Engaging process models and realistic expectation management are essential to build trust in process mining as a new organizational capability.

Operationalizing BPM is not just dealing with data challenges; it also requires the integration with complementary technologies. This is showcased in the chapter by Manuel Weber et al. using a small state-based hospital (250 staff) in Central Europe and the way it embeds Internet of Things solutions into its internal healthcare processes (Weber et al., 2024). The framework facilitating this integration covers social and technical elements and can be reused far beyond the boundaries of this single case.

In a similar way, Urszula Jessen and co-authors present the case of the European *ECE Group*, a company focused on the design and construction of shopping centres, and how this organization integrates process mining and machine learning techniques to identify critical issues (Jessen et al., 2024). The design and impact of the so-called 'process analysis pipeline' is shown using the example of the accounts payable process. By creating object-centric event logs and engaging a network of experts, the entire process from raw data to alerts is supported and challenges such as accountability and workarounds addressed.

The trade-offs between research models that are light on assumptions and practical BPM application also materialize in the design of emerging BPM solutions. This is evidenced in the chapter by Prerna Agarwal and Renuka Sindhgatta using the example of integrating ML-based decision support within *IBM*'s workflow engine (Agarwal & Sindhgatta, 2024). The authors present their operational decisions to enable bias removal, reduced computational costs, dealing with data drift and integrating feedback from knowledge workers.

3 Democratize: The Scale of BPM

Scaling BPM is not just a quantitative question of dealing with a very large number of processes; it is also about the qualitative increase in capability of the organizational entity in charge of BPM. The chapter on the related journey of the *Austrian Getzner Werkstoffe* is an illustrative example for how an organization gradually scaled up its Operational Excellence Department, the 'Getzner House of OPEX' with the aim to create a truly process-centred corporation (Eggarter et al., 2024). Magdalena Eggarter and her two co-authors provide a compelling narrative for how Getzner reached transparency over more than 500 business processes and successfully followed a roadmap defined by its own maturity model. The authors stress the development of BPM literacy as well as the importance of democratizing BPM across the entire organization.

A significant driver of scalable BPM is global activity as it is the case with *Cooxupé*, a significant Brazilian coffee cooperative that exports coffee into more than 50 countries. However, it is not just the consideration of regionally diverse process requirements but the scaling up of the intensity of BPM—from documenting procedures to truly improving process performance—that makes the chapter by Luiz Ribeiro and his co-authors so very interesting. The case of Cooxupé is a compelling story for how large-scale BPM requires the context-specific orchestration of diverse methods and techniques and the integration of project and process management to derive at a BPM approach that suits the unique organizational requirements (Ribeiro et al., 2024).

Scaling BPM matters in particular when you are the *Versorgungsanstalt des Bundes und der Länder, VBL*, Germany's largest provider of supplementary pensions (Appel et al., 2024). Driven by the mandate to digitize its business processes, Martin Appel and his team of co-authors describe how VBL used Bitkom's maturity model digital processes 2.0 and its embedded three stages innovate, design and transform to determine the adequate degree of digitalization across its landscape of business processes.

The ultimate scale up of BPM occurs when an organization manages all its operations using process management solutions. This is exactly the idealized state described by Sérgio Haas and Nivea da Silva Haas as described in the case of *Instituto Espírita Batuíra de Saúde Mental*, a small not-for-profit hospital in Brazil (Haas & da Silva Haas, 2024). This case ultimately describes ambitious Hospital Process Management (HPM) showing how a single low-code BPM system replaces a previous ERP solution. The chapter outlines not only how metrics and risks have been considered but also how this has not just been a technical but also a cultural shift for the organization.

4 Culturalize: The Adoption of BPM

Not all BPM initiatives succeed, and rebranding BPM after a first negative experience is a challenging undertaking. Using the example of the *Enervie Group*, a regional utility provider in Germany, Ralf Plattfaut et al. provide an interesting narrative for how process mining can be used to kick-start BPM within a sceptical organization (Plattfaut et al., 2024). The initial pilot and subsequent roll-out of process mining across the most critical end-to-end processes is described and how this built BPM capability and new BPM credibility and materialized in a dedicated, well-accepted and successful process mining centre of excellence.

Another example for the cultural impact of process mining in this book is the use of process mining for the optimization of the cost-benefit ratio in maintenance processes. For this, Riccarda Mark and Illario Angilletta present the innovative project of battery life cycle optimization at the *Deutsche Bahn Connect GmbH*, a provider of complementary mobility solutions looking among others after 13,000 rental bicycles (Mark & Angilletta, 2024). Here, various data sources (ERP, IoT) are used to improve predictive battery maintenance. It is interesting to note that despite the technical details in this chapter, the authors stress that the greatest effect has been 'psychological' as stakeholders shifted their established perspective from confidence to evidence.

Culturalizing BPM rests on the way how BPM is organized and governed, and this is the story of the Swiss Endress+Hauser Group Services AG, a global provider of measurement instrumentation, services and solutions for industrial process engineering. In their chapter, Jan vom Brocke et al. present a BPM governance matrix organized in three activity groups and four responsibility dimensions to provide transparency to the way BPM is organized (vom Brocke et al., 2024). The results show among others how such an approach facilitates an early conversation about BPM and the inclusion of a bottom-up BPM momentum.

Though we have categorized each of the cases in this book, to only one of the four identified challenges, our readers will notice that in most cases, references are made to a variety of these challenges in each of the 16 cases in this book. This only demonstrates the multidimensional nature of converting BPM into a reality.

While we have no doubt that BPM professionals will benefit again from this addition to the existing set of 53 BPM cases already documented in the previous two editions of 'Business Process Management Cases', we also assume that these insights into BPM realities will be an inspirational source of new and rewarding research questions for our academic colleagues.

As editors of this book, we are standing very gratefully on the shoulders of many people and their institutions.

Most of all, we would like to thank the authors of the cases featured in this book for taking the time to consolidate and reflect the experiences made so that others can benefit from their lessons learned. Also, we are very grateful for the continuing support for the international Business Process Management community and the many colleagues who served as a member of the program committee, reviewing the chapters and providing such valuable feedback on developing the chapters in multiple rounds of revisions. Namely, members of the program committee included (in alphabetic order) Saimir Bala, Jonas Bokstaller, Jörg Becker, Benoît Depaire, Johannes De Smedt, Claudio Di Ciccio, Dirk Fahland, Maria Fay, Kathrin Figl, Gregor Kipping, Henrik Leopold, Sonia Lippe, Fredrik Milani, Stefan Schönig, Markus Otto, Ralf Plattfaut, Peter Trkman, Merih Seran Uysal, Amy Van Looy, and Bastian Wurm. Last but not least, we would like to thank Gregor Kipping, Research Affiliate at ERCIS—The European Research Center for Information Systems—and a PhD student at the University of Liechtenstein, for his amazing work coordinating the editorial process. We are also grateful for the generous support of the University of Münster to apply professional language editing to the book throughout.

The third volume of BPM cases has been a great team effort. The 16 new cases complement the 53 cases from volume 1 (vom Brocke & Mendling, 2018) and volume 2 (vom Brocke et al., 2021) and bring the case collection to a total of 69 BPM cases from many well-known organizations across industries and around the world. We are very grateful for the opportunity to compile such a rich account for BPM experience from practice, and we hope all readers will enjoy the cases and find them inspiring.

References

Agarwal, P., & Sindhgatta, R. (2024). Deploying predictive models for a process-aware decision support system. In J. vom Brocke, J. Mendling, & M. Rosemann (Eds.), *Business process management cases* (3). Springer.

Appel, M., Arica, M., Britze, N., Danneberg, M., Möbus, M., Schießl, K., & Schulze, A. (2024). Digitization at VBL with Bitkom's maturity model digital processes 2.0. In J. vom Brocke, J. Mendling, & M. Rosemann (Eds.), *Business process management cases* (Vol. 3). Springer.

Brockhoff, T., et al. (2024). Process mining in textile production: Insights from Penn Textile Solutions. In J. vom Brocke, J. Mendling, & M. Rosemann (Eds.), *Business process management cases* (Vol. 3). Springer.

Davenport, T. (1993). *Process innovation: Reengineering work through information technology.* Harvard Business School Press.

de Ruijter, M. (2024). The reality behind the theory: Process mining in action. In J. vom Brocke, J. Mendling, & M. Rosemann (Eds.), *Business process management cases* (Vol. 3). Springer.

De Vos, S., De Smedt, J., Wuytens, C., & Verbeke, W. (2024). Leveraging process mining to optimize internal employee mobility strategies. In J. vom Brocke, J. Mendling, & M. Rosemann (Eds.), *Business process management cases* (Vol. 3). Springer.

Eggarter, M., Keiser, K., & Franzoi, S. (2024). Toward a process-centered organization: The operational excellence journey at Getzner. In J. vom Brocke, J. Mendling, & M. Rosemann (Eds.), *Business process management cases* (Vol. 3).

Haas, S. L., & da Silva Haas, N. T. (2024). Total BPM: What does a company that uses 100% BPMS look like? In J. vom Brocke, J. Mendling, & M. Rosemann (Eds.), *Business process management cases* (Vol. 3). Springer.

Hammer, M., & Champy, J. A. (1993). *Reengineering the corporation: A manifesto for business revolution.* Harper Business Books.

Hompes, B., & Dees, M. (2024). Detecting and mitigating the event log mutability problem at the Dutch Employee Insurance Agency (UWV). In J. vom Brocke, J. Mendling, & M. Rosemann (Eds.), *Business process management cases* (Vol. 3). Springer.

Houy, C., Fettke, P., Loos, P., van der Aalst, W. M. P., & Krogstie, J. (2010). BPM-in-the-large—Towards a higher level of abstraction in business process management. In M. Janssen, J. Pries-Heje, & M. Rosemann (Eds.), *E-government, e-services and global processes* (pp. 233–244). Springer.

Indihar Štemberger, M., Buh, B., Milanović Glavan, L., & Mendling, J. (2018). Propositions on the interaction of organizational culture with other factors in the context of BPM. *Business Process Management Journal, 24*(2), 425–455.

Jessen, U., Sroka, M., & Berti, A. (2024). Towards user-oriented process mining: A collaborative approach to minimize late payments in accounts payable process. In J. vom Brocke, J. Mendling, & M. Rosemann (Eds.), *Business process management cases* (Vol. 3). Springer.

Mark, R., & Angilletta, I. (2024). Process mining in battery life cycle. In J. vom Brocke, J. Mendling, & M. Rosemann (Eds.), *Business process management cases* (Vol. 3). Springer.

Plattfaut, R., Vollenberg, C., François, P. A., Aberman, M., Nacke, J., & Coners, A. (2024). Process mining as a driver for business process management: The case of the Enervie Group. In J. vom Brocke, J. Mendling, & M. Rosemann (Eds.), *Business process management cases* (Vol. 3). Springer.

Ribeiro, L. R. B., de Pádua, S. I. D., Aredes, E. L., & Corrêa Ferreira, J. R. (2024). Towards the full application of BPM: The case of the Brazilian coffee cooperative Cooxupé. In J. vom Brocke, J. Mendling, & M. Rosemann (Eds.), *Business process management cases* (Vol. 3). Springer.

Schmiedel, T., vom Brocke, J., & Recker, J. (2015). Culture in business process management. How cultural values determine BPM success. In J. vom Brocke & M. Rosemann (Eds.), *Handbook on business process management: Strategic alignment, governance, people and culture* (International handbooks on information systems) (Vol. 2, 2nd ed.). Springer.

Stoiber, C., & Schönig, S. (2024). The smart vending cabinet: Leveraging the industrial internet of things for business process improvement. In J. vom Brocke, J. Mendling, & M. Rosemann (Eds.), *Business process management cases* (Vol. 3). Springer.

van Montfort, J., Bernard, H., & Fahland, D. (2024). From process mining to thinking assistants in logistics. In J. vom Brocke, J. Mendling, & M. Rosemann (Eds.), *Business process management cases* (Vol. 3). Springer.

vom Brocke, J., & Mendling, J. (Eds.). (2018). *Business process management cases. Digital innovation and business transformation in practice.* Springer.

vom Brocke, J., & Sonnenberg, C. (2015). Value-orientation in business process management. In J. vom Brocke & M. Rosemann (Eds.), *Handbook on business process management: Strategic alignment, governance, people and culture* (International handbooks on information systems) (Vol. 2, 2nd ed., pp. 101–132). Springer.

vom Brocke, J., Mendling, J., & Rosemann, M. (Eds.). (2021). Digital transformation. Strategy, processes and execution. In *Business process management cases* (Vol. 2). Springer.

vom Brocke, J., Weber, M., Baumgartner, C., Roettcher, A., & Segerlund, S. (2024). On the development of the BPM governance matrix: The case of Endress+Hauser. In J. vom Brocke, J. Mendling, & M. Rosemann (Eds.), *Business process management cases* (Vol. 3). Springer.

Weber, M., Kipping, G., vom Brocke, J., & Schweitzer, M. (2024). Adopting the internet of things (IoT) technology paradigm in a state hospital. In J. vom Brocke, J. Mendling, & M. Rosemann (Eds.), *Business process management cases* (Vol. 3). Springer.

Michael Rosemann is the Director of QUT's Centre for Future Enterprise and a Professor for Information Systems at Queensland University of Technology. His areas of research are Business Process Management, innovation systems, trust and the future of learning. Dr Rosemann is the author/editor of eleven books, more than 400 refereed papers, Editorial Board member of nine international journals and co-inventor of US and EU patents.

Dr Rosemann is known for his work in areas such as BPM maturity models, context-aware BPM, explorative BPM, rapid process redesign and process modelling. Dr Rosemann has presented his work at major global BPM conferences and delivered keynotes in more than 30 countries.

His research projects received funding from industry partners such as Accenture, Cisco, Infosys, PwC, Rio Tinto, SAP and Woolworths. Dr Rosemann is also the Honorary Consul for Germany in Southern Queensland and the Vice President Strategic Partnerships for the global Association for Information Systems.

Jan vom Brocke is the Director of the European Research Center for Information Systems (ERCIS) and a Professor and Chair of Information Systems & Business Process Management at the University of Münster in Germany. He has published in leading journals such as *Management Information Systems Quarterly* (MISQ), *Information Systems Research* (ISR), *Journal of the Association for Information Systems* (JAIS), *Journal of Management Information Systems* (JMIS), *Management Science*, and *MIT Sloan Management Review* (MIT SMR). He is the author and editor of seminal books, including the *International Handbook on Business Process Management*, *BPM—Driving Innovation in a Digital World*, *Green Business Process Management*, and the *Business Process Management Cases* volumes 1, 2, and 3. Jan vom Brocke is a Visiting Professor at the University of Liechtenstein and an Academic Research Fellow at Massachusetts Institute of Technology (MIT), Center for Information Systems Research (CISR). He has been named a Fellow of the Association for Information Systems (AIS), a Fellow of the École Supérieure de Commerce de Paris (ESCP) Center for Design Science in Entrepreneurship, a Schoeller Senior Fellow at Friedrich Alexander University (FAU) in Germany, a Distinguished Professor of Process Science at the National University of Ireland, Maynooth University (MU). Professor vom Brocke is an invited speaker and serves as trusted advisor to many companies as well as governmental institutions.

Jan Mendling is the Einstein-Professor of Process Science with the Department of Computer Science at Humboldt-Universität zu Berlin, Germany. He is also adjunct professor with Vienna University of Economics and Business, Austria, Principle Investigator at the Weizenbaum Institute, Berlin, Germany, and Co-Founder of Noreja Intelligence GmbH. His research interests include various topics in the area of business process management and information systems. He has published more than 500 research papers and articles, among others in Management Information Systems Quarterly, ACM Transactions on Software Engineering and Methodology, IEEE Transactions on Software Engineering, Journal of the Association of Information Systems, European Journal of Information Systems, Information Systems, and Decision Support Systems. He is the founding co-Editor-in-Chief of Process Science and co-author of the textbooks Fundamentals of Business Process Management, Second Edition, and Wirtschaftsinformatik, 12th Edition.

Part II
Economize: The Return on BPM

Leveraging Process Mining to Optimize Internal Employee Mobility Strategies

Simon De Vos, Johannes De Smedt, Chris Wuytens, and Wouter Verbeke

Abstract

(a) *Situation faced*: The significance of human resource (HR) analytics in facilitating data-driven decision-making for managing internal employee mobility has been emphasized by the recent increasing competition in attracting and retaining the best employees referred to as the war for talent. Existing HR analytics methods typically provide support for operational and tactical decision-making. However, there is a need for long-term strategic decision support. Additionally, as current methods for managing internal mobility are being challenged, the development of new appropriate HR analytics methods is necessary.

(b) *Action taken*: In collaboration with KU Leuven, Acerta Consult implemented process mining techniques to address this issue. Specifically, process discovery techniques were applied to the event logs of HR data to generate employee journey maps (EJMs) that depict the different historic paths employees have taken within an organization.

(c) *Results achieved*: These EJMs demonstrated the difference between idealized career paths and the actual complexity of employee mobility. These discrepancies have the potential to reshape the incorrect assumptions held by HR managers. The data-driven insight gained through these EJMs can assist HR professionals by providing decision support for a wide range of cases including the identification of infrequent growth paths, analyzing hard-to-fill positions, and better understanding the causes of turnover.

(d) *Lessons learned*: The process perspective on internal mobility provides valuable insights for HR managers and was able to shed light on the general complexity of careers. As a result, this perspective can serve as a foundation for

S. De Vos (✉) · J. De Smedt · W. Verbeke
KU Leuven, Leuven, Belgium
e-mail: simon.devos@kuleuven.be; johannes.desmedt@kuleuven.be;
wouter.verbeke@kuleuven.be

C. Wuytens
Acerta Consult, Brussels, Belgium
e-mail: chris.wuytens@acerta.be

© The Author(s), under exclusive license to Springer Nature Switzerland AG 2025   15
J. vom Brocke et al. (eds.), *Business Process Management Cases Vol. 3*,
https://doi.org/10.1007/978-3-031-80793-0_2

further analyses, including predictive and prescriptive modeling, while taking into account HR-specific constraints and challenges.

1 Introduction

In recent years, many organizations have focused on utilizing the vast amount of data available to support decision-making in their daily activities in order to gain a competitive advantage. Like other business areas, HR departments are now attempting to use data to support their operational, tactical, and strategic decisions.

As reported by the Financial Times, the global trend of increasing competition for talent in the job market is evidenced by the all-time low unemployment rates in the eurozone (6.6% of the workforce) and the high number of job openings in the US (roughly two per unemployed worker) (Raval, 2022). In response, companies are offering higher wages and benefits to attract and retain employees, leading to increases in the cost of goods and services. Employers are implementing strategies to address high turnover rates, which include incentives such as bonuses and career development opportunities. To support the development of these strategies, HR analytics is more relevant than ever in terms of attracting and retaining good employees.

Organizations like Acerta are facing these challenges in HR analytics and investigate questions such as *How can companies optimize their employees' career paths?* or *What paradigm should they start from?* This business case takes a process perspective on internal mobility, specifically the implementation of process mining techniques, to support HR managers at Acerta Consult. Together with their research partners at KU Leuven, they are internally exploring the capabilities of applying process mining techniques to HR data. With the insight from this case, they aim to further broaden the range of HR analytics services offered to their clients.

Acerta is a major HR service provider in Belgium with 25 offices across the country. They serve a diverse range of customers, including starters, self-employed, SMEs, and large companies, managing administration for one million employees in the Belgian market. Acerta has 1600 employees, a 20% market share, and services 350,000 self-employed workers and 40,000 companies in Belgium, resulting in a yearly turnover of 260 million euros. Acerta Consult, the company's consulting branch with 450 employees, offers services such as recruitment and selection, outplacement, legal, and training.

Specifically, we applied process mining techniques to longitudinal career data to discover employee journey maps (EJMs) and as such examine internal employee mobility. The technical details of this approach are explained in Sect. 3.1. The behavioral nature of careers requires the use of dynamic methods for modeling, making process mining techniques a suitable method for analyzing internal mobility. These techniques can be effectively combined with existing human experience to provide insight based on data to support, rather than automate, decision-making.

This article summarizes how to conceptualize and implement considerations of internal mobility as a process, through some example HR-related use cases from

Acerta. Section 2 first provides an introduction to the field of HR analytics and explains why data-driven methods are needed for strategic decision support. Next, it presents the specific problem statement concerning the current internal mobility management methods and discusses why a process perspective is beneficial. Section 3 describes the actions taken, the methods used to implement the process perspective envisioned for managing internal mobility, and the data structure. The results are discussed in Sect. 4 and the challenges faced and lessons learned from the case are discussed in Sect. 5.

2 Situation Faced

To maintain its position as one of Belgium's leading providers of HR services, Acerta Consult stays current with the latest developments in data-driven support for strategic HR decisions and maintains a focus on employee mobility. The first part of this section explains why we need a solution for strategic decision support and discusses the growth and evolution of HR tech, accompanied by the challenges of adoption. To highlight the usefulness of our process analytics approach as a solution, the second part outlines the issues with current methods of internal mobility management in relation to the specific case study of Acerta.

2.1 Need for Strategic Decision Support

The use of technology within the HR field is not a new phenomenon, but the HR tech domain has evolved significantly in recent years and is becoming active in an ever-expanding range of applications. In the 1990s, HR processes were successfully integrated within enterprise resource planning systems (ERPs), whereas we now see HR-specific information systems (HRISs) often being used. This has led to the development of solutions for specific operational domains, such as recruitment, performance management, onboarding, training and development, payroll administration, compensation and benefits, alternative workforce planning, reporting, and internal communication. In short, operational HR applications and their corresponding tech industry are booming.

However, the adoption of HR tech for strategic decision support remains limited (Boudreau & Cascio, 2017; Fernandez & Gallardo-Gallardo, 2020). Based on a comprehensive review of the relevant literature (Boudreau & Cascio, 2017; Fernandez & Gallardo-Gallardo, 2020) and the extensive experience of Acerta as an HR services provider, we have identified three challenges that contribute to the lagging adoption of data-driven decision support in HR compared to other fields.

First, there is a self-evident gap in the knowledge and abilities of the data science teams who create analytical tools and the HR departments that are to use them. This disparity often leads to challenges in both the development and adoption of these tools. Second, employee data is sensitive and the data that is available on employees is often limited, making it difficult to apply advanced methods that require large amounts of data, for example, machine learning. For example, to construct a system for automated CV screening, a vast amount of training data is necessary. However, on account of the sensitive data and limited availability, this requirement might not be fulfilled in practice. Third, HR professionals are typically charged with making tactical and strategic decisions over the medium to long term, with outcomes that are difficult to quantify and observe. These decisions are typically made based on unstructured and varied sources of information, as well as expertise and experience. In contrast, data-driven methods are typically used to support repetitive operational decisions with clear short-term outcomes, for which homogeneous and structured data sources are readily available. As a result, HR professionals may be difficult to support with the arsenal of tools that is typically used by data scientists in other domains.

In response to these challenges, we propose applying process mining techniques to longitudinal HR data. The EJMs offer three key advantages that align with HR practices and resources. First, the process mining tooling in the form of dashboards is easy to use and allows HR practitioners to work with analytical instruments by bridging the gap between the data-related knowledge and skills of the HR departments and the data science teams. Second, as we were not searching for the best process model but using EJMs for data representation that will be interpreted by an HR professional, process mining techniques can be applied to smaller amounts of data. Third, by analyzing longitudinal data, this approach, complemented by the expertise of HR professionals, is well suited to supporting medium- to long-term decision-making with difficult-to-quantify outcomes. In summary, the proposed approach offers a useful solution that addresses three typical challenges that we have identified in the use of data-driven techniques for strategic HR decision-making.

2.2 Problems in Current Internal Mobility Management

Currently, internal mobility at Acerta is managed using a certain amount of HR professional expertise and intuition in combination with evidence-based techniques from more traditional academic HR literature. However, with this management approach, we uncovered two additional challenges specific to internal mobility. In addition to the general issues in HR tech previously mentioned, these two challenges highlight the need for data-driven insight into internal mobility.

The first challenge we pinpointed was the recent changes in managerial formats. Like many organizations, Acerta is increasingly moving away from rigid organizational structures and delayering hierarchy. Therefore, the traditional career ladders that steered the internal flows of employees have become less evident and less standardized. In addition, a shift toward focusing on the skills of individuals and the management of their competencies is taking place, reinforcing the aforementioned trend toward less standardization in internal mobility. As a result, traditional methods of managing employee pathways are being increasingly challenged.

The second challenge that we identified is known as the *fragmented process knowledge* problem (Dumas et al., 2013). This problem arises when domain experts, such as HR professionals, have a limited understanding of the overall process of managing mobility within an organization. However, HR professionals typically have a very detailed understanding of their specific responsibilities. The HR-employee ratio can vary depending on factors such as the size and complexity of an organization, but is roughly 1:50, i.e., 1 HR professional per 50 employees, in Acerta's case. Furthermore, Acerta's HR data reveals that the average tenure of an HR professional is around 4 years, based on their specific role and seniority level. The fragmented process knowledge of internal mobility among various HR professionals hampers centralized control, hindering its effective management within the organization.

3 Action Taken

KU Leuven and Acerta took action by considering internal employee mobility as a process. In this section, we first explain how HR concepts can be translated into process concepts and how we used process discovery techniques. Then we discuss the data required from a technical and practical perspective.

3.1 *Process Mining as a Solution*

Process mining incorporates the process perspective into data mining and machine learning and helps organizations further comprehend their business processes (van der Aalst, Process Mining: Data Science in Action, 2016). It involves analyzing event logs to uncover the underlying process models, bridging the gap between traditional model-based process analysis and data-centric analysis methods. By analyzing historical event data, process owners like HR professionals can gain insight into business processes, such as, in this case study, internal mobility, where career paths are the individual traces.

In order to understand the behavior contained within an event log, automatic process discovery techniques were utilized to construct a model. Various approaches could have been employed for this purpose (van der Aalst, Process Mining: Data Science in Action, 2016). However, implementing process mining in real-world scenarios is a challenging task. In the case of internal mobility, we see many process variants and the data is typically censored because process instances, i.e., careers, take a long time. Additionally, traces for internal mobility processes usually contain few activities compared to those found in other settings (Van Eck et al., 2015). As a result, its implementation at Acerta was a highly iterative process and we emphasized the need for close collaboration between process analysts and business experts.

This case study deploys process discovery techniques for data representation and visualization rather than for building the best model. Moreover, in the context of employee journey mapping, it is not only important to identify common paths taken by employees but also important to consider less frequent and obvious paths. Thus, directly-follows graphs (DFGs) were utilized as the preferred method of representation as they are the de facto standard in the industry (van der Aalst, A practitioner's guide to process mining: Limitations of the directly-follows graph, 2019). However, as there are some potential risks associated with using DFGs and frequency-based simplification, it is important for practitioners to have a thorough understanding of how these process models are generated (van der Aalst, A practitioner's guide to process mining: Limitations of the directly-follows graph, 2019). To address this, Acerta arranged information sessions to provide active guidance during deployment.

We generated EJMs on internal mobility by translating concepts from the field of process mining into HR concepts as follows:

- A case is conceptually equivalent to an employee. Over time, the employee can transition from one function to another, undertaking a journey.
- An activity translates to occupying a function within an organization. It is carried out by an employee and is characterized by a timestamp indicating when the activity starts and ends. In our particular HR context, there is no overlap or parallelism in the activities of an employee as each employee can only have one function at a time.
- A trace covers all the activities performed in a particular process instance by a specific case. Therefore, it is equivalent to an employee journey. Each trace is defined as the ordered set of subsequent functions that an employee occupies throughout their career within an organization.
- Applying process discovery techniques to an event log consisting of longitudinal HR data is conceptually the same as discovering EJMs. The event log is defined as the collection of traces and, therefore, contains information on all employee journeys. An EJM is the aggregate of all the paths employees have taken within an organization.

3.2 Data Requirements

Typically, an event log in the HR setting has the structure as visualized in Table 1. An event in a career path is a tuple $\left(u_i, t_i^s, t_i^e, v_i, x_i\right)$ where u_i is a unique identifier for an employee, holding the function v_i from time t_i^s to time t_i^e. On top of control flow information, employee u_i has features x_i which can include among others degree, branch of study, gender, date of birth, and the full-time equivalent.

An employee profile $\mathcal{D}_i \subset \mathcal{D}$ of the person u_i consists of the combination of $|\mathcal{D}_i|$ tuples where $|\mathcal{D}_i|$ is the number of functions that the employee has occupied within

Table 1 Synthetic example data $\mathcal{D}$ in the format of an event log

u	t^s	t^e	v	x_1	x_2	x_3	x_4	x_5
1	10/2014	06/2016	Researcher Jr.	MSc	Physics	F	1975	1
1	07/2017	02/2019	Researcher Sr.	MSc	Physics	F	1975	1
1	03/2019	07/2022	Research team lead	MSc	Physics	F	1975	1
2	09/2009	02/2016	Accountant Jr.	BSc	Finance	M	1981	0.8
2	03/2016	07/2022	Accountant Sr.	BSc	Finance	M	1981	0.8
3	06/2016	03/2019	Research team lead	PhD	Electronics	M	1977	1
3	04/2019	07/2022	Research dir.	PhD	Electronics	M	1977	1
4	…	…	…	…	…	…	…	…

the organization. Consequently, an employee profile $\mathcal{D}_i$ consists of the *visited* functions and personal information x_i of person u_i.

In order to gain access to this career data in event log format, Acerta faced several challenges when undertaking the HR analytics project. The first hurdle to overcome was the issue of data protection. Several stakeholders were involved in the project and each had their own interests to defend. For example, HR professionals were enthusiastic about moving forward with the project, while the legal department was, understandably, more cautious about sharing confidential data. In order to comply with the General Data Protection Regulation (GDPR), employment contracts had to be amended to allow for the use of employee data for analytical purposes. Second, there was the issue of data collection. Despite the substantial amount of available data, it was dispersed across several sources. For instance, data on previous employment was stored in different locations to the personal employee information and assessment interview results. As a result, this required an additional step of pooling the data together. Third was the issue of data cleaning. Processes in other contexts tend to be relatively short compared to career path data, which was set to a time frame of 10 years. As this period is longer than other typical data analysis projects, impurities entered the data as a result of, among other things, internal restructurings, changes in job titles, and the merging or division of positions.

4   Results Achieved

In this section, we discuss the outcomes attained using our proposed approach at Acerta. First, the achieved results are discussed in their most general form. Our approach allows for the automatic discovery of EJMs, which describe and quantify internal mobility within an organization in a data-driven way. This leads to new insight for HR professionals. Then, we demonstrate how such EJMs can be used to solve specific HR cases.

4.1   General Results

Our approach takes the descriptive character of EJMs as a starting point. These maps are mainly useful for control flow analysis, i.e., the internal movement of employees. Additionally, extra filtering techniques can be applied to personal features like educational details, office location, and salary bracket.

Figures 1 and 2 present two EJMs, represented by DFGs, that contain the activity *func 177*. To generate these visuals, we use the tool Disco by Fluxicon. They are anonymized examples of internal employee mobility at Acerta and demonstrate the usefulness of a good EJM. In addition to other functions, we include two special activities: *before_data_capture* indicates that the individual was already an employee of the organization prior to the start date of data capturing, and *leave*

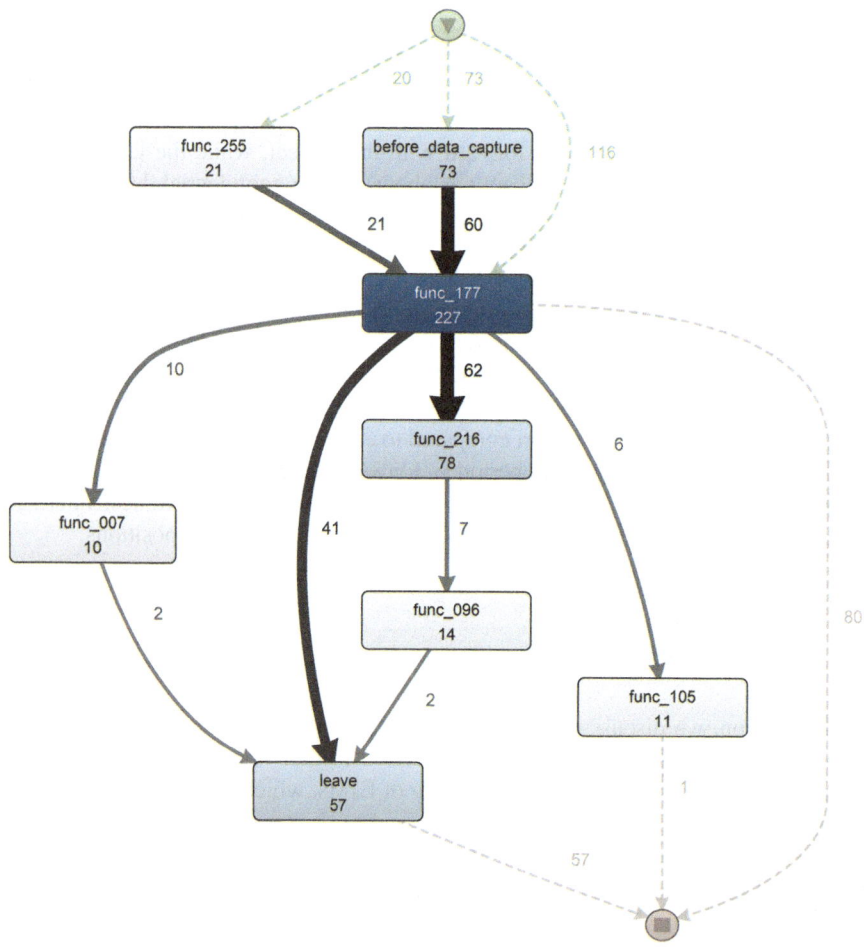

Fig. 1 A simplified EJM with career paths that contain the activity *func 177*

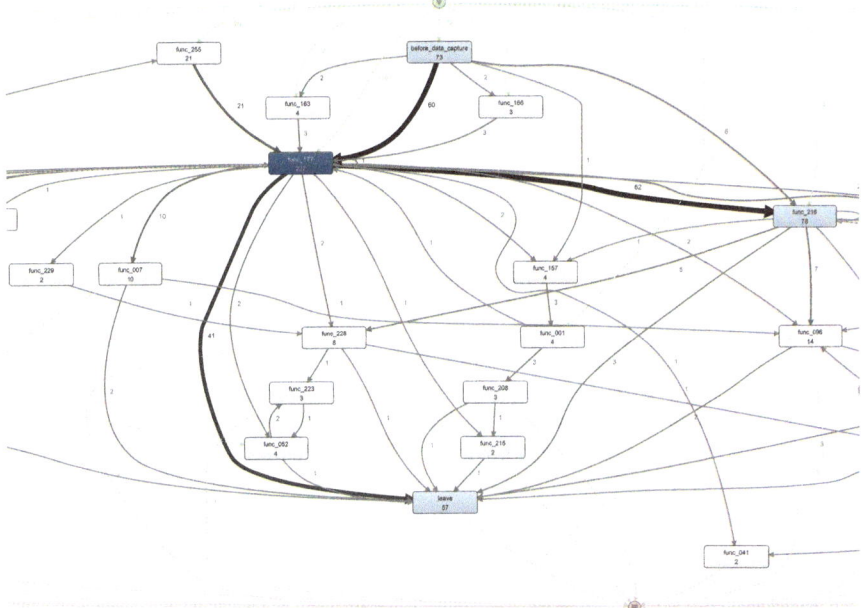

Fig. 2 An EJM displaying what career paths containing the activity *func 177* truly look like

represents an employee leaving the organization and occurs instantaneously. The transition between a function and the *sink* suggests that the individual is still active in this function at the end of the data-capturing period.

Figure 1 shows what internal mobility, according to HR professionals, looks like *by design*. In this figure, we filter on traces containing the activity *func 177* and displayed only 15% of the most frequent activities. Hence, the EJM only shows a selection of the most frequent traces. When we showed this to the HR professionals at Acerta, they agreed that this was a plausible map of the internal mobility in that company. To add nuance to this, although HR professionals often recognize that this representation is a simplification of reality, they find it challenging to pinpoint what exactly the more complex reality looks like. This figure shows a typical traditional, linear career path from junior to senior to expert positions. These are typical vertical movements with little variation.

However, in reality, Fig. 2 shows that paths are more complex. We filter on traces with the activity *func 177* and displayed 50% of the most frequent activities. The data reveals a wide range of career paths observed within the organization with less linear and more varied behavior. Most employees follow unique paths, frequently transitioning between unexpected and less obvious activities, rather than progressing through the traditional career ladders depicted in Fig. 1.

Growth paths do not always align with expectations, as Fig. 2 shows a more diverse set of transitions than Fig. 1. In this way, EJMs can help break HR managers' incorrect assumptions. It should be noted that even Fig. 2 is still a simplification of reality as it only displays the 50% most frequent activities. The full EJMs are too detailed to be included as a figure in this article.

When both a process model and an event log are provided, the discrepancy between the two highlights the value of data-driven techniques. This discrepancy can be linked to conformance checking, where the goal is to find similarities and differences between the behavior modeled and the behavior observed.

After making this connection with conformance checking, process redesign became the logical next step. The differences between Figs. 1 and 2 allowed the HR professionals to face the facts and deal with the as-is situation. This, in turn, allows them to implement well-thought-out and well-informed changes to their strategic HR management concerning internal mobility by, for example, focusing on active efforts to stimulate transitions between management functions and more technical functions. There are two main reasons why redesigning a business process can be beneficial, as discussed by Dumas et al. (2013). The first reason is that the nature of organizations is often organic and business processes naturally evolve over time, in general, becoming more complex, which leads to a decline in performance. This also applies to policies related to internal mobility that change over time. The second reason is that business environment are constantly changing, and HR strategies must be flexible in response.

4.2   Concrete HR Cases

In this subsection, we present a condensed overview of the insight obtained from the analysis presented in the previous sections in relation to the implementation at Acerta and their expert input. We make this tangible with a selection of examples.

1. *Detection of infrequent and less obvious paths.* In process analytics, the optimal workflow from the first to the final step is often the most efficient and effective. Process managers are interested in identifying and analyzing this workflow in order to optimize the process. In contrast, HR professionals are regularly interested in the opposite, in identifying infrequent and less obvious paths to explain questions such as unexpected success stories of internal mobility, transferability of skills, and atypical growth paths.
2. *Hard-to-fill positions.* Analysis of the in- and outflows of selected positions can identify favorable employee properties or profiles to attract talent in the future. For instance, when it is difficult to hire someone for a business intelligence team leader role, our longitudinal approach can look at the past experiences and future plans of employees who previously held that role. This will help us identify the qualities of employees who are likely to stay in the position for a long time.
3. *Vertical vs. lateral movements.* Both types of career moves can be beneficial for employees. Acerta stimulates both the exploration of different paths and the level of interaction between them. Examples of how our method can help here include

detecting the prevalence of vertical movement and the typical positions between which lateral movement occurs.

4. *Paths that lead to turnover.* Internal mobility can impact turnover behavior in various ways. If employees have opportunities to move within a company and find more fulfilling or suitable roles, they may be less likely to leave the company altogether. Furthermore, if internal mobility opportunities are limited or employees are not satisfied with the available roles, they may be more likely to seek opportunities elsewhere, resulting in higher turnover rates. Our approach helps Acerta understand and quantify the link between internal mobility and employee turnover behavior.

5 Lessons Learned

This story of co-creation between KU Leuven and Acerta is unique in terms of the field of application of process mining. To close this chapter, we discuss our learnings and the challenges we faced when adopting process-driven HR analytics and then conclude with a short closing word.

5.1 Challenges

Data The data in this case study on process discovery techniques in HR analytics is very sparse as it covers 1600 employees, 250 job titles, and only around 4000 job transitions over a 10-year period. This means that the majority of employees have only one or two jobs in their internal career, resulting in very short traces. Additionally, the trace length distribution is highly skewed, which can further complicate the analysis. Hence, we emphasize that DFGs are used for data visualization and representation purposes rather than for finding the best process model. Another difficulty is the observability of the data. While 10 years of event data may seem like a long time, careers are often much longer, with some starting before the data capture began. This resulted in a large number of unobserved prefixes in the traces, which can potentially result in incorrect EJMs. Conversely, many cases will still be ongoing when the data collection ends, causing these cases to be censored. A third challenge is the availability and quality of the data. In order to accurately represent employee journeys, a long period of data capture is required. However, data from this far back in time is often not available, and even when it is, it may contain inconsistencies because of organizational changes and the splitting or merging of certain functions.

In addition to these technical challenges, there are also legal considerations to take into account. The GDPR sets strict constraints on the use of personal data and the upcoming European AI Act will impose additional restrictions on the use of

AI-driven applications in HR, such as employment, management of workers, and CV-sorting software (European Commission, 2021). These constraints must be carefully considered in order to ensure compliance and avoid legal issues.

Adoption Process discovery techniques are effective for analyzing internal mobility but implementing them can be challenging on account of stakeholder interests. In any organization, there are numerous stakeholders with different interests and concerns. This can make it challenging to gain consensus and move forward with projects, particularly when it comes to sharing sensitive data. In this case study, the HR manager was eager to get started but the legal department was understandably cautious about sharing confidential data. Only after several discussions and explanations of the tool and its capabilities did the stakeholders agree to move forward. This experience highlights that simply having a method available is not enough; stakeholders must understand it and see its value. A solution here is to start with a specific problem and make the deliverable tangible.

5.2   Insight Gained

It is important to note that there may be differences in the focus and interests of *traditional* process analysts and HR professionals when it comes to these techniques. While process analysts may be more interested in the technical aspects of the processes themselves, HR professionals may be more focused on the implications for employees and the organization as a whole.

These techniques have been shown to partly support the existing knowledge and practices at Acerta. However, they have also provided new insight in the sense that they were able to correct several incorrect assumptions the managers had. This highlights the complementary nature of process discovery techniques and existing knowledge and expertise in HR. However, it is also important to recognize that the use of analytics in HR is not without its challenges and constraints.

As such, it is crucial to carefully manage expectations when using process discovery techniques and other analytical approaches in HR. It is important to make it clear beforehand what these techniques can and cannot do and, thereby, avoid making overly optimistic or unrealistic claims about their capabilities. While these techniques can provide valuable insight based on existing data, they should not be seen as a substitute for creative and thoughtful HR policies. Instead, they should be viewed as a tool that can help HR professionals better understand and optimize their existing processes.

5.3 Conclusion

KU Leuven and Acerta Consult collaborated on the development of an HR analytics method by treating internal employee mobility as a process and providing a more objective approach to strategic decision-making. The article discussed the method's development, challenges, and lessons learned, highlighting its positive reception at Acerta and potential for future development as a service. The method can provide valuable insight for managing employee mobility in HR analytics where the adoption of data-driven techniques is currently lagging behind other fields.

Acknowledgments This project was funded by the Flemish Government, through Flanders Innovation Entrepreneurship (VLAIO, project HBC.2021.0833).

References

Boudreau, J., & Cascio, W. (2017). Human capital analytics: Why are we not there? *Journal of Organizational Effectiveness: People and Performance, 4*(2), 119–126.

Dumas, M., La Rosa, M., Mendling, J., & Reijers, H. (2013). *Fundamentals of business process management*. Springer.

European Commission. (2021, April). EUR-Lex – 52021PC0206 – EN – EUR-Lex. Brussels. Retrieved December 2022. https://eur-lex.europa.eu/legal-content/EN/TXT/?uri=celex:52021PC0206. Accessed date: december 15th, 2022

Fernandez, V., & Gallardo-Gallardo, E. (2020). Tackling the HR digitalization challenge: Key factors and barriers to HR analytics adoption. *Competitiveness Review Journal, 31*(1), 162–187.

Raval, A. (2022, September). Talent wars: Why businesses have to battle to hire the best. *Financial Times*.

van der Aalst, W. (2016). *Process mining: Data science in action* (W. van der Aalst, Ed.). Springer.

van der Aalst, W. (2019). A practitioner's guide to process mining: Limitations of the directly-follows graph. *Procedia Computer Science, 164*, 321–328.

Van Eck, M. L., Lu, X., Leemans, S. J., & Van Der Aalst, W. M. (2015). PM: A process mining project methodology. In *CAiSE* (pp. 297–313). Springer.

Simon De Vos is a Ph.D. student at the Department of Decision Sciences and Information Management at the Faculty of Economics and Business of KU Leuven, Belgium. He holds a Master of Science in Business Engineering and an Advanced Master of Artificial Intelligence, with a focus on engineering and computer science. His research focuses on human resource analytics and the broader applications of data science. He has presented his work at numerous international scientific conferences, including ECML-PKDD and ICPM. In collaboration with Acerta Consult, he is committed to building a bridge between academia and industry.

Johannes De Smedt is an assistant professor in the Department of Decision Sciences and Information Management at the Faculty of Economics and Business of KU Leuven, Belgium. He holds a Ph.D. in Information Systems Engineering and previously held the Dixons Carphone (Senior) Lectureship in Business Analytics at the University of Edinburgh. His research interests include the analysis of temporal data, including sequence mining, as well as process analytics geared toward process model forecasting and XAI in predictive process monitoring. He has published in major outlets including IEEE Transactions on Knowledge and Data Engineering, Knowledge-Based Systems, Decision Support Systems, and more. He is also a program committee member for numerous conferences including the International Conference on Business Process Management, Advanced Information Systems Engineering, and Process Mining.

Chris Wuytens is the managing director of Acerta Consult and he is a professor of human resources at the KU Leuven and VUB. He is also a guest lecturer at Antwerp Management School. His research areas include employee-customer relationships and self-determination theory. He finished his Ph.D. in 2020 at Antwerp University and he is a strong believer of combining academia and practice.

Wouter Verbeke is an associate professor in the Department of Decision Sciences and Information Management of the Faculty of Economics and Business at KU Leuven, Belgium. His research is situated in the field of data science for business decision-making and is driven by real-life applications in operations management, pricing, fraud, credit risk, and human resources management. In 2014, he won the distinguished EURO award for best article published in the European Journal of Operational Research in the category "Innovative Applications of O.R." His work has been published in established international scientific journals such as IEEE Transactions on Knowledge and Data Engineering and the European Journal of Operational Research. He has authored two books, entitled "Fraud Analytics Using Descriptive, Predictive and Social Network Techniques" and "Profit-Driven Business Analytics," published by Wiley. He is a member of the editorial board of Decision Support Systems, Business Information Systems Engineering, the Journal of Business Analytics, and INFORMS Journal on Data Science.

The Reality Behind the Theory: Process Mining in Action

Marieke de Ruijter

Abstract

(a) *Situation faced*: Despite most large, complex service organizations being on a journey to simplify and digitize their business, process mining tools are not getting similar traction to robotic process automation (RPA), PowerApps, workflow optimization, and chatbot technologies. Why is this and what is required to bring process mining to the forefront and help unlock true process transformation?

(b) *Action taken*: A large financial service provider invested in building a dedicated center of excellence supported by a collaborative, innovative service offering and operating model that manages data dependencies, delivers optimization and change of processes impacting the bottom line, and has scalable, efficient process mining delivering capability with clear roles and responsibilities to maximize reuse.

(c) *Results achieved*: This case study achieved up to 60% reduction in analyst effort and up to 95% reduction in subject matter expertise required to conduct a process discovery compared to traditional "as-is" discovery methods. One year in, we have 9 reusable end-to-end process assets with 40+ active users and 5–10 new active users being added each quarter. The cost per engagement has reduced by 45% while the implementation rate increased from 2 engagements per quarter to 10. Finally, the median value unlocked per engagement at the start of the second year increased by 345% compared. As a result, senior leadership is championing the process mining capabilities.

(d) *Lessons learned*: True value comes when people in the business use the capability in their day-to-day business to drive continuous improvement and transformation. Top-down support, decision-making, and alignment with delivery teams to unlock value are critical for success. Finally, ensuring there is a clear strategy and understanding of how to deliver actual value, for example, by setting up a center of excellence and an operating model with clearly defined roles and responsibilities and the right partnerships while simultaneously investing in technical talent and the best available tools.

M. de Ruijter (✉)
Process Mining & Transformation Specialist, Melbourne, VIC, Australia

© The Author(s), under exclusive license to Springer Nature Switzerland AG 2025   29
J. vom Brocke et al. (eds.), *Business Process Management Cases Vol. 3*,
https://doi.org/10.1007/978-3-031-80793-0_3

1   Introduction

In comparison to the manufacturing industry, large, complex service organizations face additional difficulties when optimizing their processes because of their virtual and complex nature. In manufacturing, when a process is not working properly, the outcome is typically tangible and directly visible. However, in the service industry, the outcome of a malfunctioning process can be hard to see unless a customer complains or the cost of manual labor begins to rise. Process mining has been available as a methodology to help address such challenges for some time now. Process mining sources data or event logs from processes that are created by systems to enable process transparency. Once mined, variance, reword, or other issues in the processes become visible.

However, despite most large, complex service organizations being on a journey to simplify and digitize their business, process mining tools are not gaining the same traction as robotic process automation (RPA), PowerApps, workflow optimization, and chatbot technologies. Why is this the case and what is required to bring process mining to the forefront where it can help unlock true process transformation?

This case study provides insight into practical experience gained while setting up and managing a process mining center of excellence for a large financial institution with over 20,000 employees and 10 million customers. It explores

(a) the limitations of the traditional BPM lifecycle and how smart, data-driven tools, technology, and new ways of working can be used to overcome these limitations; and
(b) the organizational challenges and operating model considerations that need to be considered when delivering data-driven BPM services efficiently and effectively.

2   Situation Faced

The financial institution embarked on a journey to simplify and digitize its business processes to stay competitive. However, due to its history of mergers, acquisitions, demergers, and continuous changes in technology stacks, underlying process complexity has grown exponentially and become a fundamental challenge. This complexity was compounded by increased risk of fraud, risk of data breaches, and increased regulatory scrutiny, which required more controls in processes that were already complex. While the firm had made many improvements, especially in product and technology enhancements, historically, it had been difficult to drive process standardization in this highly variable legacy environment. As such, operations were still largely manual with high variability, delays in services, high rates of rework, non-value-adding manual tasks, and swivel chairing between systems.

As described in the BPM Context Framework (vom Brocke et al., 2015), addressing process complexity requires a move beyond incremental improvement of processes toward their complete innovation, particularly through digital technology. However, the methods used for process management have not followed these developments and are essentially the same as they were when developed 20 years ago to streamline operational processes. This is hindering the success of BPM projects. Traditional BPM methods are labor-intensive and require subject matter experts (SMEs). With the strong focus on cost reduction, SMEs are scarce and no longer readily available to support traditional process documentation. Traditional BPM methods are also expensive to maintain and their reusability is limited due to their static nature. They are also subjective in nature and return different results depending on who is supporting the documentation. Furthermore, traditional BPM methods do not capture rework, which affects process performance and customer outcomes, and they are not able to objectively monitor the impact of process improvement initiatives.

The organization was seeking to onboard process mining as a new capability to overcome traditional BPM shortcomings, help its process and workflow automation team, and deliver a step change in driving process standardization in this highly variable legacy environment. Process mining leverages data to partially automate process discovery, redesign, and monitoring processes, which reduces the need for scarce subject matter experts, creates reusable assets, and offers an objective view of the processes, their variance, and rework. However, there are a range of challenges that have hindered the uptake of process mining in comparison to similar, more established automation capabilities. Process mining on its own will deliver interesting insight but it will not deliver actual process changes. Moreover, the success of process mining is dependent on having access to the right data, which can be challenging in large, heavily regulated, and legacy-heavy service organizations. Over the last 20 years, intensive research has been conducted into various process mining techniques. However, the research on process mining has mostly focused on devising new or better algorithms. There are a few exceptions in which the focus was on process mining from the perspective of application in industrial practice (vom Brocke et al., 2021). This case study shares the experience of what is required to embed process mining in such an organization and, thus, provides a practical perspective on application in industrial practice.

3   Action Taken

The organization decided to invest in building a dedicated center of excellence that would be able to develop methodologies and an operating model to deliver process mining capability at scale across the organization. The following steps were implemented:

1. Build a strategy and scalable, efficient delivery factory with a team that has the right skills and follows a repeatable methodology.
2. Identify the right processes for optimization and automation.

3. Ensure the necessary data is available.
4. Secure executive sponsorship and invest in training and change management to ensure successful adoption and integration of the technology.
5. Establish clear goals and metrics for measuring success.

3.1 Build a Scalable and Efficient Delivery Factory

When building a scalable and efficient delivery factory or center of excellence (CoE), there are several things to consider, such as how decisions are being made in the organization, who are the customers that will benefit from the process mining services, what are their specific needs, what services should the CoE offer to meet these needs, and what is required to deliver the services faster and cheaper than the traditional BPM methods can. These are contemporary challenges in many organizations and the related body of knowledge is still rather limited (see Reinkemeyer et al., 2022).

3.1.1 Decision-Making and Operating Model Structure

In this case, business prioritization and process transformation ownership were spread across different divisions/business units. When deciding on the operating model structure, three options were considered:

1. Decentralized/BU managed structure—decisions in BU, methodology in BU, each BU develops its own functions and methodology, high level of duplication of roles, disparate processes and policies.
2. Centralized decision-making in CoE (with input by the lines of business)—change is CoE-led, high level of standardization.
3. Hybrid—a combination of options 2 and 3.

It was determined that in this case, a hybrid structure or hub and spoke model was the option that best aligned and leveraged the existing governance and delivery structures (see Fig. 1).

The CoE or central hub is responsible for building, rolling out, and maintaining the process mining foundations, while the peripheral spokes are responsible for prioritization, implementation, and transformation. Teams within the business support the CoE in managing the IT infrastructure, IT operations, and vendor-related activities. At the center of the hub, there is a small and nimble CoE team that is organized around a small core team that can be scaled up or down depending on demand to keep costs and overheads as low as possible (Fig. 2). The core team consists of the following:

- CoE lead—Responsible for the CoE strategy, pipeline management, partner and vendor management, CoE budget, and overall CoE governance.

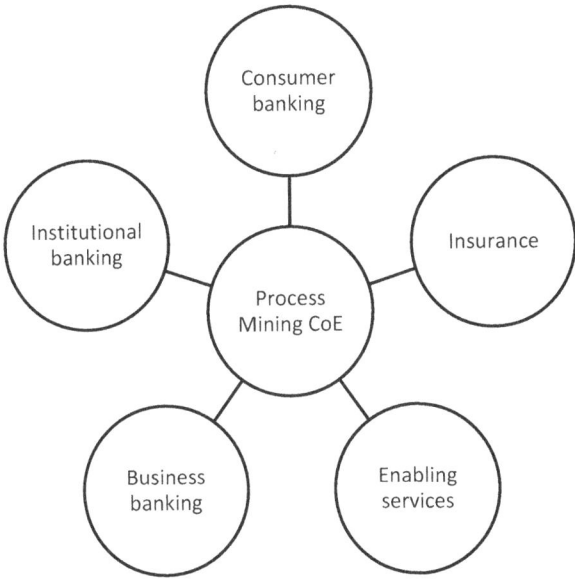

Fig. 1 Process mining operating model structure: hub and spoke model

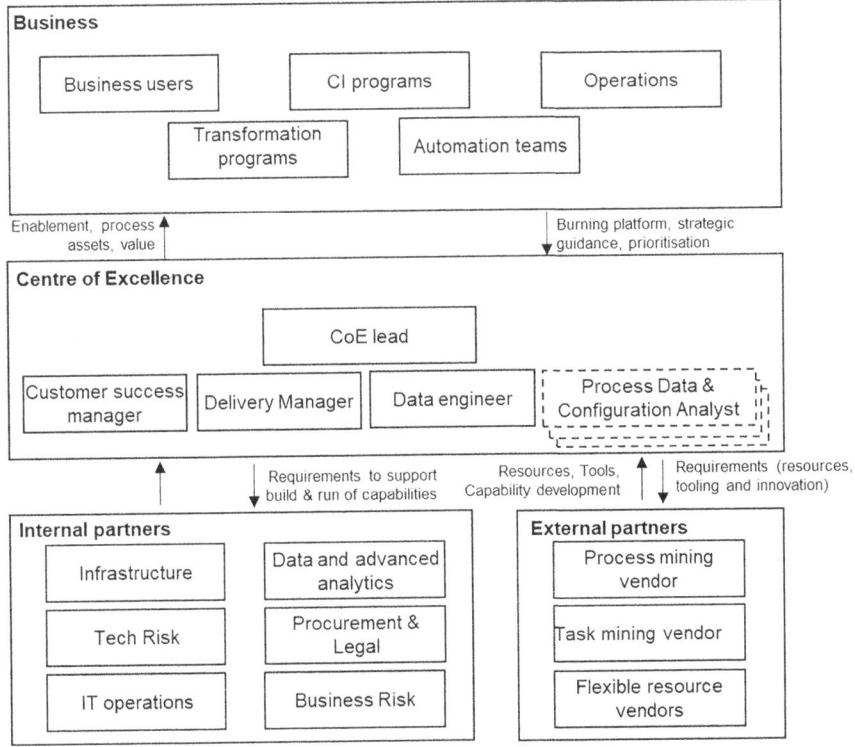

Fig. 2 Summary process mining operating model structure

- Customer success manager—Responsible for working with the business to unlock value and identify opportunities and reuse opportunities for process mining assets, building an active process mining community, and training and enabling users throughout the business.
- Delivery manager—Responsible for timely and cost-effective delivery of process mining projects, building reusable approaches and methodologies, knowledge management, and managing the flexible resource pool.
- Data engineer—Responsible for secure data extraction, preparation, and ingestion in process mining tools and working closely with data source/system specialists.
- Data and configuration analyst—This is a flexible role that can be scaled up or down leveraging other teams in the organization of flexible vendor resources.

The peripheral spokes are typically business areas or improvement teams that fulfill the following roles:

- Executive sponsorship—accountable for day-to-day operations, setting strategic direction, deciding on business priorities, owning the burning platform, providing direction and sponsorship, and holding the budget.
- Business leads—responsible for running day-to-day business or improvement projects, managing teams, coordinating SMEs, and validating insights.
- Business analysts—operational business users supporting day-to-day operations or improvement programs translating data into recommendations and (re)designing processes, working with data and analytics to define processes and use cases, key requirements, dashboards, and key performance indicators (KPIs).

3.1.2   Customer Requirements and Service Offering

To build a scalable and efficient process mining delivery factory, it was important to understand the internal customers and their requirements. The consumers of the process mining services identified were divided into five different internal customer groups:

1. Executive decision-makers—set strategic direction and priorities, own, and determine budget.
2. Operational team managers—responsible for day-to-day delivery and people management.
3. Improvement and transformation teams—deliver simplification and digitization to reduce costs and improve customer experience.
4. Compliance managers—ensure we are meeting regulatory requirements, minimize risk, and ensure controls are in place and working.
5. IT application managers—simplify the application landscape and reduce system costs.

When assessing the internal customers' needs, it was evident they were closely aligned with the BPM lifecycle model which consists of discovery, analysis, redesign, implementation, and monitoring phases (Dumas et al., 2018). The identify and quantify phase provides a reliable baseline that helps prioritize what matters most, that is, what provides the biggest return on investment. There is often no shortage of improvement ideas but determining which ones should be taken forward and implemented is a recurring question that the business was struggling with. Next, the performance must be quantified, which involves determining volumes, cost, effort, and effectiveness related to controls and applications used in the processes. Processes and process performance must then be compared across teams, brands, regions, best practice, etc. The impact of the model change must be assessed prior to implementation including by obtaining greater clarity on business cases and benefit profiles. The newly implemented process should be proactively monitored to compare what should be happening to what is actually happening in the process. Finally, the impact of implemented changes on processes, for example, training, new policy, automation, etc., must continue to be monitored.

In addition to their needs, the customer groups expressed "how" these services should be provided, which was translated into CoE service design principles:

- Easy to use and fast to deploy—Can we do this in days rather than months?
- Designed to use data so that it is not difficult for SMEs to uncover process opportunities—Can we use technology rather than human glue and avoid opinions?
- Developed to be used and consumed by enabled users in the business—Can this be put in the hands of business experts?
- Developed as an asset with the intention of being reused to optimize return on investment.
- Procuring mining licenses centrally at competitive prices to enable the cheapest cost per implementation in the business.
- Delivered partnered with data, lean design, and business SMEs to enable the most relevant and impactful insight—Can we leverage what exists rather than duplicating and building everything from scratch or in an ivory tower?
- Be innovative and market leading—Can we push the envelope by partnering with (software) vendors shaping their product roadmap to take the emerging process and task mining technology to the next level to deliver the CoE's vision and its capability roadmap?

Table 1 summarizes the services that were developed based on the customers' requirements and the alignment with the BPM lifecycle.

The services were developed, built, and rolled out across the organization in a phased approach over 12–18 months (see capability roadmap in Table 2).

Table 1 Process mining services aligned to BPM lifecycle

BPM lifecycle		What to deliver	Services to offer
Discovery	As-is process model	Automated process discovery	Process mining (where there is workflow and system data) Task mining (where data does not exist)
Analysis	Insight into weaknesses and their impact	Enable business users to derive insight and unlock value from automated process discovery	User training I 30 m lean review Customer success management
Redesign	To-be process	Drive intelligent process redesign	Simulation I big rock simulation hackathon Linking architecture, process, and task mining
Implement	Executable process model	Governance embedded into programs or teams that can decide on and deliver implementation	Implementation and value realization tracker
Monitor	Conformance and performance insights	Regular performance and conformance updates and action-oriented predictive notifications	(Near) real-time process performance updates Predictive insights/ performance notifications

Table 2 Capability roadmap

3–6 months	6–12 months	12–18 months	18+ months
Introduce automated process discovery	Embed regular process performance updates	Drive intelligent process redesign	Action-oriented predictive process mining
Process performance baselining Data-driven process discovery Process-driven benefits modeling	Business-led mining insight and applications Process performance monitoring	Process compliance adherence monitoring Process simulation Embed process and task mining in architecture	Predictive insights/ performance notifications
Ongoing innovation			

3.2 Identify the Right Processes to Target

Process mining is a powerful tool that can help businesses identify areas for improvement in their processes. However, it can be overwhelming knowing where to start with such a vast amount of data. In order to prioritize and target processes most suitable for process mining, it is important to first identify the processes that are critical to the success of the business (see also Rott & Böhm, 2022).

In our case, a conscious decision was made to focus first on processes that were directly tied to revenue and customer satisfaction. From there, the complexity, volume, and ability to make data available quickly were key considerations. Furthermore, processes with a high volume of data that can be made available quickly or complex workflows are often the best candidates for process mining. Finally, the potential impact of improving each process was considered. Processes that had the potential to significantly improve efficiency or reduce costs were prioritized over those with a lower impact. By following these steps, the CoE was able to effectively prioritize and target which processes to mine first, prove impact, and build momentum across the business.

3.3   Ensuring the Availability of the Necessary Data

Data challenges are one of the key dependencies that can hinder process mining success. Issues related to that were identified as needing to be addressed included the following:

- The data experts needed to understand the systems and source the data were often scattered across the organization.
- Data alignment to processes was often not understood by data experts alone and additional business effort is required to obtain this understanding.
- Event logs may contain sensitive customer information that would potentially expose the organization to risk if mined.

Trying to build an organization that can oversee and understand the organization's full data landscape and address the related challenges was practically impossible. The process mining CoE, therefore, had to build partnerships with key data teams and become part of the delivery organization. Once a project scope was confirmed, the right people from the right data teams in the organization were onboarded as part of the core delivery team. Without the availability of this expertise, from the start, the project would not have been likely to succeed. In addition to having the right partners as part of the delivery team, risk teams were involved in developing secure data-sourcing procedures while the CoE worked with IT infrastructure partners to align process mining tools with the organization's technology architecture.

Finally, there was one more data challenge to consider: What if the data does not exist? This financial institution is dealing with a high degree of legacy-enabled processes and data often cannot be made available. In addition, a substantial amount of work is done outside the core workflow systems. So even if data can be made available from the core workflow system, the business might perceive the insight as incomplete and not reflective of the full picture. To address this challenge, it is crucial to go beyond process mining capabilities and incorporate task mining capabilities. By deploying sensors on select user workstations, task mining generates structured data from desktop and Web applications, effectively filling in gaps for user routines that occur outside of the system. This complementary approach ensures that no essential information is overlooked.

3.4 Securing Sponsorship and Investing in Training and Change Management

Process mining is an effective way of identifying the root causes of issues and improving processes. The main benefit of process mining is that it delivers great insight. However, process mining does not deliver direct change in the process. If the value cannot be proven, process mining services can quickly be perceived as an overhead or heavy cost burden to the organization. As such, it was critical that the process mining CoE

- built partnerships that moved beyond interesting insight to deliver tangible business outcomes and
- developed a scalable, repeatable methodology that could deliver its services cheaper and faster than traditional methodologies.

3.4.1 Build Partnerships with Delivery Teams

Understanding what levers deliver process change and who in the organization is responsible for delivering the changes was a fundamental first step toward moving beyond simply providing insight. Typically, we saw process change being delivered through four levers:

1. Uplifting workforce effectiveness through training, better work instructions, performance management, etc.
2. Optimizing queues that distribute workflows across the processes.
3. Automation of process steps, for example, through robotic process automation (RPA), PowerApps, workflow optimization, and chatbot technology.
4. Delivering process, procedure, or control simplification and standardization throughout the organization.

Building a CoE that can manage and deliver all these levers from scratch would be expensive and practically impossible. When establishing the CoE and running process mining projects, a priority is to establish relationships and formalize partnerships with teams in the organization that

(a) are already equipped to deliver these changes and
(b) are interested in using insights from process and task mining to improve their delivery capability.

Table 3 Approach to process mining implementation

	Phase 1	Phase 2	Phase 3	Phase 4	Phase 5	Phase 6
Process mining	Mobilization and kickoff	Explore data	Prepare and upload data	Analyze, validate, and enable	Showcase	Implement and monitor
Task mining		Notification period	Capture period			
Duration	1 week	2 weeks	1 week	2 weeks	1–2 h	Varies
SME effort	0.5–2 h	0	0	0.5–2 h	1–2 h	

3.4.2 Develop Scalable and Repeatable Methodology

The CoE developed an innovative implementation approach that delivers results faster and more cheaply than traditional methods. It starts with supportive sponsors with a burning platform that needs to be resolved. We then build process mining assets that deliver insight to unlock value in 2–3 sprints with minimal effort (2–6 h) from business SMEs (see Table 3).

The business becomes involved during mobilization and once the data becomes available. Smart technology and innovative ways of working are then used to bring the right people together in data-driven insight and redesign sessions. Examples of this include a "data-driven 30-min lean review" and a data-driven "big rock simulation hackathon." Once the interventions have been prioritized, governance structures are in place to prioritize and execute the right delivery mechanisms. During and after the implementation phase, process impact is monitored and fed into the appropriate governance forums. The implementation phase is outside the direct control of the CoE, and during this phase, the customer success manager plays a key role in advising and ensuring process mining data is being used to unlock value.

This implementation approach is supported by clearly defined roles and responsibilities. If any of these roles are not in place, delivery will be delayed or the ability to deliver tangible business outcomes will be compromised. To avoid this, it is important to secure the following:

- Sponsorship and governance—Every engagement needs to have a sponsor and a business lead in place who works closely with the CoE delivery lead to fund and deliver the project. In addition, a governance structure that can decide on prioritization and the next steps in the implementation needs to be in place. Finally, the governance team also needs to ensure there is an implementation team in place that can execute one or more of the four delivery mechanisms.
- Mining squad—Depending on the discovery method, either a process mining squad or task mining squad needs to be mobilized (see Table 4). The squad resources are sourced from a flexible resource pool and can be scaled up or down depending on demand. This approach keeps the fixed CoE resource cost low and variable cost only increases when demand and funding are available.

Table 4 Roles and responsibilities of the mining squad

Mining squad	Responsibilities
Delivery lead (CoE)	Ensures timely and effective delivery of process mining milestones
Customer success manager (CoE)	Works with the business to unlock value from process mining assets and enable business users
Data engineer (CoE)	Data extraction, preparation, and ingestion
Source data specialist(s) (partner)	Advises on data sourcing and interpretation
Configuration lead (CoE)	Task mining configuration and sensor management
Sponsor (business)	Owns burning platform, provides direction, sponsorship and decision-making across the project
Business lead (business)	Supports project mobilization and cadence
Business process expert (business)	Process expert who validates the baseline data and codevelops insight; can be trained to use process mining tools on an ongoing basis
Business user	Business users being task mined with sensors while performing process activities

3.5 Establish Clear Goals and Metrics to Measure Success

In its first year of operations, the CoE's main objective was to build the operating model, tools, and methodologies while proving value to the business. During this phase, "proving capability and identifying value" were the main objectives. As traction with the business gained momentum, the objectives shifted from "proving capability and identifying value" to "unlocking value and delivering economies of scale." Tangible measures and targets were set to measure how the process mining CoE tracks against the objectives (see Table 5) while progress is monitored and governed through a monthly general manager-owned governance forum.

To mitigate the risk that interesting insight alone might be delivered, it is critical to manage stakeholders' expectations of what direct outcomes can be delivered from process mining and where further work is required that is outside the CoE's direct control. Table 6 articulates the typical outcomes that are directly delivered from a process mining engagement.

4 Results Achieved

In general, we have observed a significant increase in confidence when data, rather than people, informs the business on what matters most. Additionally, tangible improvements are evident when comparing traditional "as-is" discovery efforts with mining discovery efforts. For instance, we have seen up to a 60% reduction in analyst effort and up to a 95% reduction in the required subject matter expertise to

Table 5 Process mining objectives and measures

What we set out to achieve…	How we measure…	How we deliver…
Build reusable process assets	Number of reusable process assets build	Pipeline and delivery management—develop a strategic pipeline of work and build process mining assets designed to be reused
Achieve economies of scale by increasing production and lowering costs	Cost per engagement delivered Implementation rate per quarter Engagements delivered against targets	Tool and partner management—build scalable, reusable innovative tools and methodologies that can be rolled out across the organization and consumed by enabled users in the business
Unlock value from assets developed	Value identified vs. taken, forward vs. delivered % engagements aligned with transformation programs	Customer success management—train, enable, and advise users in the business to unlock value through process mining assets and develop and maintain a process mining community
Enable reuse to optimize return on investment	Users trained and enabled Annual subscriptions and users by process asset	

Table 6 Direct outcomes delivered through process mining

Typical outcomes and direct benefits from process mining to date:	
Automated process discovery	Improved confidence in business cases Improved governance Reduced analyst effort Minimize reliance on scarce SME resources Improved confidence that improvement efforts are focused on what will make the most impact
Automatic, targeted data-driven activity-based costing	
Automatic system/application usage	
FTE best-in-class performance view, which FTE works on what and how they perform	
Upstream and downstream impact of team performance I e2e process performance view	
Ongoing process monitoring—comparison capability allowing the testing of the impact of initiatives/changes	
Enabled business users with reusable process assets to drive ongoing BPM	

conduct a process discovery from start to finish compared to traditional methods (refer to Fig. 3. Process discovery comparison traditional vs. mining).

In our first year of operations, we went through a significant learning and optimization curve which resulted in strong performance against our target measures (see Table 7).

Core drivers that have enabled these achievements include the following:

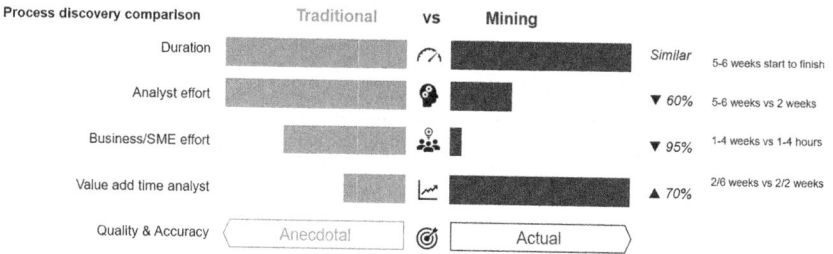

Fig. 3 Process discovery comparison traditional vs. mining

Table 7 Achievements against our measures

What we set out to achieve…	What we achieved in our first year
Build reusable process assets	Nine reusable end-to-end process assets built including mortgages, credit cards, personal loans, business lending, and merchants servicing
Achieve economies of scale by increasing production and lowering costs	Cost per engagement was reduced by 45%The implementation rate increased from 2 to 10 per quarter
Unlock value from assets developed	Value identified in the second year increased by 345% compared to the first yearAlignment with strategic transformation programs increased from 25% to 80%
Enable reuse to optimize return on investment	40+ active users, 5–10 new users added each quarter~5 different users/user groups/implementation teams per asset developed

- A strong scalable CoE and supporting partner ecosystem embedded in the organization.
- A repeatable, factory-style approach is now in place to deliver at scale.
- he right skilled resources have been recruited and onboarded.
- We have a strong vision and capability roadmap in place that supports vendors as well as the right tools to support our innovation journey moving forward.
- Based on the results they have seen, senior leadership up to the CEO and COO have been championing the process mining capability.

5   Lessons Learned

Process mining is gaining momentum and being embraced by an increasing number of organizations. More is being achieved with it every day. However, this shift has not come without its challenges. Here are six key takeaways for organizations that plan to set up a process mining program.

1. Define your process and task mining strategy: Determine what you want to achieve, how you will achieve it, how you will mature it, and how you will deliver actual value from it. Make sure there is a burning platform in the organization that you can help solve problems with its capabilities.

2. Set up a center of excellence and supporting ecosystem: Decide on the role and operating model of the CoE. Be clear on who leads and who owns what. Ensure the right teams are engaged and have the right partnerships in place to deliver at scale.

3. Invest in technical talent and best-of-breed tools: Ensure you have people with true experience and skills. Have the right breadth of people and tools that are impactful, simple to use, and fast and cost-effective to deploy.

4. Enable people in the business to unlock value: Democratization and reuse deliver economy of scale. True value comes from people in the business using the capability in their day-to-day business driving continuous improvement and transformation.

5. Embed the services in business cadence: Top-down support and decision-making are critical for success. Process mining is not a silver bullet on its own; it must be aligned with transformational programs and delivery teams to unlock and deliver its true potential.

6. Be patient: It takes time to bring people and the organization onto your journey. Find somebody who is keen to be made successful and believes in this new capability to help the organization test and learn. Make them successful so they will help bring others onto the journey.

References

Dumas, M., La Rosa, M., Mendling, J., & Reijers, H. (2018). *Fundamentals of business process management* (2nd ed.). Springer.

Reinkemeyer, L., et al. (2022). *Accelerating business transformation with process mining centers of excellence (CoE)*. Joint study report by Celonis and Fraunhofer Institute for Applied Information Technology.

Rott, J., & Böhm, M. (2022). Mine the right process – Towards a method for selecting a suitable use case for process mining adoption. *Proceedings of the European conference on information systems (ECIS 2022)*, Timisoara, Rumania.

vom Brocke, J., Zelt, S., & Schmiedel, T. (2015). *Considering context in business process management: The BPM context framework*. BP Trends.

vom Brocke, J., Jans, M., Mendling, J., & Reijers, H. (2021). A five-level framework for research on process mining. *Business & Information Systems Engineering, 63*, 483–490.

Marieke de Ruijter with a proven track record of driving innovation and transformation across multiple industries, Marieke de Ruijter currently serves as process mining and transformation specialist at one of Australia's "Big Four" banks. Her career spans diverse sectors, including financial services, fast-moving consumer goods, telecommunications, and management consulting, where she has held influential roles at prestigious organizations like ING Group, Telstra, and Ernst & Young. Before working in her current role, Marieke's leadership was pivotal in building a process innovation team of over 120 FTEs, where she spearheaded digital transformation initiatives earning several accolades. As a strategic advisor, she has guided numerous complex, multi-market digital transformation programs, such as designing a new operating model for a telecom giant in the Philippines and establishing support teams across the United States, EMEA, APAC, and China, ultimately serving over 140,000 customers globally.

The Smart Vending Cabinet: Leveraging the Industrial Internet of Things for Business Process Improvement

Christoph Stoiber and Stefan Schönig

Abstract

(a) *Situation faced*: Changing customer behavior and expectancies posed a significant challenge for a market leader of chemical products in the Scandinavian region. Previously, customers could only purchase products at certified retailers or vending machines. However, these two main distribution channels no longer met the needs of both private and business customers and, thus, suffered from individual problems. Customers were demanding, for example, online features, high availability, consultation, and guidance within their distribution process. For this reason, the distribution process needed to be reengineered.

(b) *Action taken*: A business process reengineering (BPR) project was carried out that aimed to develop a novel distribution process by merging existing processes and their advantages while extending them with additional features. Customer surveys were conducted to obtain an overview of customer requirements and problems within both current distribution processes. Based on the results, a set of design objectives for an ideal distribution process was formulated. Industrial Internet of Things (IIoT) technology was used to reengineer the distribution process radically. In this regard, existing research guided the goal-oriented leveraging of IIoT's capabilities for business process improvement.

(c) *Results achieved*: The reengineering project resulted in a novel distribution process combining the existing processes' advantages and addressing new customer needs. By including IIoT technology, a radical rethinking was able to ensure all design objectives could be addressed. In the long term, the intention is that the Smart Vending Cabinet developed will replace distribution via retailers and regular vending machines because of its additional features and capa-

C. Stoiber (✉)
University of Regensburg, Linde plc, Regensburg, Germany
e-mail: christoph.stoiber@ur.de

S. Schönig
University of Regensburg, Regensburg, Germany
e-mail: stefan.schoenig@ur.de

bilities. The prototype phase has achieved enormous benefits and highly positive customer feedback. It, therefore, significantly lowers distribution costs while increasing customer satisfaction.

(d) *Lessons learned*: The case demonstrated the value of IIoT technology for reengineering and improving business processes. By incorporating findings from current research, it addressed the formulated design objectives and met customer requirements.

1 Introduction

The distribution of chemical products for industrial and private customers in the Scandinavian region is an important field of business. Products of various kinds are produced, packed, and sold to numerous clients. In particular, selling to small businesses and private individuals is a lucrative business that is also driven by a significant number of tourists and campers. The latter group, in particular, needs nationwide access to appropriate products, which is a challenge given Scandinavia's large geographical area and relatively sparse population. With this case study, we present the development of a novel distribution process for chemical products.

The company in this case study is a global market leader in the chemical industry and one of Scandinavia's most successful producers and distributors of chemical products. The company was founded over 100 years ago, employs over 70,000 people in 2021, and has over US$20 billion in sales. In the Scandinavian countries, including Finland, it operates as a subsidiary with a significant market share. In the further course of this article, the company under consideration is referred to as *Company*.

For the distribution of chemical products, the Company uses two distribution processes, one per distribution channel throughout the Scandinavian region. Most sales are made through licensed retailers who sell the Company's products either exclusively or alongside many other products. These retailers include, for example, DIY stores and supermarkets. In addition, special vending machines are distributed throughout the region. Despite several limitations, both channels have proven valuable and, along with their underlying business processes, form the backbone of the Company's sales activities. However, when reviewing the sales numbers and customers' feedback, it became apparent that the existing distribution processes were no longer meeting the customers' expectations. While many customers appreciated some aspects of the current processes, new requirements emerged. To address the new requirements and areas of customer dissatisfaction identified, a project was initiated to reengineer and radically improve the distribution processes.

Business process improvement (BPI) is a key field in the broader area of the Business Process Management (BPM) lifecycle (Dumas et al., 2018). It is considered one of *"the most important and common titles in both literature and applications"* (Coskun et al., 2008). Among all activities associated with the BPM lifecycle, the improvement of business processes is considered to have the greatest potential to add value (Zellner, 2011; Dumas et al., 2018; Gross et al., 2021). In this regard, the radical and transformational improvement of business processes, in contrast to other incremental improvements, is referred to as business process reengineering (BPR) (Dumas et al., 2018). In this case study, the term BPI is used as a synonym for BPR, as both aim to achieve an improved state of business processes. As BPI and BPR, in particular, are often enabled by disruptive information technologies (Bhatt, 2000), the Company decided to use the Industrial Internet of Things (IIoT) as an enabler for radical process improvement. Novel research has established methods and models that (*i*) give an overview of IIoT's potential in BPI (Stoiber & Schönig, 2022a), (*ii*) provide reusable BPI blueprints (Stoiber & Schönig, 2022b), and (*iii*) support a process-oriented selection of IIoT technology (Stoiber & Schönig, 2021). Furthermore, industrial organizations are supported in the assessment of their readiness to conduct IIoT-based BPI projects (Stoiber & Schönig, 2022c). This existing research supported and guided the effective reengineering and improvement of the distribution processes.

The presented project followed the principles of the BPR approach as initially set out by Hammer (1990) and made methodologically applicable by Grover et al. (2015). More precisely, the project team followed the steps of Vakola and Rezgui (2000) that guide organizations in their BPR endeavors. This includes providing a complete understanding of the existing business processes; developing design objectives; identifying technological levers for reengineering, designing, and implementing the new process; and evaluating results.

Based on these steps, the remainder of this article is structured as follows. In Sect. 2, the initial situation faced by the Company is described in detail. Subsequently, the actions taken to address the existing challenges and problems are presented in Sect. 3. Section 4 gives an overview of the achieved results of the BPI project. Finally, the lessons learned are described in Sect. 5.

2 Situation Faced

The Company's two existing distribution channels in the Scandinavian region evolved over several decades and cover almost all of the two countries. While licensed retailers were the only distribution channel for small businesses and private customers for many years, vending machines were introduced in response to additional customer requirements (see Fig. 1). In 2019, the Company's sales department extensively analyzed sales numbers, customer satisfaction, and loyalty. This was achieved through the thorough analysis of sales data from the last 10 years and an extensive customer survey in which the Company surveyed 183 customers from different regions to identify process requirements. The 12-question questionnaires were created by the relevant sales departments and distributed as an online document. The customers were invited to indicate their satisfaction with the existing sales processes on a five-point Likert scale (Likert, 1932). They were then asked to state additional requirements they would expect from any future process.

Fig. 1 Existing distribution channels: retailers and vending machines

Table 1 Advantages and disadvantages of existing distribution channels

	Retailers	Vending machines
Pros	Customer guidance	24/7 availability
	Consultation	Process standardization
	High product variety	Multi-language
Cons	Low level of availability	Poor customer guidance
	Poor process standardization	Poor consultation
	Potential language barriers	Low product variety

The analysis showed a stagnation in sales numbers in quantity and revenue. Moreover, the surveys showed that many customers were no longer satisfied with the existing distribution processes. Depending on their preferred distribution channel, customers reported several problems and expected changes. The specific findings of this analysis for both established distribution channels are presented here and their pros and cons are summarized in Table 1.

The sale by **retailers** is the most established distribution channel in Scandinavia. Retailers provide direct customer contact and guide customers through every stage of the distribution process. This includes consultation on the products available and the required solutions. Retailers usually have large storage areas, so are able to stock a large variety of products. Nevertheless, several drawbacks were identified that lead to customer dissatisfaction and decreased loyalty.

First, each certified distribution partner has specific opening hours that the Company often cannot influence. This is highly problematic for tourists and campers in particular, as they often depend on chemical products outside normal opening hours. This decreased the sales experience significantly. Second, given this wide variety of retailer types, there needed to be a higher degree of process standardization. Despite the Company's many efforts to harmonize and standardize the distribution processes, no standard process could be developed meaning the customers had to be aware of many factors when seeking to purchase the Company's products. For example, some retailers provide online payment while others only accept credit cards or cash. Moreover, some retailers enable customers to check product availability online while others do not. Customers must collect products from some retailers in-store while at many other stores, the retailers' employees manage and check the products. Finally, various customers reported that retailers often have severe language barriers. Most tourists do not speak Swedish, Danish, Norwegian, or Finnish and seek to communicate in English. If the employees are not fluent in English, this poses a problem.

Vending machines were introduced several years ago to offer a more standardized distribution process. These machines have been specially tailored to the needs of private customers and are placed throughout the Scandinavian countries, for example, at supermarkets and service stations. In contrast to the traditional retailer distribution channel, the vending machines provide several advantages. As seen in Table 1, the advantages are directly connected to the disadvantages of retailers. Vending machines offer 24/7 availability and process standardization, including verification of product availability and online payment options. They can also be used in many different languages. However, their drawbacks are also closely connected to the advantages of retailers. For instance, they have a limited variety of products, inferior consultation opportunities, and no customer guidance.

The customer surveys conducted demonstrated that both existing distribution channels had prominent weaknesses. Furthermore, many customers stated additional requirements that neither of the existing channels provided. The three most relevant requirements were the option for (*i*) online payment, (*ii*) online verification of product availability, and (*iii*) online product reservation.

3   Action Taken

This section outlines the actions taken during the course of the BPR project. Having fully understood the advantages and disadvantages of existing distribution processes and additional customer requirements, we identified the need for a reengineered process. In response, the Company formed an interdisciplinary project team. The team consisted of seven people including the relevant process owners, sales staff, engineers, and IT specialists. The project started in 2019 and ended in 2022 with a fundamentally reengineered process in the evaluation phase.

This chapter presents the three main stages of the process revision. First, design objectives were formulated based on the analysis described in Sect. 2. These design objectives constituted the main features of the ideal distribution process. In the second step, IIoT technology was identified as a lever for BPR in this situation. Third, the distribution process was generically designed and iteratively refined by exploiting the capabilities of IIoT technology. To this end, the design phase was supported by the patterns for IIoT-based BPI in Stoiber and Schönig (2022b). These patterns provided generic IIoT solutions that address specific process challenges. The process design and application of IIoT-based BPI patterns are then performed iteratively until a feasible process and physical representation is developed.

As the Company had not regularly been using IIoT technology for BPI, a maturity assessment had to be performed. This determined whether the Company was ready to conduct the BPR project using IIoT technology. The assessment was conducted using the maturity model for IIoT-based BPI outlined in Stoiber and Schönig (2022c). The results showed that the Company had sufficient organizational capabilities to be able to integrate even advanced IIoT technologies into their business processes. This was deemed to be the case because the organization had already established responsibilities for information technology and the management of business processes. Thus, there was sufficient knowledge to proceed with the BPR project.

3.1 Formulation of Design Objectives

Based on the findings of Sect. 2, a set of design objectives were derived that constituted fundamental requirements for the new distribution process. They were formulated by the project team that analyzed and synthesized the survey results.

1. *Process standardization*: Harmonize and merge the advantages of existing distribution processes to reduce process diversity and create clearer process flows.
2. *Task automation*: Automate process tasks on the Company side to enable 24/7 availability and cost reductions.
3. *Online services and features*: Provide services to the customers, for example, online payment, online verification of product availability, consultation, multilanguage features, and online product reservation.
4. *Process stability and flexibility*: Enable real-time customer guidance throughout the process to identify problems, process deadlocks, and solutions.
5. *Economic and scalable process*: As the distribution process needed to be provided in all Scandinavian regions, it must be cost-efficient and easy to scale.

These five design objectives reflected customer feedback and constituted the focal points for the BPR endeavor. On this basis, a high-level overview was designed that represented the ideal distribution process. This ideal process was not modeled to the very last detail. Instead, the most important key points and features were summarized and the rough workflow presented.

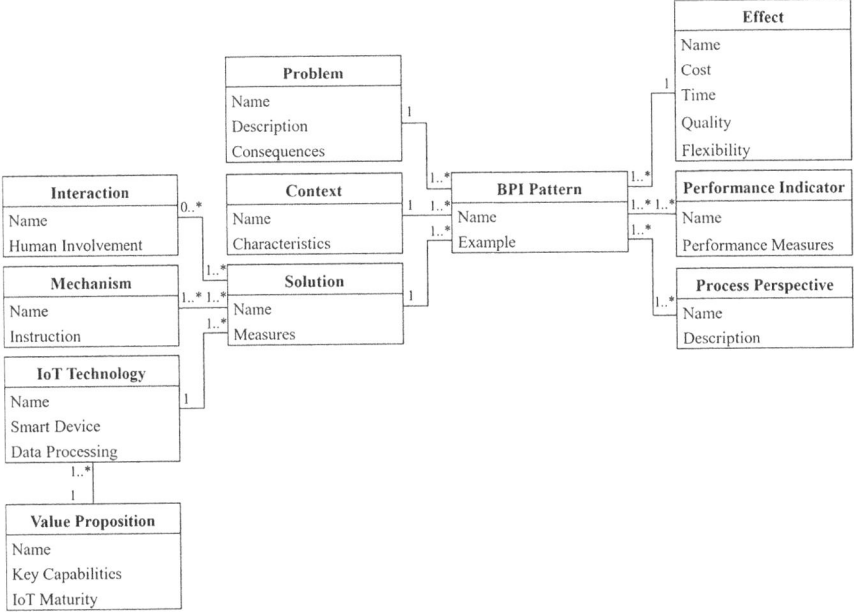

Fig. 2 Metamodel of IIoT-based BPI based on Stoiber and Schönig (2022b)

3.2   Application of Patterns for IIoT-Based BPI

Within the case study project, IIoT technology had been identified as a capable driver for the process reengineering. An in-depth analysis of IIoT showed that it would enable the design and realization of the future distribution process. However, a systematic approach was required to effectively find proper IIoT solutions for the design objectives. For this purpose, Stoiber and Schönig (2022b) developed a set of patterns that provide generic blueprints for IIoT-based BPI. These patterns are illustrated using a metamodel as shown in Fig. 2.

The metamodel comprises all elements and characteristics vital for IIoT-based BPI and proposes a solution for existing problems and challenges within processes. This includes the description of the underlying process problem or challenge that should be tackled and the wider context around the underlying reason for the problem. Furthermore, the metamodel includes a generic solution based on the IIoT technology proposed.

Within multiple workshops, the design objectives were mapped with the pattern catalog of IIoT-based BPI. Starting with the design objective descriptions, suitable problem descriptions were sought within the patterns. Eventually, five patterns were identified that would enable the realization of all design objectives. These patterns are briefly presented in the following.

- *Smart Data Processing Pattern*: The smart processing of data collected by sensors enables various customer services and features. Generally, this pattern is also the basis for the other patterns. Analyzing the current stock at vending machines and retailers using various sensors allows the availability of specific products to be checked. This data can be collected, for instance, using simple proximity sensors that show the presence of products. This is highly beneficial for customers as they can use a smartphone app to check product availability. Furthermore, such a smartphone application can facilitate payment for and consultation on the products. Additional services and features can be easily added by integrating more sensors and expanding the functionality of the smartphone application accordingly.
- *Process Task Automation Pattern*: The automation of process tasks was formulated as a central design objective as it is the prerequisite for providing low-cost 24/7 availability and decreasing sales expenses. Using IIoT technology, the most relevant process tasks that people perform at retail stores can be automated. The key is integrating actuators into the process that simulate human actions triggered by the data as it is collected and analyzed. In this way, payment and product handover can be automated. The latter can be realized by checking if a specific customer has purchased a product and then opening an access lock to allow the product to be collected.
- *Authorization and Authentication Pattern*: A successful distribution process includes several customer-specific tasks. Therefore, customers must be individually recognized in order to deliver a satisfying service. This allows for user-specific actions and prevents theft or other misbehavior. This need is usually met by sales representatives but it can also be achieved using IIoT technology. By sensing a customer's location and checking for orders placed, access to process tasks can be granted or denied. This feature can be used to ensure customers can only retrieve the product from the vending machine or retailer when successful payment has been confirmed.
- *Process Guidance Pattern*: Designing a standardized process was also a design objective. To guarantee this, customers must be guided through all process tasks. This is especially important for users who are new to the process. In this regard, order data can be used to initially create a specific process instance that includes all necessary tasks. Throughout the process execution, IIoT technology can sense the necessary process steps and guide customers using visual or audio signals. These signals can include LEDs that show which product can be retrieved by the customer after payment has been made.
- *Process Deviation Detection*: Wrongly executed tasks must be detected and corrected for a process to be stable but flexible. As human support is unavailable on-site in automated scenarios, the detection of falsely executed process tasks must be provided. In this regard, sensors can collect actual process task data and compare it with expected values, including thresholds. Thus, the IIoT application can recognize deviations and alert customers when, for example, the customer retrieves the wrong product. Combined with the process guidance pattern, this can ensure a stable and flexible process.

Having iteratively identified appropriate patterns, the distribution process was reengineered. Various process tasks and flows were adapted and simplified. This novel process comprises all the advantages of the established processes and includes additional features that were enabled by IIoT technology. The final distribution process was modeled using Business Process Model and Notation (BPMN 2.0).

4   Results Achieved

This section outlines the results of the BPR project including a description of the developed distribution channel and the reengineered business process. Moreover, the results of the first evaluation phase are described to illustrate the impact on customer satisfaction, distribution costs, and sales numbers.

4.1   The Smart Vending Cabinet

A combination of hardware and software development was required to realize the newly designed distribution process. A group of project engineers and software developers created the so-called Smart Vending Cabinet application that consists of five main components: a regular 20-foot container, a modular IIoT kit containing sensors, actuators, relays, edge nodes, and a cloud server that hosts the Business Process Management System (BPMS) provides APIs and analyzes and stores IIoT data for multiple services. In addition, a smartphone app was developed. The 20-foot container is equipped with the IIoT sensor and actuator kit and has enough space to hold various chemical products. The Smart Vending Cabinet can be placed anywhere with a power supply and network infrastructure. It does not require the presence of an on-site sales representative and has the same location requirements as the vending machines. The primary customer interface is the smartphone application which decreases the individual cost of the cabinets. This subsection describes the basic process flow at the Smart Vending Cabinet.

The first step for the customer is to purchase a product via the smartphone app. It is also possible to obtain a consultation on the chemical products available through the app if required. The availability of the various products at each Smart Vending Cabinet is displayed and payment can be made online. As a sales representative is not required, any products purchased can be collected 24/7. The corresponding cabinet reserves the goods until they are collected. Combining the *Smart Data Processing* and *Process Task Automation* patterns enabled these features.

In their next step, the customer must attend the appropriate Smart Vending Cabinet and request access to the product via the smartphone app. Alternatively, the actions can be performed in an internet browser via the Company's website. Furthermore, the cabinet can detect the customer's presence via Bluetooth using the *Authentication and Authorization* pattern. The cabinet then only opens the door via

Fig. 3 Different steps within the reengineered distribution process

the actuators when it has confirmed the customer has placed and paid for an order. This is highly cost-efficient as no additional human interface is required. This step is illustrated in the image on the left in Fig. 3.

Next, after the door is opened, the customer is shown the product they have purchased and is able to remove it. According to the *Process Guidance* pattern, light-bars show the customer which product to be removed visually. In this regard, customers new to the process or the products are supported during product retrieval. This is illustrated by the center image in Fig. 3.

To enable a stable and flexible process, errors are detected within the process and communicated to the customer. This is done according to the *Deviation Detection* pattern. For example, if the customer removes the incorrect product, the lightbar changes to red, and the customer receives push messages on their smartphone. The customer receives instructions via the lightbars and smartphone application to correct the task. The image on the right in Fig. 3 shows two push notifications. The first indicates that the customer has retrieved the wrong product and should place it back in the relevant slot. The second notification means the customer did not correctly close the cabinet after retrieving the product.

4.2   Prototype Phase and Customer Feedback

The Smart Vending Cabinet is currently in the evaluation phase. In this regard, it has been presented to all key customers of the regions where it has been deployed using newsletters and optional online presentations. During this piloting phase, the Company evaluates the distribution costs, sales numbers, and customer satisfaction to verify business viability. Until September 2022, data was collected for 8 months to compare the newly designed process with the established distribution processes.

An initial customer survey showed that satisfaction had increased substantially. However, many customers were initially skeptical because of the relatively novel IIoT technology and fundamentally different process. After an initial introduction phase of 3 weeks, which included presentations and training, acceptance increased significantly. Even customers who had previously used only one of the established channels reported being satisfied with the new process and a preference for using it in the future. Indeed, customers have yet to indicate any substantial disadvantages in the new process, which indicates that the goals set for the new process were achieved. Moreover, the customers have not reported any major additional requirements. The only relevant adaption to the Smart Vending Cabinet requested is some improvement in the customers' product consultation options.

It was also possible to collect and analyze data on the costs of the distribution process meaning costs of construction and operation could be compared in detail. This comparison showed that the Smart Vending Cabinet reduces distribution costs for comparable products by 36% compared to the retailer process: The primary reason for this is the savings in sales staff. Costs are reduced by under 9% when compared to the original vending machines, mainly due to lower technical maintenance costs.

Absolute changes in sales figures could not be identified in the period under review. However, there has been a solid migration toward using the Smart Vending Cabinet in the regions where all three channels are still available. Almost 25% of sales were processed via the new process in the 8-month pilot phase. This willingness to change distribution channel and positive customer feedback indicates a success that may gradually lead to an absolute increase in long-term sales, as competitors still rely mainly on retailers and standard vending machines.

5   Lessons Learned

Reengineering this distribution process using IIoT technology has highlighted several essential factors and learnings. First, a detailed analysis of process requirements is crucial for effective reengineering. Here, it is necessary to focus on customer expectations that must be satisfied by the processes established while still considering best practice standards and process features that need to be preserved. These requirements should be used to derive a set of design objectives that need to be considered within the design and development phase. Second, from a technical point of view, integrating IIoT technology into a business process enables the provision of novel features and services to customers. In this case study, the collection of real-time process data from IIoT devices enabled the extensive monitoring of process performance. This data could then be used to provide process guidance and detect process deviations. Therefore, the case study shows that distribution processes can also benefit from IIoT technology although it is, currently, mainly used within production or logistics processes.

In general, it became apparent that BPM can benefit significantly from introducing IoT technology and vice versa. This supports the statements made by Janiesch et al. (2020), who postulated that IoT and BPM could be mutually beneficial. During the case study, the extent to which manually executed physical processes can be supported by a combination of IoT and BPM became clear. The *Process Task Automation* pattern is the primary influence on this. Furthermore, the quality of task execution can be tracked according to the *Deviation Detection* pattern. Another relevant benefit presented relates to how to deal with new situations during the process. Thanks to the *Process Guidance* pattern, process participants can be guided through new and complex processes. Here, IoT technology helps sense situational data that is then used within the BPMS to recommend response tasks. These tasks are presented to the process participant through the IoT technology.

Finally, from a customer perspective, it was essential to properly introduce the Smart Vending Cabinet and its benefits. For small-size business customers in particular, the novel process that included modern technologies and a new smartphone application was received with skepticism. However, this initial inhibition threshold was effectively broken through by offering detailed instruction and training.

References

Bhatt, G. D. (2000). Exploring the relationship between information technology, infrastructure, and business process re-engineering. *Business Process Management Journal, 6*(2), 139–163.

Coskun, S., Basligil, H., & Baracli, H. (2008). A weakness determination and analysis model for business process improvement. *Business Process Management Journal, 14*(2), 243–261.

Dumas, M., La Rosa, M., Mendling, J., & Reijers, H. A. (2018). *Fundamentals of business process management*. Springer.

Gross, S., Stelzl, K., Grisold, T., Mendling, J., Röglinger, M., & vom Brocke, J. (2021). The business process design space for exploring process redesign alternatives. *Business Process Management Journal, 27*(8), 25–56.

Grover, V., Jeong, S. R., Ketting, W. J., & Teng, J. T. C. (2015). The implementation of business process reengineering. *Journal of Management Information Systems, 12*(1), 109–144.

Hammer, M. (1990, July–August). Reengineering work: Don't automate, obliterate. *Harvard Business Review*, pp. 104–112.

Janiesch, C., Koschmider, A., Mecella, M., et al. (2020). The internet of things meets business process management: A manifesto. *IEEE Systems, Man, and Cybernetics Magazine, 6*(4), 34–44.

Likert, R. (1932). *A technique for the measurement of attitudes* (Archives of psychology). Columbia University.

Stoiber, C., & Schönig, S. (2021). Process-aware decision support model for integrating internet of things applications using AHP. In *Proceedings of the 23rd international conference on enterprise information systems (ICEIS)*.

Stoiber, C., & Schönig, S. (2022a). Improving business processes with the internet of things—A taxonomy of IIoT applications. In *Proceedings of the 30th European conference on information systems (ECIS)*, Timişoara.

Stoiber, C., & Schönig S. (2022b). Patterns for IoT-based business process improvements—Developing a metamodel. In Proceedings of the 24th international conference on enterprise information systems (ICEIS).

Stoiber, C., & Schönig S. (2022c). Digital transformation and improvement of business processes with internet of things: A maturity model for assessing readiness. In: *Proceedings of the 55th Hawaii international conference on system sciences, HICSS*, pp. 4879–4888.

Vakola, M., & Rezgui, Y. (2000). Critique of existing business process re-engineering methodologies: The development and implementation of a new methodology. *Business Process Management Journal, 6*(3), 238–250.

Zellner, G. (2011). A structured evaluation of business process improvement approaches. *Business Process Management Journal, 17*(2), 203–237.

Dr. Christoph Stoiber received a bachelor's and a master's degree in industrial engineering from the University of Augsburg. Furthermore, he received a doctoral degree in information systems from the University of Regensburg. During and after his studies, he worked in various positions at multinational corporations such as Audi, Volkswagen, and Linde in Germany and Mexico. Since 2023, he has been the Head of Production Digitalization at EagleBurgmann and is responsible for the corporation's digitalization strategy. Christoph Stoiber has been an external researcher under the Professorship for IoT-based Information Systems (Prof. Dr. Stefan Schönig) since December 2019. His research topic is the interconnection of IoT and BPM, i.e., systematic methods and models for IoT-based business process improvement. In this capacity, he has published in renowned conference proceedings and journals in the IoT, BPM, and general IS field.

Prof. Dr. Stefan Schönig received both a master's degree (with honors) in applied computer science and a doctoral degree from the University of Bayreuth. He is a professor at the Institute of Management Information Systems at the University of Regensburg in Germany. He has previously been a post-doctoral researcher with the Institute for Information Business at WU Vienna and a tenured assistant professor at the University of Bayreuth. He has an established background in BPM/process mining and has been working in this field for over eight years. Furthermore, he has participated in several industry projects that address process mining, process analysis, process monitoring, and process intelligence. He has published extensively on BPM and Information Systems Research, both in international conference proceedings and journals. Moreover, he serves on several program committees for, among others, EDOC, ENASE, BPM, BPMDS, and as a reviewer for journals.

Part III
Operationalize: The Feasibility of BPM

Detecting and Mitigating the Event Log Mutability Problem: At the Dutch Employee Insurance Agency (UWV)

Bart Hompes and Marcus Dees

Abstract

(a) *Situation faced*: UWV is the Social Security Institute of the Netherlands. At UWV, event data was used to gain insight into the unemployment benefits process. Traditionally, event logs have been conceptualized as immutable append-only data streams. However, in the real world, process mining implementations are generated a posteriori from business process execution systems which may not store all temporal data changes. This contrast brings forth silent risks caused by the mutability of recorded process execution data. In order to investigate this phenomenon, six event logs were created covering the same *observation period* from different *reference timestamps*. The logs showed significant differences in the form of *inserted*, *updated*, and *deleted events*.

(b) *Action taken*: Once the event log mutability problem was identified and sufficiently analyzed, three potential mitigation strategies were devised. Instead of using the monthly data mart for event log creation, an intermediate data layer was constructed based on weekly mutations from the information system. Though the possibility of unobserved events was not completely ruled out, the solution provides sufficient transparency into the process and its changes over time.

(c) *Results achieved*: By structurally creating data extracts and event logs for the same *observation period* at different *reference timestamps*, we were able to identify the event log mutability problem. Having a much more detailed account of what happens to each entitlement has already been shown to have additional analysis benefits.

(d) *Lessons learned*: For analyses to be trustworthy, they should be repeatable, reliable, and reproducible. The event log mutability problem that results from current event log creation practices may prevent this. Three risk mitigation strategies were proposed as inaction is not a viable option. Since our practice

---

B. Hompes (✉) · M. Dees
Artifex Consultancy & Eindhoven University of Technology, Eindhoven, The Netherlands

Uitvoeringsinstituut Werknemersverzekeringen (UWV), Amsterdam, The Netherlands
e-mail: bart.hompes@artifexconsultancy.nl; marcus.dees@uwv.nl

J. vom Brocke et al. (eds.), *Business Process Management Cases Vol. 3*,
https://doi.org/10.1007/978-3-031-80793-0_5

also identified the event log mutability problem in other processes and organizations, we integrated it into the core responsibilities of the process mining team.

1 Introduction

Business processes perform activities to achieve business goals such as creating a product or delivering a service. Modern processes are supported by process-aware information systems (e.g., ERP and CRM systems) that store digital footprints in the form of event data. Events typically record what process activity happened when, for which process instance (case), and who was involved. The analysis of this data has made it possible to accurately analyze process performance, conformance, compliance, and productivity through process mining (van der Aalst, 2016).

Existing process mining research typically conceptualizes event logs as immutable, append-only data streams. However, in most current real-world use cases, event logs are not stored as is by the information systems but are generated a posteriori. Source data needs to be extracted and transformed from the source systems' databases to generate event logs before process mining tools can be applied (van der Aalst, 2016; González López de Murillas, 2019; Jans et al., 2019).

Information systems may not store all temporal changes in their underlying databases. Often, only a selection of the changes is recorded and not necessarily all real-world events may be reconstructed from the recorded data. As a result, due to *unobserved events*, event log extracts made at different moments in time may differ, even if they contain data pertaining to the same time period. Event logs re-extracted at a later date may show *inserted*, *updated*, or *deleted events* compared to previously created logs. As these temporal changes may reflect on previously analyzed periods, results obtained in the past may be invalidated in the future, which could impact business decisions. In short, as they are typically created, event logs are susceptible to change over time.

This case study raises awareness of the event log mutability problem described above, demonstrates the risks involved, and shows how these risks can be mitigated. The remainder of this paper is structured as follows. Section 2 describes the situation faced. Section 3 discusses the actions taken. Section 4 describes the achieved results. Section 5 concludes the paper with lessons learned.

2 Situation Faced

UWV is the Social Security Institute of the Netherlands. It executes several employee-related social insurance processes related to unemployment, illness, and disability. In this case study, we focus on the unemployment benefits process. Workers who lose their job through no fault of their own can apply for unemployment benefits by filing a claim at UWV. Accepted workers receive monthly benefits. The benefits end when the maximum duration of the entitlement is reached, when a worker finds a new job, or when a worker has been ill for a longer period. In the latter case, other types of social benefits may apply.

At UWV, a preprocessed data extract of the business process execution system supporting the unemployment process is made available at monthly intervals. The main purpose for this monthly data extract is to report on the development of the unemployment benefits process within the UWV organization. The raw data from the information system is extracted and stored on a weekly basis. During preprocessing, the weekly extracted data, which contains all the mutations in the information system, is transformed into a monthly data mart containing the last known information for each entitlement that was active or changed during the month. The monthly data mart also contains attributes that can be used to create cross sections of the unemployment benefits process. These monthly data marts are used to report on the number of new, active, rejected, and ended entitlements. In addition to reporting, the data is used to analyze the process execution of the unemployment benefits process and to answer specific analysis questions. For example, "How many customers have multiple unemployment benefits periods" and "How much time is there between the end of one period and the start of the next period?" For this purpose, the data marts are transformed into event logs used for process mining. In the event logs, each case corresponds to one entitlement, and changes in the state of the entitlement (a claim, a decision, a payment, etc.) are represented as events. The monthly event logs are used to discover process variants as well as frequency- and performance-enriched directly-follows-graphs (DFGs) (van der Aalst, 2016) to gain insight into how customers flow through the process and, ultimately, to give advice on how to improve the process from a customer perspective.

In the unemployment benefits process, the number of new, active, rejected, and ended entitlements may change over time as a result of the state of the economy or due to seasonal variations. Comparisons between different monthly event logs showed that both the DFGs and the set of process variants remained stable over time. However, while comparing event logs, we found that specific events in 1 month's data mart were altered in another. This occurs, for example, when new information is received about the employee's employment contract. An employer may not take into account a notice period while ending their employment. In this case, the official unemployment start date needs to be corrected. This may result in updating the entitlement start date from a date in 1 month to a date in the next month, which retroactively decreases the number of active entitlements for the original month and increases it for the next month. In other words, the event representing the start of the case is updated. In the monthly data mart, only the most recent version of an event is present.

In order to investigate the phenomenon described above in a structured manner, we prepared six event logs covering the *observation period* 1-1-2020 until 31-12-2020, i.e., the whole year 2020. The logs were created with six different *reference timestamps*: 1-1-2021 until 1-6-2021. We labeled the event logs *V1* to *V6*, respectively. Several differences were found between the versions, namely, *inserted*

Table 1 The number of cases, events, and changes in the number of events by insertions and deletions in the observation period 2020 in the event logs for each reference timestamp compared to the previous reference timestamp

Reference timestamp	Log version	Case count	Event count	Delta count	Inserted events	Deleted events	Updated events	% no change
1-1-2021	V1	744,118	1,528,250	–	–	–	–	100.0%
1-2-2021	V2	774,869	1,590,240	61,990	68,060	6070	2527	95.4%
1-3-2021	V3	782,122	1,609,659	19,419	23,369	3950	2266	94.2%
1-4-2021	V4	785,741	1,615,694	6035	8295	2260	1017	93.9%
1-5-2021	V5	787,358	1,617,714	2020	2893	873	404	93.8%
1-6-2021	V6	788,460	1,619,054	1340	1965	625	316	93.7%

events, *updated events*, and *deleted events*. An event is uniquely identified by its activity label and the case it belongs to. The event logs that have been created contain events for the activities *Request*, *Decide*, *Pause*, *Resume*, and *Stop*. Each activity label only occurs once for each case. The following event attributes are included in each event log. The attribute *Decision* contains the outcome of the decision on the claim, i.e., *Accepted* or *Rejected*. The attribute *Reason* contains a description of the reason why the claim was rejected or why the benefits were stopped. Each event also has a timestamp that can be changed. When event attributes are updated, their activity label stays the same.

Table 1 shows, for the event logs of each reference timestamp, the number of cases and the number of events in the third and fourth columns, respectively. In the *delta count* column, the change in the number of events in comparison to the count at the previous reference timestamp is shown. The next two columns show that the change in the *event count* is a combination of inserted events and deleted events, respectively. Updated events do not influence the count, for example, the value of one or more event attributes of the event has changed while the activity label of the event stays the same. *This observation also implies that only looking at the number of events that have changed is not enough to identify what kind of changes have occurred*. The final column contains the percentage of the events of the event log that remained the same, i.e., show no difference when compared to the log at the first reference timestamp. In the following, we refer to the version of the event log at a specific reference date by its event log version. For example, log version *V3* refers to the event log at reference date 1-3-2021.

Table 1 shows that the biggest change between the log versions, visible in the *delta count* column, takes place between the first and the second reference timestamp. This was expected as it is less likely that never-before-seen cases related to the observation period are reporting themselves and more cases will get closed as more time passes. Yet the data for the observation period shows changes even 6 months later.

At this point in the analysis, we observed that information could be missing from every event log version. This problem results when there are unrecorded changes to a data mart. When an observation period is not revisited, all changes to that period that occur after the first—and in that case sole—version of the event log will not become part of any event log, especially given that observation periods either do not overlap or entail a sliding window. In the latter case, any changes in the observation period that are no longer part of the period selected in the window are not reported. In our case, this situation would have occurred if, for example, log version *V2* was skipped. While the delta count between *V1* and *V3* would have remained $61,990 + 19,419 = 81,409$, the number of inserted and deleted events would change to 89,807 and 8398, respectively. The number of inserts between *V1* and *V3* is not equal to the sum of inserted events at *V2* and *V3*, i.e., $89,807 \neq 68,060 + 23,369$ (=91,429). Apparently, some of the events inserted at *V2* were no longer considered inserts at *V3*. This implies that inserted events at *V2* that are deleted at *V3* would not have been visible in any event log, if log version *V2* had not been made.

Next, we investigated how the share of inserts, deletes, and updates influences the event log attributes for *Timestamp, Decision, Reason,* and *Amount.* The shares of inserted, updated, and deleted events at each reference timestamp are shown in Fig. 1. Even though the number of changes decreases at each consecutive reference timestamp (as can be seen in Table 1), inserted events remain the largest group of event log mutations. The share of deleted events increases over time for all these attributes. However, the share of updated events does not show the same pattern for each attribute. For the decision attribute, the number of updated events is almost equal to the number of deleted events. While for the other three attributes, updated events only rarely occur. From Fig. 1, it is clear that inserted, updated, and deleted events can influence attribute counts in different ways.

In addition to the different ways mutations are distributed across event attributes, the impact of changes can be different for each event log version. Figure 2 shows the relative change in each event log compared to event log *V1* for three metrics: new cases, ended cases, and average duration of an entitlement. This latter metric is only

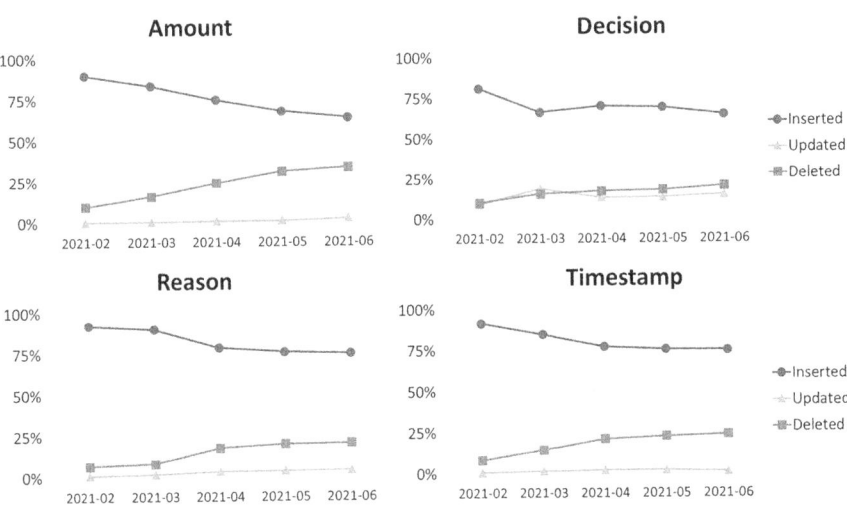

Fig. 1 The share of *inserted, updated,* and *deleted events* in each event log version for the event attributes

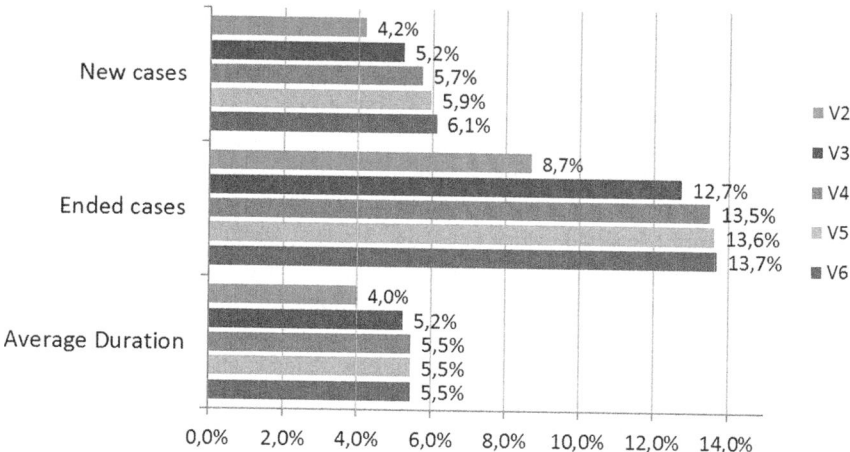

Fig. 2 Relative change in metric results compared to event log *V1*

calculated for cases that have ended. Figure 2 shows that *V6* has 6.1% more new cases than *V1*. *V2* contains 8.7% more closed cases than *V1*. The change in the average duration, compared to *V1*, stabilizes after 4 months (*V4*) at 5.5% longer. From an accountability perspective, reporting the state of the population at the end of each month complies with what is required. However, from a process analysis point of view, which is part of the BPM lifecycle (Dumas et al., 2018), not observing certain events and their effect on the metrics calculated is potentially harmful, especially when a decision is taken based on those metrics, because accounting for such changes may have led to different decisions. Existing process mining research conceptualizes event logs as append-only data streams (van der Aalst, 2016). As process activities are performed, events are recorded in the business process execution system and arrive in the event log for permanent storage. Though event data might arrive out of sequence, the log of events that have arrived is considered to be immutable (Awad et al., 2020). That is, data is assumed to flow along a linear path through time into a historical repository of events. Figure 3 represents such an immutable, append-only event log. These event logs allow for straightforward computation of aggregate results such as process models and KPIs. Though aggregate results may be updated when new events occur, previously computed aggregates over past time periods will no longer change.

The idea of immutable event logs, while conceptually sound, unfortunately, contrasts with most current real-world use cases of process mining and, in fact, with the observations from the case study. In reality, event logs are often generated a posteriori from business process execution systems using tailor-made queries or so-called *connectors* offered by commercial process mining solutions. These involve complex logic that extracts and joins together multiple source tables or even multiple source systems in order to derive events from flat data (González López de Murillas, 2019; Lu et al., 2015; Jans et al., 2019; Verbeek et al., 2010). Figure 4 represents the

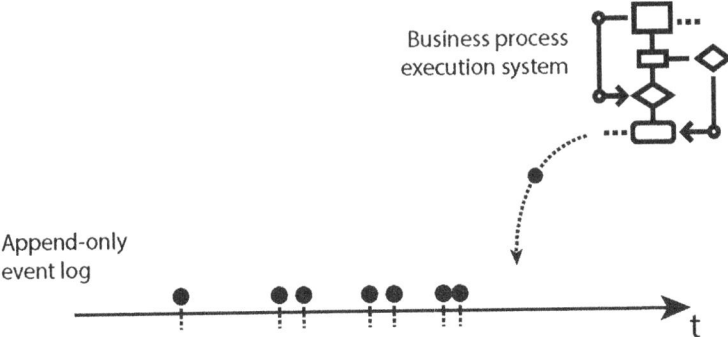

Fig. 3 Traditional process mining research conceptualizes event logs as immutable, append-only data streams. Dots represent events

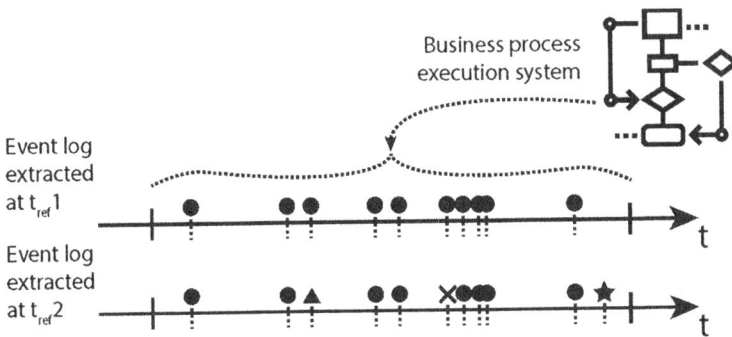

Fig. 4 The event log mutability problem visualized. Real-life event logs are extracted from information systems at reference timestamps using tailor-made queries. Dots represent events

situation where event logs are extracted from business process execution systems a posteriori. Note that in Fig. 4, data is only extracted as it was stored at the reference timestamps $t_{ref}1$ and $t_{ref}2$. Triangles, crosses, and stars represent inserted, updated, and deleted events, respectively, in the log created at $t_{ref}2$ compared with the log created at $t_{ref}1$. The reference timestamp has become an integral part of the event log creation process itself, in contrast to the situation in Fig. 3, where it merely represents the moment in time at which the event log is observed.

A problem arises from the fact that most business process execution systems do not incorporate a complete event log as they do not record all temporal changes. Rather, data is stored in nontemporal databases or—more typically—temporal changes are only recorded for a selection of key elements. Examples of business process execution systems that are often sourced for event data and do not store all temporal changes are SAP, Salesforce, and ServiceNow. For example, SAP installations typically store changes to a selection of elements in its central change tables. However, not all changes to SAP documents are maintained. Similarly, Salesforce stores changes to its first-class-citizen objects in per-object history tables. Again, only a selection of object property changes is recorded while changes to other properties are not stored. ServiceNow follows a similar design. Consequently, data elements for which changes are not recorded may cause differences between extracts made at different moments in time (i.e., reference timestamps). Unregistered and, therefore, unobserved events such as these may either be part of the process or be undesirable or non-permitted changes to the data that originate from outside of the business process context. In this work, we do not focus on the source of unrecorded and unobserved events. Instead, we look at their effect on event logs in general.

3 Action Taken

Analyzing business processes using process mining and related technologies and methodologies is a process in itself. As such, when using one of the mitigation strategies to redesign said process, trade-offs have to be made between time, quality, cost, and flexibility (Dumas et al., 2018). Once the event log mutability problem was identified and sufficiently analyzed, a project team was assembled, consisting of 4 data analysts from different UWV departments. Three potential mitigation strategies were devised to redesign the process, each at different degrees of technological complexity and required investment levels.

The first and preferred mitigation strategy is to modify the source system such that all historical data is maintained, thereby creating an immutable, append-only event log. The source system may store its data in event format directly or track changes to all (in-scope) database records. Regardless, the goal is to be able to recreate the state of the system as it was at any given point in time. In an SAP environment, for example, this would mean enabling the changelogs for all documents that are within the scope of the analysis. Similarly, in a Salesforce environment, this would mean enabling property change recordkeeping for in-scope objects. Though this mitigation strategy offers the most flexibility and requires little in terms of technological complexity and financial investment, it does require continuous synchronization efforts to maintain a full historical event log. When scope changes, it is vital to update the source system configuration to record related data changes. Additionally, this mitigation strategy may increase the load on the original system which could potentially impact system performance.

The second mitigation strategy keeps the source system and its underlying databases as is. Instead, an intermediate layer is added between the system and the event logs which is tasked with storing historical data. Changes in the source system can be tracked by monitoring its databases or internal archive logs. For example, Oracle databases keep a so-called redo-log which is a structure for recovery operations and consists of two or more pre-allocated files that store all changes made to the database as they occur. This strategy typically requires a sizeable investment in the form of additional logic or IT system(s) that need to be integrated within the existing IT landscape, therefore increasing the complexity of the overall solution. The extent of this financial and time investment depends on the details of the situation at hand. In this strategy, resource capacity can be provisioned, managed, and budgeted for separately, offering much in terms of flexibility while maintaining high data quality.

The third mitigation strategy is to store the extracted event log used for each analysis together with its results. This straightforward approach allows additional analyses to be executed on the same event data as the original analysis and facilitates their future validation. Furthermore, it complies with most audit requirements for the availability of source data. This strategy requires essentially no financial or time investment and does not add technological complexity. However, as it fails to aid the explanation of differences in data between extracted event logs made at different reference timestamps, it is the least qualitative, least flexible, and therefore, least desirable strategy and does not fully mitigate the problem.

At UWV, extracts of the business process execution system supporting the unemployment benefits process are created monthly, as described above. Any period of interest for analysis may only be observed at 1-month intervals (i.e., reference timestamps). As a result, changes to the observation period occurring between those timestamps remained unobserved. The business process execution system used in this process is considered legacy and as such warrants no new development efforts. However, the system already keeps track of all historic changes. Extractions can only be made from the system at weekly intervals because of the strain the extraction process places on the source system. The weekly exports, consisting of all mutations, are aggregated into a monthly data mart which is made available to the organization as a data mart in the UWV data warehouse.

As the source data for the monthly data mart consists of all mutations, the chosen event log mutability mitigation strategy is that of an intermediate historical data layer. Instead of using the monthly data mart for creating the event logs, a new data mart was constructed based on the weekly set of mutations from the information system. As each mutation has a mutation date and a validity start date, the state of each entitlement can be reconstructed at each moment in time. This layer also provides compliance with retention periods for this type of customer data. Although the implemented solution does not completely rule out unobserved events, it provides sufficient transparency into the process and its changes over time. Furthermore, the time and financial investment are modest and flexibility is high as there is no dependence on modification to the legacy source system. Finally, the insights into the event log mutability problem were actively shared within the organization through both the process mining working group and the newsletter.

4   Results Achieved

By structurally creating data extracts and event logs for the same observation period at different reference timestamps, we were able to identify the event log mutability problem. We realized the cause for this was that a significant number of events were inserted, updated, and deleted, between the different versions of the event log. Furthermore, we identified the accompanied risks by analyzing typical aggregate results created using event logs such as DFGs and performance metrics. We found differences in actual reported metrics and KPIs between the different event logs were much higher than anticipated and that action needed to be taken.

The project team considered the different mitigation strategies. Since the UWV source system already stored all historic mutations, no changes were needed to it. The project team decided, after considering the different mitigation strategies, to add a layer tasked for recording changes in the process data. The project team had the mandate and the business and data understanding necessary to design the new data layer. The chosen mitigation strategy allows UWV to maintain and analyze historical data in much greater detail. It allows event logs to be created that include events for changes to important process aspects, such as the unemployment benefit start and end dates, without modifying or straining the legacy source system.

Having a much more detailed recount of what historically happens to each entitlement has already been shown to have additional analysis benefits. For example, when a customer has to be transferred from one type of benefit to another, this can now be identified with more accuracy. The solution prevents the miscalculation of the benefits the customer is entitled to. Identifying this situation was not previously possible using event logs extracted from the monthly data mart. In addition to analyzing the unemployment benefits process itself, the intermediate layer has made it possible to analyze the process of mutating information related to the unemployment benefits process. This gave insight into the quality of the process of recording benefit-related information. Figures 1 and 2 also confirm that recorded information changes over time. The department responsible for managing the unemployment benefits process has been informed about our findings and started an investigation into the root causes of the unnecessary mutations.

5   Lessons Learned

In order to make analyses trustworthy, they should be repeatable and their results reliable and reproducible. As discussed above, the event log mutability problem that results from the current event log creation practices may prevent this. Business decisions that were taken based on insight gained from event log data might be invalidated when this data changes. Clearly, inaction is not a viable option. As such, three risk mitigation strategies were proposed. Undoubtedly, the first suggested strategy is the most desirable from a process analysis perspective as it supports the complete recollection of history and creation of event logs over the same observation period from multiple reference timestamps. The second and third strategies do not fully prevent the organization from missing unobserved events. However, these strategies may be desirable considering additional criteria.

In our case, the effort needed to realize the intermediate layer was considerable. First, a team of data engineers created an ETL (Extract Transform Load) process to load the raw data into the source layer of the data warehouse. Next, a team of data analysts created scripts to recreate the data mart using the loaded raw data. The result was tested and finally, the scripts were implemented in the business layer of the data warehouse. The whole effort involved three data engineers and four data analysts and took roughly 1 year of throughput time.

As a result of the findings discussed here, since becoming aware of the problem, our practice has also identified the event log mutability problem in other processes and organizations. Therefore, we have begun to include it as a primary concern in all our process mining projects and proactively discuss the associated risks and possible mitigation strategies before commencing a new project.

Organizations wondering whether they are affected by the event log mutability problem can follow a straightforward approach to verify if this is the case. For each process step in scope, one should verify whether all related changes to the data are indeed recorded. However, the optimal way to verify depends on the process and source system under investigation. Regardless of the system landscape, we advise extracting event logs of the same—sufficiently large—observation period at several reference timestamps and comparing the results using a method similar to that described in Sect. 2. This way, any unrecorded changes will show as inserted, updated, or deleted events and one of the described strategies can be implemented to mitigate the effects of the event log mutability.

The field of process mining has been growing rapidly in recent years. Many new techniques and technologies have been introduced for the analysis and monitoring of event data. Techniques to analyze the quality of event data in an event log are prevalent. Yet little research relates to the stability of event data over time as discussed in this paper. The current maturity level of process mining may yield problems that are related to and potentially even considered solved in other fields. Therefore, we expect a cross-pollination of methods and techniques from other domains to make their way into business process management. For example, it is our belief that the business process execution system that allows for the most detailed analysis of the processes it supports will prove most valuable to any organization concerned with data-driven process improvement. As such, we recommend novel business process execution systems to be developed following the event-sourcing and command-query-responsibility-segregation (CQRS) software design patterns (Pachecho, 2018). These patterns allow the different software components of the system to communicate using events, which can then be easily stored in an immutable, append-only event store. This design combines well with modern software design principles such as separation of concerns and micro-services architecture. Nonetheless, event log mutability will continue to be a core responsibility of the process mining analyst.

References

Awad, A., Weidlich, M., & Sakr, S. (2020). Process mining over unordered event streams. In *2020 2nd international conference on process mining (ICPM)* (pp. 81–88). https://doi.org/10.1109/ICPM49681.2020.00022

Dumas, M., La Rosa, M., Mendling, J., & Reijers, H. (2018). *Fundamentals of business process management* (2nd ed.). Springer. https://doi.org/10.1007/978-3-662-56509-4

González López de Murillas, E. (2019). *Process mining on databases: Extracting event data from real-life data sources.* Eindhoven University of Technology. ISBN:978-90-386-4704-3.

Jans, M., Soffer, P., & Jouck, T. (2019). Building a valuable event log for process mining: An experimental exploration of a guided process. *Enterprise Information Systems, 15*(5), 601–630. https://doi.org/10.1080/17517575.2019.1587788

Lu, X., Nagelkerke, M., van de Wiel, D., & Fahland, D. (2015). Discovering interacting artifacts from {ERP} systems. *IEEE Transactions on Services Computing, 8*(6), 861–873.

Pachecho, V. (2018). *Microservice patterns and best practices: Explore patterns like CQRS and event sourcing to create scalable, maintainable, and testable microservices.* Packt Publishing Ltd.

van der Aalst, W. (2016). *Process mining – Data science in action* (2nd ed.). Springer. https://doi.org/10.1007/978-3-662-49851

Verbeek, H., Buijs, J., van Dongen, B., & van der Aalst, W. (2010). XES, XESame, and ProM 6. (P. Soffer, & E. Proper, Eds.) (LNBIP, Vol. 72, pp. 60–75). https://doi.org/10.1007/978-3-642-17722-4_5.

Bart Hompes is a process optimization professional and PhD candidate at the Eindhoven University of Technology. Until 2018, he was co-founder and CTO of Aviliz. His research areas include process mining, business process management, and data science. Bart has (co-)authored over a dozen research articles and several book chapters. In his daily practice, he helps organizations obtain value from their data.

Marcus Dees is a customer intelligence analyst at UWV, the Social Security Institute of the Netherlands. In his work, Marcus connects present-day business problems with academic research in the business process management and the process mining domain.

From Process Mining to Thinking Assistants in Logistics

Joost van Montfort, Hilda Fabiola Bernard, and Dirk Fahland

Abstract

(a) *Situation faced*: Vanderlande Industries BV, or Vanderlande for short (VI), is a global market leader for end-to-end material handling solutions (MHS) increasing customer expectations regarding system performance while also increasing system capabilities and complexities. Although process mining fundamentally enables data-driven insight into the causes of performance problems, preexisting process mining technology assumed that processes were single object and executed in isolation. However, MHS are complex multilayered systems with multi-object processes that operate across shared equipment. Thus, despite its potential, VI's engineers found very limited room for improving MHS performance through classical process mining.

(b) *Action taken*: VI initiated and funded a long-term research collaboration between VI's process engineers and data scientists and TU Eindhoven's (TU/e's) process mining research group involving the authors. After receiving access to system data, users, and use cases, we followed the design science research method to develop and validate novel process mining techniques and tools that provide VI engineers with the information they need to increase system performance.

(c) *Results achieved*: We developed several novel process mining techniques and tools that overcome the limitation of classical process mining by analyzing all cases and their interdependencies within a system together over both time and shared equipment. Validation through case studies confirmed the effectiveness of the tools and several tools are now being industrialized. The overall insights

J. van Montfort · H. F. Bernard
Vanderlande BV, Veghel, The Netherlands
e-mail: Joost.van.Montfort@vanderlande.com; Hilda.Bernard@vanderlande.com

D. Fahland (✉)
Eindhoven University of Technology, Eindhoven Artificial Intelligence Systems Institute, Eindhoven, The Netherlands
e-mail: d.fahland@tue.nl

J. vom Brocke et al. (eds.), *Business Process Management Cases Vol. 3*,
https://doi.org/10.1007/978-3-031-80793-0_6

from the project led to the development of the concept of a "thinking assistant" that supports operators in decision-making.

(d) *Lessons learned*: The joint collaboration between industry and research not only enabled the development of a paradigm shift in process mining research, it also facilitated a transition from standard industry tooling for process mining to custom solutions designed for specific use cases. We also identified several large research challenges for process mining directly driven by customer needs.

1 Introduction

Vanderlande (VI) provides automated *material handling solutions (MHS)* for major airports and parcel and warehouse companies around the world. Vanderlande is a global market leader for end-to-end integrated solutions, including hardware, (intelligent) software, and lifecycle services. The projects executed vary heavily in complexity and size. The bigger projects can involve up to 20 km of conveyors, hold over 150K individual storage locations, and have multiple concurrent complex processes handling over 100K items a day and facilities covering a footprint of over 100K square meters.

It is Vanderlande's mission to *"Improve the competitiveness of our customers through future-proof logistic process automation."* This entails continuous investment in innovation that improves end-user experience, flexibility, scalability, reliability, and efficiency of Vanderlande's solutions over the entire end-to-end logistics process and life cycle. Vanderlande's mission is further pushed and accelerated by ongoing (global) trends such as labor scarcity, sustainability, and increasing customer expectations of proactiveness and predictability. These factors push Vanderlande to continuously gratify and simplify the operators' working environment by including solutions that also offer decision support.

In combination, these aims inspired VI to augment engineers and system operators with advanced process analytics and prediction technology. The ambition was to develop a "thinking assistant" that enabled engineers and operators to make better decisions in their (remote) daily work resulting in enhanced system performance for VI's customers.

A cornerstone in this ambition was to leverage the rich event data recorded in Vanderlande's systems using process mining (PM) technology. However, the traditional PM perspective on events in one case alone was not living up to customers' expectations and was not effective for VI's engineers. In a long-term research collaboration, a team of researchers from TU Eindhoven and VI, including the authors, developed and adopted new PM techniques that were able to consider thousands of material items traversing equipment at the same time. These techniques enabled us to detect and analyze the complex interplay between equipment, items, processes, and operators. Operationalizing these insights enhances the ability of VI's engineers and operators to ensure each bag makes it to its flight.

2 Situation Faced

A *material handling solution* (MHS) is a semiautomatic system for the short-range movement, sorting, processing, short-term storage, and distribution of items. It consists of various (semi)automatic and manual processing stations connected by automated conveyor belts. Typical examples include *baggage handling systems* (BHSs), which are the focus of the following case study, in addition to automated warehouses and distribution centers, and parcel and postage sorting and distribution systems.

Driven by increasing end-customer expectations of same-day deliveries, transparency, predictability, and flexibility, MHSs are becoming more complex from both a system design and system control perspective. In addition, VI's own project execution and systems are pushed to their limits due to the increasing growth of logistics demand and customers' expectations of service level agreements are increasing. It was determined that if it could be attuned to Vanderlande's specific company and industry needs, process mining could offer a solution for overcoming these challenges. As a starting point, Vanderlande investigated where in the end-to-end life cycle of VI's systems a process mining solution could benefit customers and the internal organizations.

Figure 1 shows the typical life cycle of a Vanderlande system indicating where the main opportunities for process mining were. Opportunities were identified throughout the entire life cycle, with the most direct and promising use cases in the operational phase.

However, MHSs have different characteristics than the processes typically addressed by traditional process mining. As Fig. 2 depicts, an MHS consists of various processes and objects that are managed by a hierarchical control system.

Examples of the various processes in a BHS that take place at an airport include check-in, transport, (manual) identification, (security) screening, sorting, loading into a container, and loading into the aircraft. These processes are not only

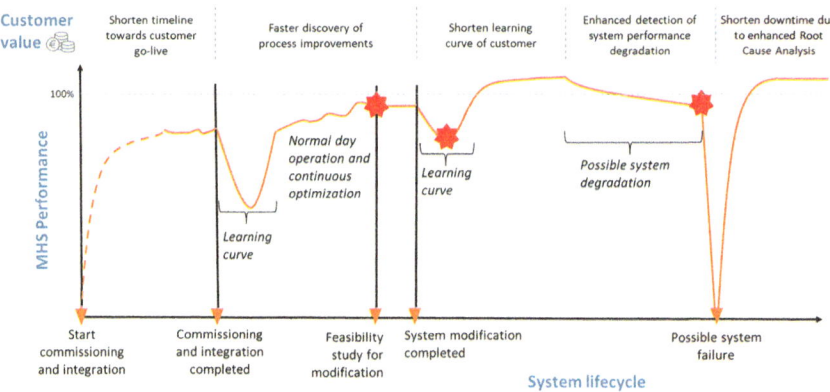

Fig. 1 Typical Vanderlande system life cycle with process mining opportunities

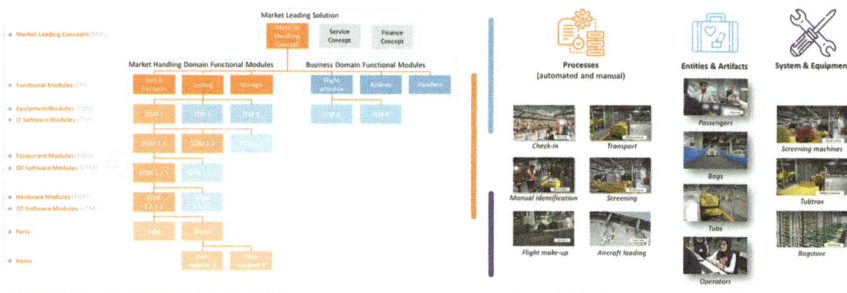

Controls hierarchy of Material Handling System   Material Handling processes and objects

Fig. 2 Typical processes and objects in a material handling system

dependent on each other but on various objects through direct interactions and the periphery of the BHS, such as operators, passengers, individual carriers that carry bags over longer distances with enhanced accuracy, and the (individual) bag(s).

Like a traffic accident on a congested road network, a small disruption within such a system and/or business context has a big impact. Although they rarely occur, situations in which (part of the) system comes to a stop unfortunately do happen and their greatest impact is on the customers.

Hence, Vanderlande's first use case was to compare traditional process mining to VI's established analysis methods in a retrospective one-off root cause analysis of an incident at a large European airport. The established analysis was performed by VI's process engineers who are responsible for the continuous optimization of the system performance at customer sites. These are highly trained and analytically savvy professionals who can perform root cause analysis and explain the outcome and complex system behavior in a manner that customers understand. The challenge was whether the same analysis could be executed faster and by less trained people using traditional process mining techniques. This initial analysis was very fruitful as it proved the potential of process mining techniques in the logistics domain. However, the traditional techniques were not living up to customers' and engineers' expectations of transparency, user-friendliness, and, above all, predictability in providing insight.

3 Action Taken

To provide Vanderlande engineers with actionable insight into the systems, VI initiated and funded a long-term research collaboration with Eindhoven University of Technology (TU/e) that began in 2016. The authors (subsequently "we") managed this collaboration which involved:

- Two fully co-funded 4-year PhD positions in the process mining research group[1] who provided 15 years experience in research into and the development of new process mining techniques.
- A (growing) team of Vanderlande data scientists who were developing, shepherding, and expanding the use and deployment of data-driven analysis techniques and machine learning within Vanderlande.
- A team of Vanderlande process engineers who were willing to engage with new data-driven analysis methods and tools (even in the form of prototypes) in the context of their own work at customer sites.
- Sponsorship from Vanderlande's leadership team.

The collaboration had a warm-up phase of 6 months and an active research and development phase according to information system design science research methods (Peffers et al., 2007).

During the warm-up phase, we jointly explored the value and capabilities of existing process mining technology through a number of use cases based on data from customer sites. The objective of this phase was to establish a common language and understanding between the domains of MHS and process mining. We considered the general and specific characteristics of individual MHS, the available event data previously recorded by the Vanderlande systems, industrial and academic process mining techniques, the typical use cases encountered by VI's engineers when working on customer sites, and how VI's engineers could be supported by process mining analysis questions.

To achieve this objective, we conducted exploratory case studies of several customer sites of varying complexity. We consolidated the findings in a series of workshops with VI's process engineers. We defined and prioritized analysis use cases by identifying what information is required to deliver additional value (in time gained and costs saved) to VI's process engineers and customers in various situations, then analyzed how existing process mining techniques addressed (or rather did not address) these use cases.

In the subsequent research and development phase, the project operated in three streams, research (TU/e), validation (VI engineers), and productization (VI data scientists), that we kept aligned using an agile process with biweekly sprints. Sprint reviews focused on knowledge exchange about current research concepts (research stream), design and properties of VI's systems or specific customer sites and engineer experience (validation), and value propositions (productization). The sprints facilitated the following cyclical research and development process.

First, we jointly selected the use cases to work on based on the findings of the warm-up phase. We then clarified the solution requirements, specifically which information a solution could add value, either for the engineer or for the customer.

The research stream set out to develop techniques to extract this information from the data available while giving freedom to how the information should be

---

[1] Officially called "Architecture of Information Systems" led by Wil M.P. van der Aalst in 2016; renamed to "Process Analytics" in 2020 led by Boudewijn F. van Dongen.

presented. As the use cases (i.e., analyses of the causes of performance problems) were fundamentally different from problems typically addressed in process mining (i.e., identifying outlier paths), research activities involved extensive data exploration and visualization to ideate new concepts for modeling and visualizing MHS dynamics. We realized research ideas in software prototypes which we demonstrated on large-scale real-life datasets during sprint reviews. The validation allowed the research stream to iteratively improve the fit with the intended use cases and helped the validation and productization stream plan of their activities and onboard stakeholders.

The matured research prototypes were documented and handed over to the productization and validation stream, then to train skilled process engineers for their use. Process engineers applied the prototypes in specific case studies in small-scale projects at customer sites with the aim of assessing their effectiveness in an industrial context. The findings then either initiated a new research cycle for this technique or moved the technique to productization. The productization stream then used the prior design and evaluation insights to develop a software solution using VI's development processes. This solution was validated again and further improved through their application by Vanderlande engineers at customer sites.

Evaluation cycles of research and product prototypes exposed process engineers and customers to new visualizations and analyses of MHS, which regularly unlocked new analysis questions and objectives. Specifically, after foundational research results were established, new use cases were successfully addressed in 6-month master projects at TU/e.

4   Results Achieved

The long-running nature of the collaboration had a transformational effect on problem understanding, the scope of use cases, and process mining research and techniques—with developments in the latter significantly expanding the former.

We developed new visualization and analytical techniques for detecting performance outliers, enabling benchmarking of equipment and systems (Köroglu, 2019), and detecting outlier cascades that led to dynamic bottlenecks (Toosinezhad et al., 2022), thus enabling process engineers to perform root cause analysis quickly.

With a growing awareness of the most recent research at Vanderlande and an enhanced business domain understanding at the TU/e, these initial steps prepared us for more advanced use cases focused on:

1. *Reducing the commissioning and integration time of our systems*, i.e., "Does our system meet the agreed-upon in-system times?" or "Where are the bottlenecks in the system expected and can they be overcome using an enhanced system configuration?"

2. *Enhancing our consultancy services with more advanced analytics capabilities*: "Can we detect underperforming process steps?" "Are our systems properly balanced so we are working at maximum system capacity?"
3. *Providing decision support to (remote) control room operators responsible for the daily monitoring and control of our systems*, i.e., "What could we do so this baggage item will make it to its flight on time?"

These use cases propelled our research and prototypes toward advanced analytics. We extended the object-centric process mining paradigm by adopting knowledge graphs to integrate system design models, equipment configuration, and event data from multiple, interconnected processes. This multidimensional representation of an entire MHS enables interconnected analysis of material transport and logistics processes, routing, and equipment behavior. Subsequent application at a large European airport led to the identification of routing rules that negatively impacted performance in a different part of the system (Chu, 2022). Such capabilities allowed VI to reduce commissioning and integration time enabling the acceleration of the go-live time for the customer and the ramp-up period after the go-live.

Next, we report how the technical results generated value for three different use cases and how they culminated in the concept of the "thinking assistant."

4.1 System Map Visualization: Reducing Time to Insight Gained

Vanderlande's test and integration engineers are responsible for integrating all control layers of the baggage handling solution at each customer's site and ensuring the optimal performance of the system at go-live. To achieve this goal, they design and execute a series of tests in the system under deployment to observe where system performance still needs to improve the time to go-live.

The tracking event data recording the movement of bags in the system enabled a data-driven analysis of points of attention. While classical exploratory data analysis and classical process mining enabled computing relevant KPIs and the visualization of the flow of bags in the system and potential bottlenecks, both techniques failed to contextualize analysis results in the overall system design. For instance, process maps discovered from tracking event data have thousands of nodes in an automatically generated layout while engineers were used to designing and planning actions using system design diagrams. The amount of information and the lack of alignment with context information slowed engineers seeking insights.

To help engineers understand test results faster, we developed a *system map visualization*. It overlays the process map generated by process mining on the system design diagram as shown in Fig. 3. Compared to a process map, the system map visualizes performance information in the context of the system design, which enables engineers to relate performance problems visualized in specific areas to the underlying equipment. This enabled the engineers to detect suboptimal

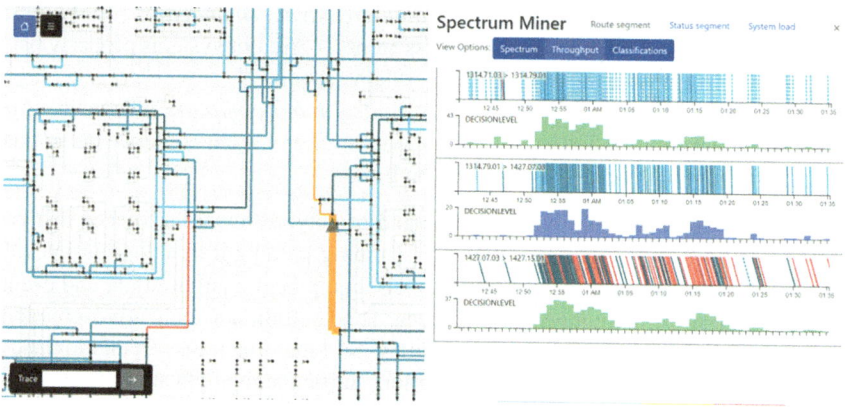

Fig. 3 System map and performance spectrum

configurations in different parts of the system more quickly as fewer tests were required to design, plan, execute, and analyze the process. This has led to the following feedback from VI's test/integration engineers: "Would not have found these issues otherwise" and "Reduced time analyzing missing reports. Over time, the time gained is exponential!!!" This demonstrates that the availability of system maps as an analysis tool reduced the internal costs for Vanderlande and led to earlier go-live times for customers, strengthening their business case for automation.

4.2 Performance Spectrum: Understanding System Behavior

Vanderlande's process engineers are responsible for the continuous optimization of the system after go-live and support customers becoming acquainted with their systems. Completing this task requires process engineers who are fully familiar with the system's overall behavior and how the system's behavior is affecting the process. Thus, the engineer must be able to understand how the system responds to gradual or sudden changes in load, for example, in peak traffic moments, as well as where, how, and why performance problems arise and affect bags. Moreover, the engineer must be able to communicate this understanding to customers who do not have the same technical background as the engineer.

Classical process and system maps can reveal process steps with low performance, for example, by highlighting edges with on-average higher processing times or by animating the movement of cases over process and system maps (Leemans et al., 2014). While instrumental in providing an overview of the system, these techniques did not perform as expected in generating understanding of any temporary changes, drifts, and short-term bottlenecks that are often hidden by global averages and are difficult to locate in an animation (Denisov et al., 2018). The techniques also failed to convey how performance problems in different parts of the system were related (Toosinezhad et al., 2022).

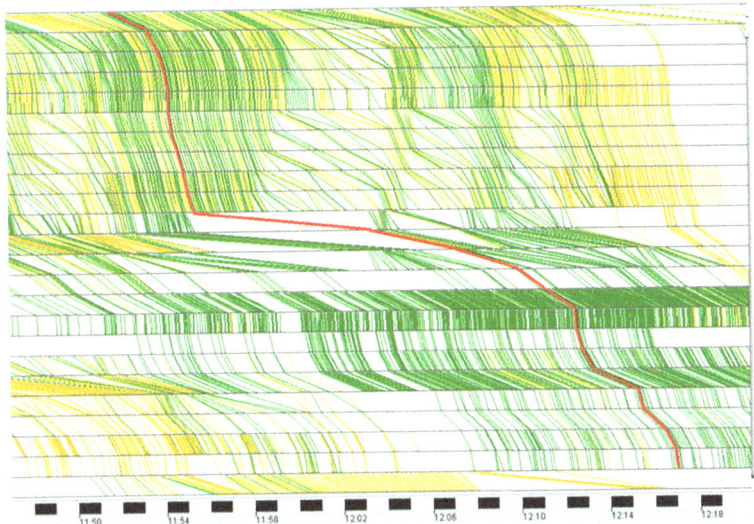

Fig. 4 Performance spectrum from a maximum load test

To enable analysis and visualization of time-bounded performance phenomena, we developed a visual analytics technique called the *performance spectrum*, which maps the movement of cases, for example, bags in the system, as shown in Fig. 4.

We implemented the performance spectrum using an interactive tool with an intuitive UI for visualizing how the underlying equipment, such as conveyor belts, handles cases over time. The tool then intuitively visualizes the characteristics and changes in load, processing time, and transport times. With this tool, we were able to locate the causes of performance problems in large-scale baggage handling systems without relying on experts with intimate knowledge of the underlying system or multiple years of experience. The integration of the performance spectrum with the system map, shown in Fig. 5, facilitates the process engineers' conversations with the customer about the system and its performance that are supported by the underlying data. This transparency builds trust and intimacy. Feedback from the process engineers emphasized that "We showed bags to customers in the process mining application and they really like the way we showed the information."

4.3 Knowledge Graphs: Integration of Multiple Processes

Vanderlande's integration engineers are responsible for configuring the system, including routing and load balancing rules, to ensure optimal performance for the customer, both at and after the system go-live point. Optimizing routing and load balancing requires understanding, integrating, and improving multiple interrelated processes, such as item transport processes, resource allocation, and routing processes, as well as equipment behavior including maintenance, failure, and recovery.

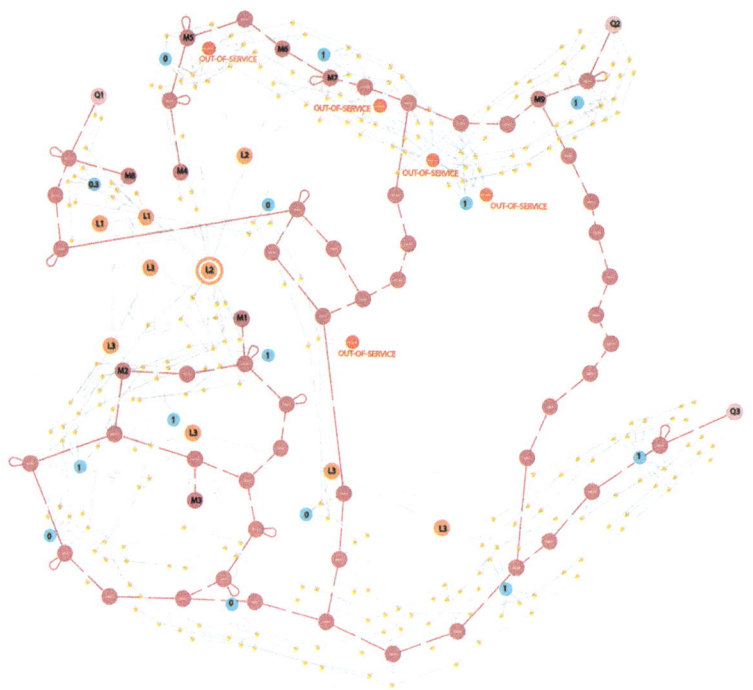

Fig. 5 Part of an event knowledge graph of a baggage handling system

Understanding where and how one of these processes negatively impacts another process is a time-consuming task that requires guidance and support in order to locate the root causes in configurations that cause suboptimal performance.

To overcome the limitations of classical process mining techniques that are limited to analyzing a single process, we adapted event knowledge graphs (Fahland, Process Mining over Multiple Behavioral Dimensions with Event Knowledge Graphs, 2022b) in order to integrate and model the event data of multiple processes together with the system design diagrams in a common data model (Chu, 2022).

Using the graph database system Neo4j, we automatically constructed event knowledge graphs for several larger airports by integrating existing data sources. We were able to leverage graph-based querying and graph visualization for faster exploration of specific dynamics of interest and determining how these originate in resource allocation and routing processes as shown in Fig. 5. Their visualization proved intuitive for integration engineers to understand after a short introduction. Furthermore, graph-based querying and aggregation facilitated the rapid implementation of existing key performance indicators (KPIs) and the development of new KPIs, which was previously a more time-consuming task (Chu, 2022).

Feedback from the integration engineers highlighted that the event knowledge graph provided new insight into several KPIs and the underlying dynamics for which the integration engineers are responsible, such as the efficiency of various processes. It also supported analysis tasks they already performed providing insight that helped identify actions for optimizing system performance: "This helped us find where tubs were being routed incorrectly and adjust the software configuration to prioritize/penalize certain actions."

4.4 Thinking Assistants: Integration and Proactive Service

The results described in the preceding use cases were achieved by integrating various event data sources with domain knowledge and explicitly modeling multiple processes and interconnected dynamics over time. While effective in their own right, these techniques increase the amount and complexity of information an engineer or operator has to engage with. This raises the need for proactive services that support operators and help them see, in any given situation, the relevant information for understanding which problems exist, what causes them, and how to resolve them.

To address this need, we developed the research concept we called the "thinking assistant." The thinking assistant can be considered an example of an AI-augmented process management system (Dumas et al., 2022). It defines, at its core, a system knowledge graph that organizes object and event data from the various processes and equipment in the system in multiple interconnected layers, grounded on system design information as shown in Fig. 6.

The system knowledge graph can be enriched with further information through pattern detection and forecasting models, for instance, cascades of undesired emergent system behavior like load peaks or blockages that propagate over the

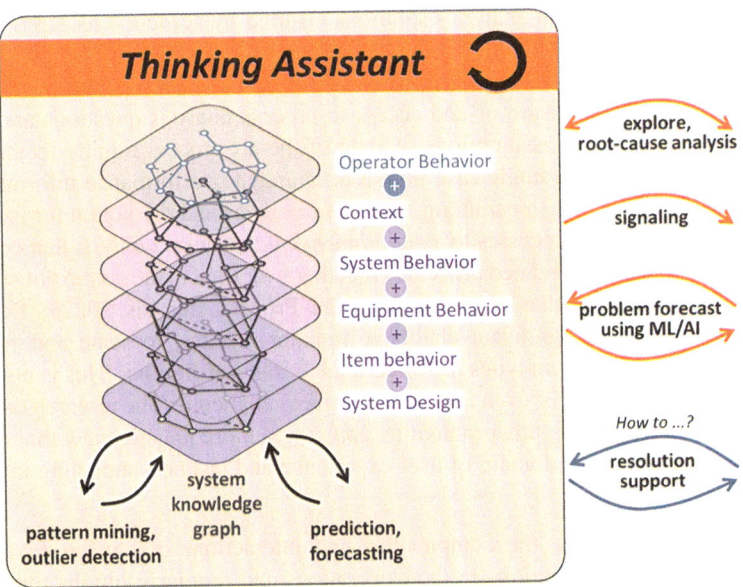

Fig. 6 Thinking assistant concept

system and affect unrelated cases (Toosinezhad et al., 2022). The engineer or operator is notified about undesirable behavior (Köroglu, 2019) and can explore the situation through graph querying (Chu, 2022). The operator can invoke forecasting algorithms and models of the integrated data to get insights into how the system may behave in the near future. Any resolution actions initiated by the operator are recorded and can be recommended in similar situations in the future based on their effectiveness in handling the situation.

In the mid and long term, the increased predictability enables us to offer high-value-adding proactive services such as (remote) monitoring and optimization services. In this phase, we are currently building prototypes that allow us to empathize with Vanderlande's end customers. Some initial responses from OEM support engineers were as follows: "I think this is really great. It can help us as Vanderlande process engineers but, in the end, also the control room operator. The operators have to use five screens to find out what is wrong and go through them, step by step, to collect bits and pieces of information. If this could pinpoint what bag a flight is waiting for and what the alternatives are, they can make much faster decisions."

5 Lessons Learned

The significant advancements in Vanderlande's capabilities to improve system performance are the results of two key factors. A decisive, long-term commitment to a research collaboration with a process mining research group enabled the development of an entirely new process mining technology that targets the unique process challenges of logistics. The willingness to transition from mainstream process mining technology to custom analytics solutions inspired by academic research prototypes ensured increased adoption by engineers and operators for solving their highly complex tasks.

Conversely, the exposure of and access to process analysis questions and data that did not satisfy the assumptions of state-of-the-art process mining techniques (such as the focus on a single case notion or aggregate performance information) was essential in realizing a paradigm shift from analysis and prediction for isolated cases in single-object processes to a *multidimensional process analysis* that considers all cases of multiple related processes together over time in the context of system design information (Fahland, Multi-dimensional Process Analysis, 2022a). Beyond this advancement, a significant challenge remains. That is to scale and further embed the successful prototypes in Vanderlande's daily operations. This is not only a technical challenge; it is, even more so, a business challenge. The research domain can contribute to solving this problem by applying a more holistic view that incorporates expertise in the domain of user experience and business modeling into the equation:

1. Customers recognize the complexities and interactions of *various layers* of material handling solutions in their operations and require solutions that opti-

mize and increase *overall system performance*. Closing this gap requires further research techniques that reflect reality and are able to model and visualize system complexity *as it is*, for example, through object-centric process mining (Aalst, 2019) and multidimensional process mining (Fahland, Multi-dimensional Process Analysis, 2022a).

2. Users are very much interested in decision support and automation, i.e., the integration of predictions into their operational systems. When showing how predictions could be integrated into their UI (decision support), customers confirm that integrating this intelligence directly into the system (decision automation) is preferred.

3. For decision support and decision automation to become a reality, process mining and the underlying techniques need to become *(near) real time*. For decision support, a latency of seconds is acceptable. For decision automation, milliseconds are preferred.

4. Most existing process mining visualizations are abstract models of reality. It is mentally difficult to overlay this data onto actual physical processes, especially when considering the high data volume found in logistics environments. Enhanced visualization will accelerate the use of process mining beyond the administrative domain.

Acknowledgments We thank Wil M.P. van der Aalst for his vital role in initiating and advising this collaboration and Shane O'Seasnáin for planting and nurturing the seeds of the "thinking assistant" concept.

References

Aalst, W. M. (2019). Object-centric process mining: Dealing with divergence and convergence in event data. In *SEFM* (pp. 3–25). Springer.

Chu, V. (2022). *Using event knowledge graphs to model multi-dimensional dynamics in a baggage handling system*. Eindhoven University of Technology.

Denisov, V., Fahland, D., & Aalst, W. M. (2018). Unbiased, fine-grained description of processes performance from event data. In *BPM* (pp. 139–157). Springer.

Dumas, M., Fournier, F., Limonad, L., Marrella, A., Montali, M., Rehse, J.-R., et al. (2022). AI-augmented business process management systems: A research manifesto. *ACM Transactions on Management Information Systems, 14*(1), 1–19.

Fahland, D. (2022a). Multi-dimensional process analysis. In *BPM* (pp. 27–33). Springer.

Fahland, D. (2022b). Process mining over multiple behavioral dimensions with event knowledge graphs. In J. Carmona & W. M. Aalst (Eds.), *Process mining handbook* (pp. 273–319). Springer.

Köroglu, Ö. (2019). *Outlier detection in event logs of material handling system*. Eindhoven University of Technology.

Leemans, S. J., Fahland, D., & Aalst, W. M. (2014). Process and deviation exploration with inductive visual miner. In *BPM (Demos)* (pp. 46–50). Springer.

Peffers, K., Tuunanen, T., Rothenberger, M., & Chatterjee, S. (2007). A design science research methodology for information systems research. *Journal of Management Information Systems, 24*(3), 45–77.

Toosinezhad, Z., Fahland, D., Köroglu, Ö., & Aalst, W. M. (2022). Detecting system-level behavior leading to dynamic bottlenecks. In *ICPM* (pp. 17–24). Springer.

Joost van Montfort is the service design lead of Vanderlande's digital service factory. With a background in industrial engineering and management science, his passion for data was aroused during a multiyear assignment at London Heathrow. Afterward, he established the data science and data service development team, which is now accelerated as the Digital Service Factory within Vanderlande's technology department. It aims to connect Vanderlande's global installed base and leverage the data obtained to create new insight and digital solutions for Vanderlande's customers. He builds bridges between technology and business, accelerating Vanderlande's service journey by developing new digital solutions. These focus on continuously improving the operational performance of Vanderlande's systems and enhancing the operational, tactical, and strategic decision-making at customer sites. Given the complex nature of Vanderlande's systems and the hundreds of decisions made per day by a multitude of operators in various domains, "thinking assistants" are considered necessary to the realization of Vanderlande's ambition.

Hilda Fabiola Bernard is a Senior Product Owner in Vanderlande's Digital Service Platform. She has a background in Software Engineering and Data Science. She worked as a Software Engineer, building prototypes and first-time implementations of healthcare products, where she discovered the field of data science. To follow this passion, she moved to the Netherlands to pursue a master's degree in computer science, specializing in Data Science at Eindhoven University of Technology(TU/e). Her interest in Process Mining and Process Optimization techniques led her on a journey in the process science world with TU/e and Vanderlande, including a short stint as a PhD student (for one year) and later as a data scientist at Vanderlande. With work experience as a software engineer and data scientist, and her passion for building solutions based on business needs, she is currently leveraging her experience to build software for data science that supports the optimization of Vanderlande systems' processes. With the move to more proactive solutions, these tools and techniques are crucial for Vanderlande's success.

Dirk Fahland is an associate professor in process analytics on multidimensional event data at Eindhoven University of Technology (TU/e). His research area is the analysis and improvement of complex, distributed systems through event data, process mining, and explainable models. Dirk has contributed to research in process management and mining since 2008 in over 80 journal, conference, and workshop publications with foundational results in process modeling, discovery, analysis, and repair. His current research specifically studies cause-effect relations and emergent behavior in networks and dynamic systems as a whole. The insight gained through numerous industrial projects led to the idea of encoding behavioral information in event knowledge graphs, a cornerstone of a new generation of "augmented BPM systems."

Process Mining in Textile Production: Insights from Penn Textile Solutions

Tobias Brockhoff, Merih Seran Uysal, Anahita Farhang Ghahfarokhi,
Leon Reinsch, Thomas Kordtokrax, Andreas Meister, Franz Schütte,
Tugsan Vural, Mahsa Pourbafrani, Thomas Gries,
and Wil M. P. van der Aalst

Abstract

(a) *Situation faced*: In the textile industry, each individual manufacturing step is typically highly optimized. Nevertheless, inter-manufacturing step dependencies usually have great potential for further optimization. Penn Textile Solutions GmbH collects its manufacturing event data in a dedicated database on the completion of each manufacturing step. However, the data are not used to generate a holistic view of the process. In this study, we apply process mining to leverage the data, generate insights, and visualize a manufacturing production process that is focused on a single machine—the tenter frame.

(b) *Action taken*: We first focused on measuring working hour-aware time intervals (i.e., not considering off days and holidays). Then we split the analysis phase into two major parts—the manufacturing process and the quality control process. We then analyzed both parts using process models as a structuring element. For the manufacturing process analysis, we first conducted a working hour-aware analysis of lead times, process times, and machine utilization. Using a hybrid discovery approach, we discovered a process model at the

Funded by the Deutsche Forschungsgemeinschaft (DFG, German Research Foundation) under Germany's Excellence Strategy-EXC-2023 Internet of Production-390621612. We also thank the Alexander von Humboldt (AvH) Stiftung for supporting our research.

T. Brockhoff (✉) · M. S. Uysal · A. F. Ghahfarokhi · M. Pourbafrani · W. M. P. van der Aalst
Process and Data Science, RWTH Aachen University, Aachen, Germany
e-mail: brockhoff@pads.rwth-aachen.de; uysal@pads.rwth-aachen.de; mahsa.bafrani@pads.rwth-aachen.de; wvdaalst@pads.rwth-aachen.de

L. Reinsch · T. Gries
Institute for Textile Technology, RWTH Aachen University, Aachen, Germany
e-mail: thomas.gries@ita.rwth-aachen.de

T. Kordtokrax · A. Meister · F. Schütte · T. Vural
Penn Textile Solutions GmbH, Paderborn, Germany
e-mail: t.kordtokrax@penn-ts.com; a.meister@penn-ts.com; f.schuette@penn-ts.com; t.vural@penn-ts.com

machine level, used it to define production stages, and investigated the latter in more detail. Finally, we analyzed the quality process based on a model-induced case classification.

(c) *Results achieved*: We successfully created a process model that described the manufacturing process well. Using this model, we compared cases within and between production stages. While we were able to identify critical stages, the analysis revealed significant variance that was not straightforward to explain, even when taking the impact of COVID-19 into account. The accompanying analyses of resource load, idle times, process time, and lead times were an initial means of making machine utilization accessible. Our results sparked discussions, and by comparing results, we were able to identify the bottlenecks.

(d)*Lessons learned*: Closely integrating stakeholders helped us define realistic, realizable goals. While presenting intermediate results increased trust and understanding in the subsequent stages, it also led to interesting, unexpected discussions. Regarding the application of process mining, we found it helpful to structure the analysis using process models. However, we also recognized the limitations of existing techniques to analyze flexible processes at a detailed level. A major challenge we overcame was how to map the process in a way that took the production context into account so that we could better classify the results.

1 Introduction

The textile industry is one of the oldest industrial sectors, providing work for millions of people worldwide (Annapoorani, 2017). While most of the production has been relocated to Asia, Europe is still the leader in high-quality, special textiles, and digitalization and Industry 4.0 have been identified as key enablers for sustaining its leading role (Kemper et al., 2017). While the individual process steps are highly optimized, a holistic view of the process chain has the potential to identify further opportunities for optimization. Despite this, adoption has been slow (Kemper et al., 2017). In this case study, we investigate the application of process mining techniques to analyze the textile production process at Penn Textile Solutions GmbH (Penn). Penn is a German manufacturer producing innovative textiles to meet the demands of international customers. The production at Penn covers each step between the rolls of yarn and the finished textiles. However, the scope of this work is limited to the treatment of the knitted textile and the final quality control stage.

As described in van der Aalst (2016), traditional process mining is based on *event logs*, that is, on collections of so-called *events*. Each *event* is a recording containing information on three major concepts: A *case notion*—in our case, a textile ID—links events to a business case. An *activity notion*, in our case manufacturing operations, describes what has been done, and a *timestamp*, here the time when a manufacturing operation was performed, provides an order for the events. Following these concepts, a high-level, schematic illustration of the production is depicted in

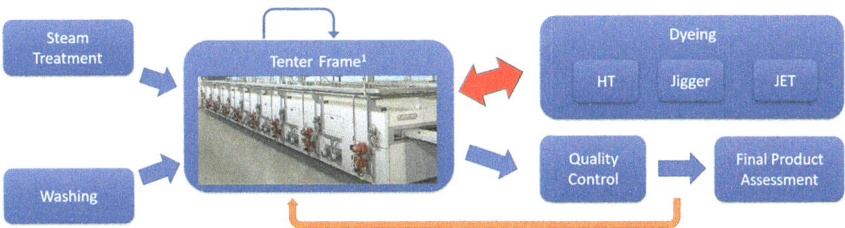

Fig. 1 Schematic illustration of the main production steps at PS. Operations performed at different machines frequently involve processing at the tenter frame (http://www.fi-tech.com/View. aspx?page=textilesproducts/tenterframesandovens). The arrows depict typical process flows. The tenter frame is used repeatedly within each case

Fig. 1. It shows the tenter frame as the central machine involved in various production steps. Two important subprocesses are dyeing, where we can distinguish between different modes, and quality control, where the textiles and colors are tested. Notably, the tenter frame is used multiple times within each case.

We applied process mining to analyze the performance of the production and quality control processes. Moreover, Penn was particularly interested in how the required rework, as determined during quality control, affects the manufacturing process. In the long term, the insight generated can be used to improve the scheduling of orders and reduce setup costs and lead times. As depicted in Fig. 1, a major challenge to answering these questions lies in the tight coupling between machines and activities. The tenter frame is required for multiple production steps for each textile, and these tasks may also differ for different textiles. While considering the low-level activities would result in an overly complex control flow, only considering the machines consolidates the control flow and, consequently, the performance analysis. However, it introduces loops centered on the tenter frame, which need to be considered carefully during the analysis. Furthermore, from a performance perspective, there are strong dependencies between the textile orders because of the shared resources, that is, machines. In our analysis, we need to consider multiple textile orders with large variations in both their manufacturing process and the order of the steps involved.

In the following, we elaborate on the situation faced including how data is currently being used at Penn as well as on the event data collected and the challenges it presented. Afterward, we present a high-level overview of the actions taken and how the project was conducted. The details of each step will be presented along with the results achieved. Finally, we highlight the lessons learned.

2 Situation Faced

At the beginning of the project with Penn, the production department had been collecting data in a dedicated database. The data was used to query fundamental statistics but it was not exploited to generate holistic insight and, ultimately, steer the process. On-site decisions (e.g., scheduling orders) were based on domain knowledge. Therefore, Penn's main interest was exploratory—What can be done with the data?—and geared toward analyzing the production planning. However, the available domain-specific information was not yet sufficient for automating the planning. Therefore, we aimed to evaluate the as-is situation.

Although the system was not designed to support process mining, most of the information required—that is, case identifier, activity concept candidates, and task completion timestamps—was directly available. Only the data on quality control steps and a few additional attributes, such as human-readable activity descriptions, are needed to be extracted from additional tables. A snippet from the composite event data, including the most important concepts used during the project, is depicted in Table 1. The Partie column represents an order and corresponds to the *case ID* in process mining terminology. KoststNr identifies the *cost center (CC)* which corresponds to a machine type (e.g., CC-20 is the tenter frame). The first digit also identifies a specific CC type (e.g., a leading three describes CCs related to dyeing). The CC ID together with the KststLfNr column can be associated with a human-readable task description given in column KstText1. The start timestamp was computed using domain knowledge (e.g., based on the complete timestamp, the textile's length, and the machine speed). Finally, the columns LaborID and SchauID reference the quality control and final product assessment subprocess, respectively.

The full dataset also contained domain-specific attributes, which are often specific to certain production tasks. However, not all machine configurations were logged. Therefore, rather than analyzing domain-specific decisions, we focused on performance. A major challenge for a detailed performance analysis is the control-flow variability in the dataset. Table 2 gives an overview of a few fundamental statistics on the data. The number of distinct activities is high, and there are many variations in how a textile is processed. The most frequent variant covers only 6% of all cases while, together, the five most frequent variants cover 23% of the event log. As a detailed performance analysis requires that all cases are considered, this variability is particularly challenging. Moreover, the data contain many loops involving the tenter frame, which is used multiple times within each individual case. Furthermore, the tenter frame is the most expensive machine; therefore, its load should be high, and the tenter frame was thereby an anticipated bottleneck.

3 Action Taken

In this use case, we applied process mining techniques to generate insight into the manufacturing data. As indicated in Sect. 2, we focused on the performance dimension where sub-aspects were identified together. Given Penn's interest in an exploratory analysis, details on intermediate steps were also presented and discussed. Figure 2 depicts a detailed illustration of the steps taken. At a high level, we identified three steps: data extraction and preprocessing, analysis of the manufacturing process, and analysis of the quality control process. Each step entailed discussing

Table 1 Reduced snippet of the manufacturing data

Partie	Zeile	KststNr	KststLfNr	LaborID	SchauID	KstText1	Start	Complete
7004	0	10	1			Steaming	DD.MM.YYYY hh:mm	DD.MM.YYYY hh:mm
7165	0	10	1			Steaming	...	...
7165	1	12	1			Washing	...	...
22,426	3	30	1			HT dyeing	...	...
22,426	4	20	17			Finishing	...	...
22,426	5	90	2	394,759		Quality control	...	...
22,426	6	60	1		817,491	Examination	...	...

Table 2 Fundamental event log statistics using task descriptions as activity notion

Statistic	Value
#Cases	14,417
#Events	101,482
#Activities	40
#Variants	2851

Top 5 variants

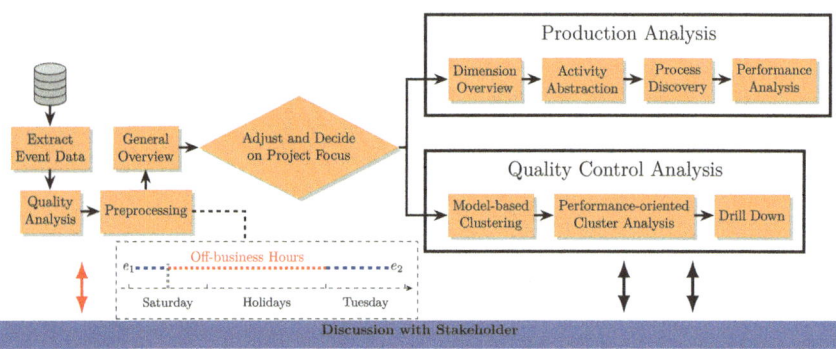

893 traces 6,19% of the log	Dämpfen	Fixieren, Bäume...	HT Färben	Appretieren nass in nass	Qualitätskontrolle	Fertigwarenschau
822 traces 5,70% of the log	Dämpfen Breit waschen	Fixieren, Bäumen, dur...	HT Färben	Appretieren nass in nass	Qualitätskontrolle	Fertigwarenschau
622 traces 4,31% of the log	Breit waschen	Fixieren, Bäumen, dur... HT Färben	Appretieren m...	Qualitätskontrolle	Fertigwarenschau
586 traces 4,06% of the log	Breit waschen	Fixieren, Bäumen, dur... HT Färben	Appretieren nass in nass	Qualitätskontrolle	Fertigwarenschau
402 traces 2,79% of the log	Fixieren, Bäume... HT Färben	Appretieren nass in nass	Qualitätskontrolle	Fertigwarenschau

Fig. 2 Overview of the steps taken during the analysis. We distinguish three parts: preprocessing—particularly measuring business hour-aware time intervals—and initial overview, performance-oriented analysis of the production and performance-oriented analysis of the quality control process. The analysis was closely accompanied by discussions with Penn

the results with Penn, and considering the importance of these discussions was one of the lessons learned. In particular, we highlight the discussion of intermediate results during the preprocessing phase.

As depicted in Fig. 2, we first identified the relevant tables based on domain knowledge and extracted an event log as shown in tabular form in Table 1. Then we analyzed the data quality while focusing on the potential for performance analysis and discussed the initial results with the company. The subjects discussed ranged from relatively technical insight (e.g., the distribution of missing timestamps depicted in Fig. 3a) to more relatable statistics, such as the distribution of manufacturing operation completions on a particular day (see Fig. 3b).

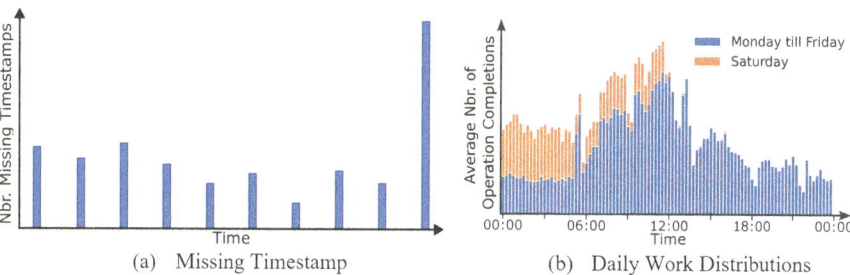

Fig. 3 Example of timestamp-related results discussed in the initial project phase: (**a**) The distribution of missing timestamps based on the latest observed timestamp of the associated case. (**b**) The daily average number of completed operations. The capacity of the manufacturing line changes over the day

The steps showed that the data quality was high. Many missing timestamps were associated with cases for which the latest event was recorded close to the end of the extraction window. This can be explained by information not yet being filled in completely. We later decided to drop these events. The daily distribution of timestamps in Fig. 3b reflects that Penn is, on working days, working in three shifts (i.e., 8 h per shift, 24 h per day). On Saturdays, work is only conducted for half of the day. Moreover, it shows that the capacity of the production varies over the day. The activity level at night is lower than during daytime. This makes measuring business hour-aware time intervals challenging. As illustrated in Fig. 2, we accounted for holidays when measuring case durations. However, to effectively evaluate waiting times, the current capacity would need to be considered.

In general, Fig. 3b sparked discussions on when and how work is conducted. However, missing timestamps and high intraday activity-level variance rendered the analysis of the scheduling difficult. In addition, the start timestamps were derived based on the complete timestamps and were, therefore, not precise. For an accurate analysis and automated planning, additional information would be required. Accordingly, the focus was shifted to an investigation and visual assessment of the overall performance of the manufacturing and quality control process. In doing so, we again robustly measured and compared time intervals. As there was no precise information on capacity changes during the day, this was not considered.

3.1 Production Model Discovery

To investigate and measure the performance of specific production stages, we first structured the production using a process model. Based on this process model, we identified specific parts of the process of interest and investigated them using a *model-based performance spectrum (PS)* (van der Aalst et al., 2020). A PS is a visualization of per-case throughput times for user-selected sections of a process model. Each case is represented by a line whose endpoints correspond to the timestamp indicating when it entered or exited that part of the process. Therefore, PS is suitable for analyzing performance on a low level.

We only used the process model to structure the process and analyze its performance. The control flow and potential deviations were mostly uninteresting from a domain expert's perspective. Considering the level of granularity in the event data at hand, the upfront assumption is that control flow decisions made on the shop floor are easily explainable. Valuable insight into control flow would require more detailed consideration of the activities and the incorporation of, for example, machine configurations. The model for the performance analysis was designed as follows:

(a) Specify five activity label candidates on different abstraction levels, specifically task descriptions, aggregated task descriptions (domain knowledge), CCs, CCs grouped by function, and CCs grouped by function and loop unrolling.
(b) Process discovery using the inductive miner algorithm (IM) (Leemans et al., 2013) and a grid search over activity candidates, sub-logs containing the frequent variants covering [25, 50, 75, 85, 100] percent of the log, and IM noise thresholds [0.1, 0.2, 0.4].
(c) Evaluate by investigating fitness, precision, and F1-score.
(d) Manual extension based on the inspection of alignments (Adriansyah et al., 2011).

We tested loop unrolling to better unravel the process around the tenter frame. If the tenter frame is repeatedly used at almost the same position within the process, loop unrolling might better capture the different phases.

3.2   Quality Control Analysis

When analyzing the quality control process, we applied a clustering-based approach to assess the effects of control flow variance on quality control lead times. To this end, two to-be models (according to domain experts) were created that described the expected behavior when quality control and final product assessment were conducted without objection, as well as when rework was required and conducted as expected. We then analyzed lead times after splitting the log into three classes, one for each of these models and one log for the remaining, unfitting cases. The aim was to analyze whether cases that deviate from the well-structured control flow defined by the models exhibit worse lead times. If so, better structuring the quality control and rework workflows would be valuable.

4   Results Achieved

In this section, we discuss and report the results achieved based on the actions taken. Our focus is on the production and quality control analysis. Due to confidentiality, we frequently leave out precise axis tick labels in the examples provided.

4.1 Production Analysis

The goal of the production analysis was to identify and evaluate the subprocesses and behaviors responsible for the performance variations. We started from the hypothesis that scheduling orders and adapting the schedule of tasks—for example, due to rework—was a main driver for lead time variance. To underpin and refine the hypothesis, we started with a brief analysis of two additional, potentially important factors—namely, machine/resource utilization and process times. By analyzing the machine utilization, we verified that there were no obvious inefficiencies in the scheduling (e.g., machine idle time), and by analyzing the process times, we verified that the impact of product-specific properties on lead times was low.

Two high-level results of this initial analysis are depicted in Figs. 4 and 6. Figure 4a shows the CC load in terms of the number of completed tasks within a sliding window of 48 hours. Note that we applied a working hour-aware sliding window to compensate for Sundays, part-time work on Saturdays, and holidays. The figure confirms that the utilization of critical resources, such as the tenter frame (CC-20, red), is high. The period of high variance in the middle of the figure can be attributed to the effects of COVID-19, while shorter outlier periods were caused by misclassified off days. Figure 4b focuses on the tenter frame and depicts the utilization achieved and the utilization's upper limit. As the data were not available, setup times were not considered.

Other than the period affected by COVID-19, the utilization achieved is relatively stable but still not yet perfect. Finally, the comparison of order lead times to total process times in Fig. 6 shows that processing time contributes little to the overall lead time. Again, we measured working hour-aware time periods with noise sometimes causing short or even negative process times.

As illustrated in Sect. 3, we followed a hybrid approach to discover a process model based on which we could structure the subsequent analysis. We determined that the model based on CCs would be most suitable. Considering the task

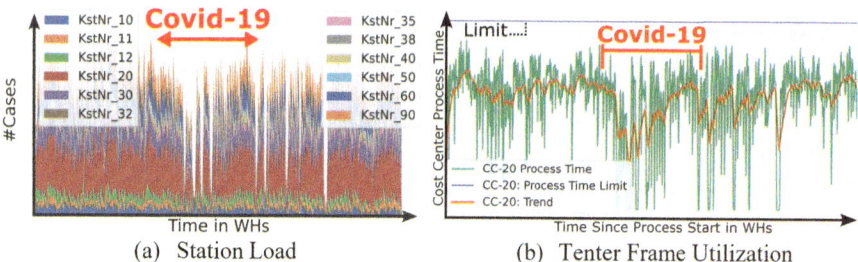

(a) Station Load   (b) Tenter Frame Utilization

Fig. 4 Working hour-aware overview of CC load and capacity utilization of the tenter frame: (**a**) a stacked plot showing a two-day sliding window of the number of completed tasks. The resource utilization of critical machines (e.g., tenter frame (red) and HT dyeing (purple)) is high. (**b**) The achieved daily tenter frame utilization (turquoise), the trend line (orange), and the theoretical maximum (purple) do not consider setup time

descriptions led to large models, even though fitness and precision were decent. Aggregated task descriptions faced the problem that previously distinct activities, which usually occurred at different positions in the process, could not be properly handled by IM. Grouping CCs did not create significant improvement over the CC baseline and straightforward loop unrolling had a negative effect because a few CCs repeatedly occurred at different positions for different tasks. The resulting process model, as well as the tools used in the hybrid model discovery, are depicted in

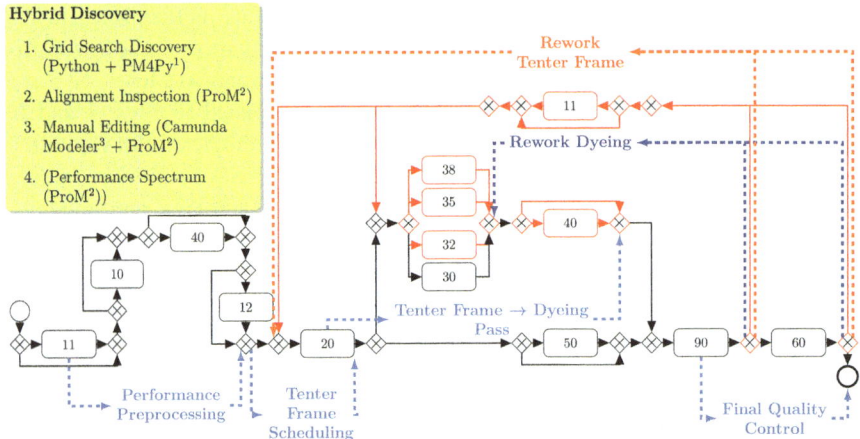

Fig. 5 Tools (PM4Py: https://pm4py.fit.fraunhofer.de/; ProM: https://promtools.org/; Camunda Modeler: https://camunda.com/download/modeler/) and steps of the hybrid discovery approach and the resulting BPMN model. Each task corresponds to a processing step at a CC. The manual extensions of the model are highlighted in red. The dashed lines illustrate the sections of the model that were analyzed in relation to their performance using PS

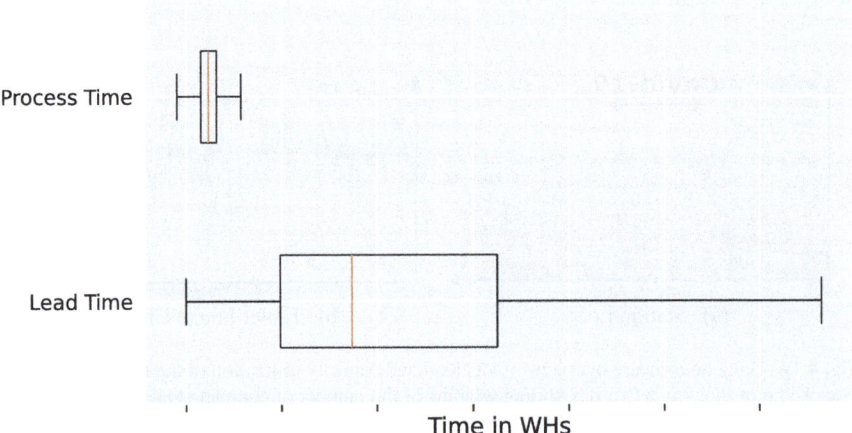

Fig. 6 Comparison of lead times to total per-case process times

Fig. 5. After inspecting deviations in ProM, we added three less frequent dyeing procedures, explicitly modeled the (infrequent) rework, and accounted for CC-11 and CC-40 being used in multiple positions, which IM cannot handle natively. Based on this model, we defined six stages of interest:

(a) Initial processing of the textile before the first run on the tenter frame.
(b) Rework that is directly scheduled for dyeing.
(c) Time until a preprocessed textile is scheduled on the tenter frame.
(d) Rework that directly requires processing on the tenter frame.
(e) A single tenter frame run with subsequent dyeing.
(f) Completion of the final quality control and product assessment stage.

For each stage, we computed a model-based performance spectrum based on the model depicted in Fig. 5. The resulting spectra are depicted in Fig. 7. It shows that any of the defined stages can be associated with high lead times. While the average load of the tenter frame is high (comp. Fig. 4a), Fig. 7a, c suggest that this is partially the result of scheduling many orders. In a significant number of cases, preprocessing is started and completed much later. Moreover, preprocessed cases may need to wait to be processed on the tenter frame. Once an order is scheduled on the tenter frame and for dyeing, this process stage is usually completed without major delays (comp. Fig. 7e). However, there are some exceptions (e.g., sample products). As expected, rework can require a significant amount of time. In particular, rescheduling products on the tenter frame can cause a bottleneck (comp. Fig. 7d). Finally, Fig. 7f shows that finalizing the order and conducting the final product assessment step can have a major impact on lead times.

Our analysis confirmed that there was a high level of resource utilization, resulting in the tenter frame being a main bottleneck. Moreover, by structuring the analysis through a process model, we visualized the impact of scheduling rework on the tenter frame and compared it to the impact of other production stages. The analysis

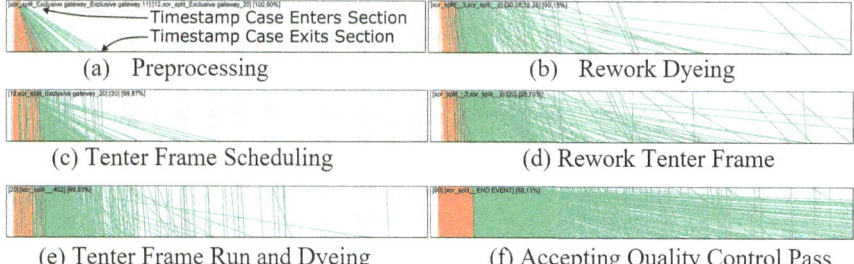

Fig. 7 Performance spectra for the sections defined in Fig. 5. Each spectrum shows the working hours relative to the case's start on the x-axis. The left column shows spectra related to manufacturing sections, while the right column focuses on quality control and rework. The orange lines reflect the 80% of cases with the lowest lead times, while the turquoise lines reflect the 20% with the highest lead times. Important causes for delay were identifed as (**f**) time till customer acceptance and (**d**) rework scheduled on the tenter frame

provided evidence that high resource utilization is partly achieved by having many pending products at the same time. However, a primary driver for long lead times seems to be the finishing stage.

4.2   Quality Control Analysis

As quality control and final product assessment can have a big impact on lead times, the final step of the analysis focused on this stage. First, we filtered the event log so that it only contained the last production step preceding quality control and the production steps that occurred during the quality control stage. The resulting log was classified by replaying it on the models depicted in Fig. 8a, c. We then analyzed the lead times for each cluster, focusing on the unfitting cases in particular. An overview of the lead times is depicted in Fig. 8b. As expected, lead times for the final stage were higher for orders that required rework. However, the overall lead time did not increase for the unfitting cases. In fact, allowing for additional flexibility did result in lower lead times than the rework process defined by the model presented in Fig. 8c. At this point in time, we have not completed analyzing the process to identify generalizable recommendations based on this observation. However, drilling down into the final stage lead times revealed that customer response times play an important role and vary among customers. Further details on this are omitted here to maintain confidentiality.

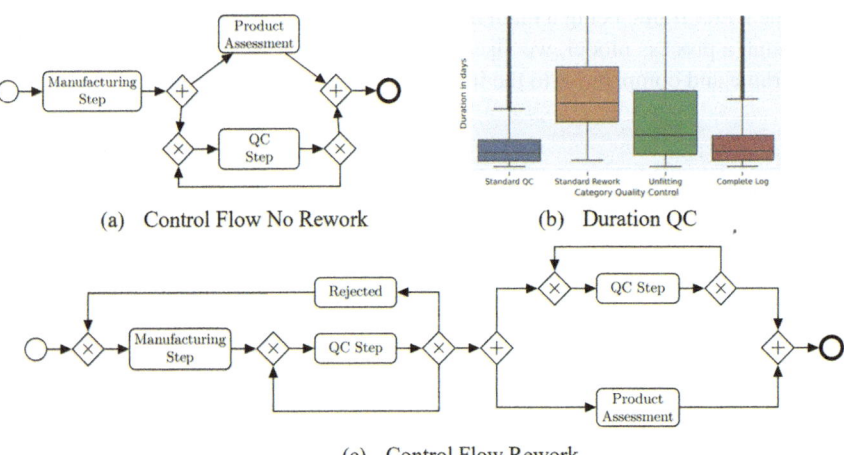

Fig. 8 Classification of cases according to whether rework is required, the order is finalized without objection, or neither of the former applies. The models used for classification are depicted in (**a**) and (**c**). Note that (**a**) contains a case-dependent optimization of simultaneous, early quality control. The lead times of the final production stages are compared in (**b**)

5 Lessons Learned

In this section, we elaborate on the lessons learned over the life cycle of the project—that is, project setup, event data preprocessing and overview, and in-depth process analysis. As discussed in Sect. 2, with Penn being interested in advancing their digitalization, the initial scope was an exploratory analysis. Even though there were specific questions, such as how to improve the scheduling, the extent to which they could be answered was unclear given the available data. For example, an analysis of the scheduling process might require additional information on when orders would have been available (rather than only seeing them once they were scheduled), precise process times, and setup times and costs. Thus, the initial project was scoped as a larger exploratory analysis showing, relating, and quantifying insight into the performance of the process. Rather than defining potentially unrealistic objectives upfront, we, together with Penn, iteratively defined sub-aspects of interest for the analysis. Given the current results, realistic objectives for the next stage will be better defined. We found that it can also be helpful to sketch intermediate steps and results. For example, the distribution of task completions during the day, shown in Fig. 3b, has been used as a sanity check for timestamps and for defining working hours. While these results can sometimes lead to somewhat unexpected discussions, for example, Fig. 3b sparked a discussion on when certain tasks were performed, intermediate results such as these also helped increase trust (e.g., when the behavior experienced aligns with the analysis) and understanding of subsequent stages. For example, Fig. 3b shows outliers relating to the usual working hours, which can lead to negative working hour-aware timespans. Having previously seen Fig. 3b makes this problem more accessible for stakeholders.

Thereby, the project increased trust and interest in applying process mining to gain new insights. Yet the cautious approach did not result in significant on-sight changes. Rather, it sparked discussions and increased stakeholder awareness of the process. We presume that real change would require the incorporation of additional domain-specific information and constraints. For example, specific production decisions are currently made based on operator experience. Taking the opportunity provided by a follow-up project, which would potentially require less domain knowledge, we discussed broadening the scope. Creating transparency for the integration of procurement, production, and sale was considered an interesting topic for future work. A data-driven approach based on event data could help connect less strongly coupled departments.

During our analysis, we focused, in particular, on model discovery and detailed performance analysis using performance spectra. We used process models to structure the process for the performance analysis. The control flow modeled was, itself, from a domain perspective point of view of relatively little value. In fact, this might generalize to other production processes. In contrast to virtual business cases where, depending on the configuration of the information system, many actions might be enabled at any point in time, in this case study, each production case has a physical state that restricts the next step. Furthermore, it is often impossible to undo an operation; therefore, performing tasks in the incorrect order can irrecoverably destroy the product. Moreover, production operations can have complicated physical effects that are dependent on low-level machine configurations. Medium-level task descriptions are, for instance, insufficient to predict rework. For example, to predict rework based on the model shown in Fig. 6, it is highly likely that factors such as tenter frame configurations, product colors, and textile properties would need to be incorporated. Consequently, the modeled control flow gives little insight into individual cases. In fact, it might be assumed that the order of task executions is valid as it is. Nevertheless, we found the model to be useful for structuring the analysis and for concretely discussing production stages. Finally, we applied automatic model discovery in a grid search to effectively test configurations and activity concepts to come up with an initial model which we then manually edited based on conformance diagnostics.

Regarding the detailed performance analysis, we identified limitations in existing process mining techniques. Orders were scheduled by a domain expert and no obvious inefficiencies, for which no reasonable explanation exists, were found. Assessing and evaluating the performance is difficult as it is context-dependent. At a detailed level, the state of the production depends on the number of available orders, the size of the orders, setup costs related to colors, the type of orders which influence the conducted tasks, and the due dates. While determining the next stages of the analysis based on discussions of intermediate results helped us adapt to the limitations of the data and led to "*interesting*" insights, we encountered difficulties converting specific retrospectively obtained insights into action. Identifying opportunities for optimization in an already optimized process requires consideration of a broader context and many additional implicit constraints.

References

Adriansyah, A., van Dongen, B.F., van der Aalst, W.M.P., 2011. *Conformance checking using cost-based fitness analysis*. 15th international enterprise distributed object computing conference.
Annapoorani, G. S. (2017). Social sustainability in textile industry. In *Sustainability in the textile industry* (Textile science and clothing technology). Springer.
Kemper, M., Gloy, Y. S., & Gries, T. (2017). The future of textile production in high wage countries. *IOP Conference Series: Materials Science and Engineering, 254*(20), 202002.
Leemans, S. J. J., Fahland, D., & van der Aalst, W. M. P. (2013). *Discovering block-structured process models from event logs – A constructive approach*. PETRI NETS.
van der Aalst, W. M. P. (2016). *Process mining – Data science in action* (2nd ed.). Springer.
van der Aalst, W. M. P., Tacke Genannt Unterberg, D., Denisov, V., & Fahland, D. (2020). *Visualizing token flows using interactive performance spectra*. PETRI NETS.

Tobias Brockhoff is a research assistant in the Process and Data Science Group at RWTH Aachen University. He obtained his bachelor's and master's degrees in computer science from RWTH Aachen. His research interests include process mining and focusing on probabilistic approaches for comparative process mining. As a member of the Cluster of Excellence "Internet of Production," he is also interested in applying and developing process mining techniques in production contexts.

Merih Seran Uysal worked as an IT consultant in the industry on numerous projects after completing her computer science diploma at RWTH Aachen University. After a couple of years, she began working as a research associate and doing her PhD at RWTH Aachen University. After completing her PhD, she started working as a group leader at the newly established Chair of Process and Data Science and supervising PhD students. She took full responsibility for managing activities of the Cluster of Excellence project "Internet of Production," acting as the coordinator for industrial projects and being responsible for the acquisition of industrial partners. She is also a lecturer at the Business School of RWTH Aachen. Her research focuses on process mining applied in industry, comparative process mining, process mining of uncertain event data, and process matching and similarity for business process models. She has published 47 peer-reviewed publications and given 26 talks at companies, conferences, and universities.

Anahita Farhang Ghahfarokhi received her bachelors in automation engineering from the Isfahan University of Technology, Isfahan, Iran, in 2015, and a master's degree in industrial management from Tehran University, Iran, in 2019. In 2019, she began working as a research assistant in the project Internet of Production (IoP) at RWTH Aachen University. Her research interests include data science, process mining, and Industry 4.0.

Leon Reinsch worked as a research assistant at the Institut für Textiltechnik of RWTH Aachen University. He obtained his bachelor's and master's degree from RWTH Aachen in Mechanical Engineering and specialized in textile machinery. As a member of the Cluster of Excellence project, "Internet of Production," he participated in interdisciplinary research on applied digitalization. Since 2023, he has been working at Reifenäuser Reicofil as a digital engineer in the R&D department.

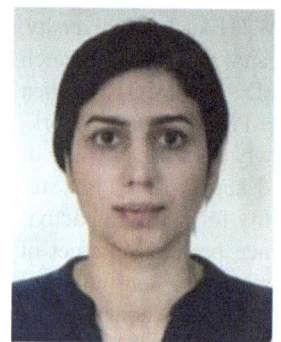

Mahsa Pourbafrani is a research assistant in the Data and Process Science Group of RWTH Aachen University. She is a last-year PhD student under Professor van der Aalst's supervision. Her research focuses on forward-looking process mining, which employs data science methods to turn data into actionable insights. The actions are taken using simulation, what-if analysis, and predictions in process mining regarding the performance metrics of processes. She is also a scientist working on the "Internet of Production" project under the Germanys Cluster of Excellence, which aims to combine process mining and machine learning techniques to support operations and decisions in production lines.

Thomas Gries was born in Cologne, Germany, in 1964. He received his Dipl. Ing. degree in Mechanical Engineering and a Dipl. Wirt. Ing. degree from RWTH Aachen University, Germany, in 1989 and 1992, respectively, and a Ph.D. degree from RWTH Aachen University in 1995. From 1995 to 2000, he worked at the Lurgi Zimmer AG, Frankfurt/Main, Germany, as the Head of the Department and Central Division of Technologies for Fibres. In 2001, he became a professor of textile machinery at RWTH Aachen University and the Director of the Institut für Textiltechnik (ITA).Since 2013, he has been an honorary professor with Lomonosov Moscow State University, Moscow, Russian Federation. He has authored and coauthored more than 3000 publications (thereof 1500 scientific papers) and held more than 625 presentations (thereof 140 presentations as keynote or invited speaker), mainly at international congresses.

Wil M.P. van der Aalst is a full professor at RWTH Aachen University, leading the Process and Data Science (PADS) group. He is also the chief scientist at Celonis, a part-time affiliate with the Fraunhofer FIT, and a member of the Board of Governors of Tilburg University. His research interests include process mining, Petri nets, business process management, workflow management, process modeling, and process analysis. van der Aalst has published over 900 articles and books and is typically considered to be one of the top 15 most cited computer scientists with an H-index of 173 and more than 130,000 citations. van der Aalst is an IFIP Fellow, IEEE Fellow, and ACM Fellow and has received honorary degrees from the Moscow Higher School of Economics and Hasselt University.

Adopting the Internet of Things (IoT) Technology Paradigm in a State Hospital

Manuel Weber, Gregor Kipping, Jan vom Brocke, and Mirco Schweitzer

Abstract

(a) *Situation faced*: We are here reporting on a project from a small state hospital in the Rhine Valley (Central Europe). The hospital is currently in the preplanning phase for its main building and is aiming to systematically elaborate on and analyze the needs and requirements of its entire information and communication technology (ICT) infrastructure. Adopting the Internet of Things (IoT), they expect to generate innovative solutions for their patients and internal stakeholders by transforming their internal processes.

(b) *Action taken*: Based on an IT management workshop and several exchanges with the practitioners, we co-developed the IoT implementation framework. Grounded in research and motivated by practical use cases, the practitioners applied the framework to guide the implementation process in the healthcare context. In the course of numerous evaluation cycles and after considering social and technical elements, we were able to achieve a holistic understanding of IoT in the state hospital.

(c) *Results achieved*: Our results show that the framework is suitable for systematically managing and guiding the adoption of IoT at the organizational and process levels. Furthermore, the framework helps understand the interplay between the social elements (people, structure) and technical elements (technology, task) and better align the needs of the various employees adopting and using IoT.

M. Weber (✉)
Liechtenstein Business School, Department of Information Systems & Computer Science, University of Liechtenstein, Vaduz, Liechtenstein
e-mail: manuel.weber@uni.li

G. Kipping · J. vom Brocke
European Research Center for Information Systems (ERCIS), University of Münster, Münster, Germany
e-mail: gregor.kipping@ercis.uni-muenster.de; jan.vom.brocke@uni-muenster.de

M. Schweitzer
State Hospital, Rhine Valley, Switzerland

© The Author(s), under exclusive license to Springer Nature Switzerland AG 2025
J. vom Brocke et al. (eds.), *Business Process Management Cases Vol. 3*,
https://doi.org/10.1007/978-3-031-80793-0_8

(d) *Lessons learned*: The IoT technology paradigm is a multilayered and complex concept, requiring an integrated multi-view perspective during the adoption process. It should be implemented and used within carefully selected and suitable processes. A systematic and coordinated introduction is necessary in view of the high financial and operational risks. The IoT implementation framework raises awareness of the impact and sharpens the identification and evaluation of use cases by internal stakeholders. Finally, the framework triggered and guided the discussions and, ultimately, contributed to improved communication and collaboration at the project level.

1 Introduction

Rapid changes in the environment, society, technology, and regulations in healthcare are creating ever more challenges for healthcare organizations. Modern information technology (IT), such as the Internet of Things (IoT), promises innovative business models and processes (e.g., Tesch et al., 2017) and even sustainable solutions (Beier et al., 2018). IoT can also positively contribute to firm performance (Tang et al., 2018) and the agility and flexibility of organizations (Chakraborty et al., 2019). However, the benefits and added value for the organization are often uncertain. This is a challenge for the professional management of expectations, goal setting, the availability of resources, and other dimensions. As a result, IoT-enabled services or products require careful advance assessment and systematic planning before implementation (Lee & Lee, 2015). The subject appears to be complex, and few researchers have reported on drivers for the successful management of such adoption and implementation processes (e.g., Kodali et al., 2015; Mahajan & Gupta, 2020).

In this chapter, we are reporting on a project from a state hospital in the Rhine Valley (Central Europe). Their main building no longer satisfies the needs of the stakeholders, especially the healthcare staff and patients. Therefore, the hospital management is currently in a pre-project phase planning the construction of a new building. As part of this phase, all requirements for the new hospital building will be systematically recorded. This includes the replacement of the entire information and communications technology (ICT) infrastructure. The hospital sees this as an opportunity to implement modern IT, such as the Internet of Things (IoT), and hopes to realize a wide range of medical and facility management applications. Against this background, we observed that the responsible project managers did not fully understand what was necessary for the successful adaptation of their existing processes. They were not fully aware of social and technical factors relevant to realizing IoT solutions and the dynamics involved in these kinds of implementation processes. They were also interested in the managerial implications of successfully embedding this technology paradigm into the existing ICT landscape and organizational boundaries.

With the co-development of the *IoT implementation framework*, we supported the project managers as they came to grips with this multilayered and complex topic. The basic idea was to support the project managers in launching initial use cases introducing the IoT technology paradigm and providing them with a mental model to improve their shared understanding. The structured derivation and description of IoT use cases provided should then provide senior management with a foundation for launching initial pilot tests and releasing monetary resources. Furthermore, we hoped that our framework would serve as a common basis for discussion that would make all project stakeholders more aware of the social and technical dimensions of this technology paradigm.

2 Situation Faced

The case organization is a state-funded hospital located in the Rhine Valley, Central Europe. The hospital annually reports approximately 2000 inpatient discharges, 11,000 outpatient cases, and 7000 treatments. The hospital employs around 250 medical and administrative staff and provides general medical services to both local residents and people from across the border. The hospital is embedded in a functioning ecosystem, with partners that offer rescue and ambulance services, specialists, therapy centers, and laboratory facilities.

In 2019, hospital management decided to build a new building at a new location nearby. The existing facility is no longer state of the art and the hospital has reached its capacity because the population in the region has also been increasing. From a technological, organizational, and medical perspective, many existing devices and concepts need to be renovated and redesigned. The hospital is currently in the pre-project phase. Thus, the project team is collating all the requirements and needs of the various departments and divisions. Hospital management and their sponsors consider the new build an opportunity to deploy modern IT that improves the patient experience and both the medical and facility management processes. They also realized that this pre-project phase was a beneficial time to adopt IoT. Without the new building project, the procurement and implementation of such a radically new IT system would have been challenging to implement while carrying out of daily business and would have required significant investment and resources. This phenomenon has already been recognized within the academic literature. Tyre and Orlikowski (1994) referred to this as the "window of opportunity," a period in which new technology is adopted and manipulated into the organizational social context. Second, according to the project managers, the adoption of IoT is contingent on the expectation that it will add value to the relevant processes and services. However, prior to this project, the state hospital had no experience using IoT. As one (leading) project manager mentioned, "*(…) new medical treatments and processes either could not be implemented at all or could not be implemented successfully because of adverse (organizational, note) structures (project manager).*"

Next, as the hospital is a state-funded institution, procurement procedures must, by law, be transparent and tenders must be carried out in accordance with a true and fair principle. Therefore, the subject matter was too complex and multilayered for the IoT technology paradigm to be implemented without any guidance. Implementing IoT in organizations is a challenging and multidimensional task that involves a high level of financial investment and impacts various levels. The benefits are often unclear and companies need strategies to help them adopt this technology paradigm successfully. Hence, a coordinated and structured approach is essential. The hospital generally intends to deploy IoT solutions to add value to customers (patients) and other stakeholders such as facility managers and visitors. Conscious of its smallness, the state hospital is not aiming for a large-scale solution, especially because such investments in IoT are subject to public attention regarding data privacy and cybersecurity. However, the project managers had identified several areas in which IoT "makes sense" in terms of adding value for their internal stakeholders (and target groups). However, as implementing IoT raises several complex questions, there are potential risks and challenges, as well as managerial implications that have not yet been fully answered for the team. Accordingly, there is a risk that an uncoordinated implementation could overlook aspects of these multilayered issues. One of the project managers mentioned, *"Our vision is to use IoT to track certain patients and medical devices for specific purposes. However, we are not aware of how to systematically use and adopt IoT – it's new for us (...)"* (Weber et al., 2022, p. 3).

The practitioners were interested in how to implement the IoT technology paradigm and the impact it would have on the processes affected. In this way, they considered the adoption of IoT not just as an end in itself but as a means to improving processes and providing even better service to patients: *"We aim to implement IoT as a future technology for our new building. However, lack means what is important during this implementation and which factors are decisive – also, for which processes does IoT make sense"* (Weber et al., 2022, pp. 3–4).

We encountered further decisive topics and challenges. In addition to the architectural design of the new building, the understanding of organizational spaces must be clarified as part of this endeavor. For example, there was a need to address how organizational space influences human actions when selecting new technology. In the course of this workshop, we identified valuable and perhaps also paradoxical situations related to IoT and the construction of their new building: *First*, although the hospital raised concerns about the possibility of increased cyberattacks in the future in general, they want to use IoT to collect more data about devices and patients for increased transparency across patient and medical devices. As one of the project managers said, *"Data protection must be guaranteed in the context of healthcare (...). Data is the gold of the future in healthcare (project manager)."* *Second*, IoT leads to increased datafication and digital connectivity of people and medical devices in the hospital context. As a result, the behavior of people or social groups within the organization becomes more visible and transparent. Within this IoT implementation (design) process, the managerial implications relating to existing structures and processes would have to be reconsidered. In the course of the relocation and construction project (their new building), the spatial (physical) divisions and separations must influence the positioning of IoT sensors to ensure interference-free connectivity and the correct localization of devices and people. *Third*, although the hospital considers the impact of architectural design on the healing process and patient well-being, they are aware that the excessive use of IoT entails increased electromagnetic radiation.

As the practitioners reported, hospital staff could be resistant to the implementation and use of IoT. There was a risk that they would be unwilling to learn the new skills required or adapt to the new processes. In addition, hospital staff may not have the necessary training and skills to operate and maintain IoT devices and systems. Lack of training can lead to errors, misinterpretation of data, and miscommunication. In this context, IoT devices may need to be integrated with existing hospital systems. This can be challenging and may require IT staff to work closely with clinical staff to ensure the systems work together effectively. Moreover, IoT devices and systems collect and store sensitive patient data raising privacy and security concerns. Therefore, patients may be reluctant to use IoT devices if they perceive them as intrusive or if they are unsure about how their data will be used and stored. Overall, the successful adoption of IoT in healthcare may require a patient-centered approach that considers patient needs, preferences, and concerns.

Finally, during the collaboration with the state hospital, we were not able to consider all stakeholders, challenges, or limiting factors relevant to this endeavor. This preplanning phase aimed to identify and evaluate individual use cases in the context of IoT adoption. To this end, we have not taken a patient or supplier perspective in this chapter and have, therefore, explicitly not addressed them.

3   Actions Taken

First, we argue that the IoT adopted should not be isolated from the existing IT and infrastructure from a technical point of view. Therefore, a well-structured and coordinated introduction of this new IoT technology is of great strategic importance. Further, the project managers did not consider IoT as critical to the hospital's current operations. Instead, they considered IoT an additional resource that would generate added value for different target groups (users). They wanted to adopt this IT to strengthen their position within their health ecosystem. Next, implementing the IoT technology paradigm depends on successfully aligning and configuring technical and social elements across the organizational layers and within the structures over time.

In an online conference held via Zoom, the first two authors held an initial exchange with the two project managers in mid-January 2022 with the aim of understanding "the big picture" of this construction project and what needed to be taken into account when replacing the entire ICT landscape. Two weeks later, the first author was invited to a physical workshop, the overarching goal of which was to conduct an initial requirements analysis. Two project managers and four department heads formed the core project team. During the pre-project phase, the core project team engaged with other external companies, such as electricians and builders (who were not present at the workshop). In total, 11 practitioners participated in the workshop including two external IT experts who led the workshop. The external experts advised the project team on the procurement of the hardware and the first author took handwritten notes during this workshop as a silent observer. He had no active part in this workshop beyond noting the decisions, opinions, and relevant input of the practitioners. Later that same day, the notes were transcribed electronically. The second author reviewed the notes and checked the document for consistency. In general, the practitioners broadly discussed the following three topics: first, the hospital's new and adapted vision statement; second, the availability and requirements of new technologies and ICT infrastructures in the form of a target-actual comparison, such as 5G, cloud storage, mobile devices, and IoT; third, which processes would be affected, including procurement, and medical and administrative services. They then prioritized these topics according to three categories: (i) priority implementation, (ii) implementation where possible, and (iii) non-priority implementation.

We found that the development of an IoT implementation framework, in the form of a visual inquiry tool, would positively guide and support the project managers and associated stakeholders as they adopt the IoT technology paradigm at the organizational and process level. In collaboration with the state hospital, we have already looked at the adoption of IoT from an academic perspective. Based on this research, we derived the dimensions and elements (Fig. 1) and substantiated them with research-based evidence. Specifically, the dimensions and elements are based on theories from business informatics and organization science. To take a brief look at Fig. 1, the horizontal axis consists of the phases proposed by Porter and Heppelmann (2015): monitor, control, optimize, and autonomy. In essence, this phase aims to determine the extent of the IoT rollout and the intervention between the physical and virtual (digital) elements of the IoT system as a whole. In contrast, the vertical axis represents the organizational or enterprise architectural layers (Hewlett & CEA, 2006). We made minor adaptations here. We replaced the element "technology" with "infrastructure" to account for sensors or hardware. The technology, as such, is instead reflected at the center of this draft. We visualized the IoT paradigm as a socio-technical system (Schroeder et al., 2020). Next, we depicted the organizational boundary with the dashed frame. The underlying rationale for this is motivated by two theories: *First*, by referring to the adaptive structuration theory, we aimed to account for the reshaping and redesigning of the IoT technology paradigm during its adoption process by the users in their social context. *Second*, by referring to the socio-technical theory, we aimed to consider the interaction between the two subsystems (social and technical).

We asked the project managers for their assessment of these dimensions and elements and how useful they thought they would be for their purposes. They responded that the designation of the two dimensions could be misleading to the users. The same applies to the time dimension, shown outside the organizational boundaries (dashed lines). We also discussed the benefits of applying these elements when evaluating practical use cases. We concluded that the placeholder "Alignment over

Time" would not increase or add value for the users of this framework. Finally, we added the placeholder "Data" to the vertical axis and visualized as part of the IoT system in the center of the framework.

Consequently, Fig. 1 did not meet the needs of the end users in this project. However, inspired by these dimensions and elements, we were able to develop the *IoT implementation framework* presented in Fig. 2. We received feedback regarding the distribution of roles and responsibilities when introducing IoT in an organizational context. In response, we determined that governance should be more explicitly evident in the framework. Although "People" and "Task" were already included, they did not give an indication of the roles and responsibilities during the IoT implementation process. Finally, they requested that we reverse the order of the two elements, "Data" and "Application," because the infrastructure, such as sensors, will collect and provide data that feeds into the application.

One of the project managers reported, "*For me, the processes are missing (…). If we are already discussing process optimizations, why don't we integrate them into the framework (project manager)?*" This requirement was also identified in one of the online sessions. Furthermore, we observed that the selection of processes suitable for IoT applications was also challenging for the project managers, as they

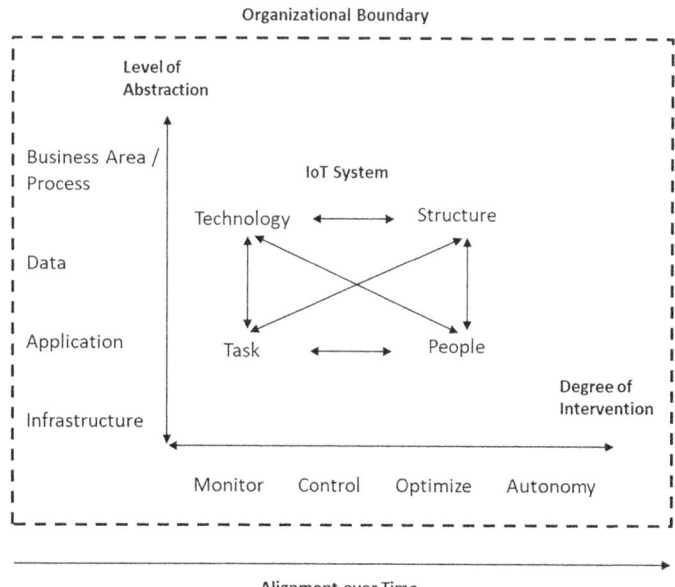

Source: Adapted from and based on Bostrom and Heinen (1977), Hewlett and CEA (2006), Porter, and Heppelmann (2015), and Weber, Kipping, and vom Brocke (2022).

Fig. 1 Dimensions and elements relevant for using IoT. (Source: Adapted from and based on Bostrom & Heinen, 1977; Hewlett & CEA, 2006; Porter & Heppelmann, 2015; Weber et al., 2022)

lacked a process map and architecture that provided a systematic view that supported the selection of processes for IoT applications. In several meetings, the logistics or patient flow management processes were addressed and seemed to be at the center of the project group's focus. For example, IoT could be used in the context of the intra- or interhospital transportation of goods and medicine. External suppliers could benefit from tracking inventory in real time and triggering automatic orders. Finally, during our meetings, we agreed to look at internal use cases first in order to limit the scope of the review. External stakeholders should only be considered if the state hospital can usefully implement IoT within the organization.

Based on the stories told in the workshop and other exchanges with the practitioners, we decided to transfer these dimensions and elements (in an adapted form) into MS Excel. In the process, we attempted to explain and define them in more detail using short notes. These notes were intended as fill-in guides for users interested in specific IoT use cases. For better readability of Fig. 2, we have hidden these notes here. The idea was that the individual fields of the framework could be filled in and described in more detail by the relevant party. Our secondary goal was to increase awareness of socio-technical elements within the IoT adoption process and, thus, improve communication and coordination among the relevant stakeholders.

The project managers used the framework to showcase and sketch one of the discussed use cases (see Fig. 2): room occupancy management. After filling out this table, we discussed the results in light of the feasibility and dependencies of other ICT systems. We chose to share this specific use case because it is relatively easy to understand and seems intuitive to us. At the time of application, none of the users had any experience with this case study. The idea was to link patient flows and room occupancy to provide monitoring for the nursing unit and facility management network.

4 Result Achieved

One of the main results was the development of the *IoT implementation framework* (see Fig. 2) as a mental model that would facilitate the shared understanding of the project stakeholders. As the IoT paradigm and its underlying technology are complex and multidimensional, our framework laid a foundation that would also be informative for the project managers and the associated stakeholders, such as the heads of the IT and logistics departments. The framework also laid a foundation that will support the practitioners assessing the benefits of IoT in specific use cases. The framework also facilitated an exploration of options on how to integrate IoT into the hospital's processes. However, the project managers mentioned that it would be even more useful if there was an existing and mature process architecture available. Such a systematic view would help them identify the processes for which IoT really makes sense. In order to partially meet this requirement, a placeholder for processes has been provided in Section B of the framework. As processes can take many different forms, we repeatedly discussed which processes could be implemented with

IoT Implementation Framework
Sketching an Exemplary Use Case: Room Occupancy Management

A	Use Case	
1	Needs	Resource-oriented planning of room occupancy (mainly patient rooms); coordination with horizontal and vertical processes
2	Goals	Efficient and targeted use of occupancy of existing patient rooms in long-term care
3	Requirements	Duration, type, use of space and medical needs of patients
4	Stakeholders	Patients, nurses, doctors, facility management

B	Organizational Levels	
5	Process	Related processes: patient onboarding, medical and nursing procedures, patient offboarding
6	Data	Number of patients per room, maximum occupancy rates, length of stay
7	Applications	Software application to map the room occupancy, number of rooms, alternate rooms
8	Infrastructure	Sensors for data collection; software application for visualization of rooms and occupancy plans

C	Degree of Intervention	
9	Monitor	Real-time monitoring of room occupancy and data-driven processes for facility management
10	Control	---
11	Optimize	---
12	Autonomy	---

D	IoT System	
13	Technology	Tablets for mobile displays, sensors for motion detection in lounges
14	Task	Room reservations; booking management; coordinate with medical needs and space availability during high season
15	Structure	Access only for caregivers and facility management
16	People	Active users: caregivers, facility management, accountants and controllers (using the data for internal calculations)

Source: Own Illustration.

Fig. 2 Applying the IoT implementation framework. (Source: Own illustration)

IoT during the review sessions. Key factors include the degree of digitization of the process as well as the frequency of execution and ability to generate adequate process logs that can later be evaluated. One of the department heads added the fact that a distinction should be made between management, core, and support processes. This division system has been used in management research for decades and this is a useful division for the state hospital to be aware of as they gain the experience of implementing IoT for the first time. In this context, they discussed which processes would be suitable for applying the framework.

Given that they not only want to redesign organizational structures and processes in the course of developing the new building but also want to strengthen the focus on the patient, this framework enables them to redesign or even improve their healthcare operations and supporting processes. The socio-technical approach supports the adoption of a process view by providing an overview that combines people, their tasks, and the technology used in the process. Finally, as one of the future steps, one of the department heads was assigned the task of elaborating a process landscape and identifying specific processes that could benefit from the use of IoT.

Moreover, the project managers stated that the traditional view of organizational space as a fixed, physical space has changed. New technologies, the changing nature of relationships between people, and the ongoing change of organizational structures are challenging. Applying IoT entails new ways of working that must be reflected in high-performance structures. In this respect, the framework must also be presented to the employees involved. According to the head of the IT department, it is not enough to present the dimensions and elements (see Fig. 2); it is also necessary to prepare concrete training materials.

Sketching the use cases also led the practitioners to consider what impact the IoT devices (e.g., sensors) would have on the design of the new building. While the new (building) architecture should make patients feel more comfortable and, thus, contribute to their healing process (e.g., shielding them from radiation), the architects will need to use materials that do not interfere with the wireless connections of the IoT devices. According to the project managers, the new technologies will have to be adapted to the infrastructure of the building. For example, the hospital stakeholders were thinking about a "healing architecture" that would not favor the connectivity of IoT as they intend to install special radiation-protected walls. Working in the other direction, the server landscape also affected the architectural requirements of the basement complex. These issues necessitated a discussion on how to reconcile physical architecture with digital architecture as they cannot be detached from each other and must be closely coordinated. Applying the IoT paradigm can, therefore, make both processes and human behavior visible in the physical space.

Finally, the practitioners discussed issues and possible solutions for avoiding and resolving these conflicting requirements. They identified the need to make a sophisticated assessment of the benefits and risks of using this technology. This assessment should also consider the processing of personal data. As a state-funded hospital, they are subject to even higher transparency, quality, and legal criteria, which require them to plan this endeavor systematically and with the utmost care.

5   Lessons Learned

We view the *IoT implementation framework* as a living document and tool for planning and realizing IoT solutions. The project members, as well as process stakeholders, can use it to present and demonstrate their digitalization endeavors using IoT. Hence, the framework serves as a communication and collaboration facilitator and an effective means of coordinating such endeavors. Using this framework, other stakeholders can create a shared understanding of any digitalization initiative from a socio-technical perspective. Although this framework artifact is primarily intended for project managers, the success of any IoT application or system will heavily depend on whether the users perceive the realized solution as useful. Also, the successful use of the IoT system or application might be determined as well as influenced by a multiuser perspective.

The isolated view of IoT from a purely technical perspective would have posed a risk to user and business acceptance. However, the application of a socio-technical and managerial perspective has led to a greater understanding of these complex issues. As depicted in Fig. 2, we only considered intraorganizational issues and excluded external stakeholders. However, our practitioners noted that external stakeholders must also be involved in the use cases and processes concerned in the subsequent stages. On a larger scale, the state hospital can, therefore, become part of an IoT ecosystem.

We applied a socio-technical and managerial perspective to the implementation of the IoT technology paradigm. As IoT often involves various combinations of software and hardware elements, the practitioners had to sharpen their focus on specific use cases. In addition, each stakeholder's specific needs, requirements, and goals had to be considered, sometimes in isolation.

The practitioners also learned to first describe the expected or intended goals before even thinking of adopting new IT. The acquisition of new IT for popularity reasons does not lead to satisfactory results, especially given the high risk of significant misinvestment. According to the practitioners, adopting IoT alone does not bring any benefit per se. The processes that are improved or even revolutionized in the process must always be taken into account. In this respect, process changes must be anticipated constantly. Especially in the case of new construction projects, the planning phase often lasts for years. The *IoT implementation framework* does not currently incorporate possible interconnections between existing IS within the hospital. Hence, its usefulness must be interpreted with caution. As the hospital is still in the planning phase and the new building has yet to be constructed, the practitioners were only able to perform an artificial evaluation using this mental model.

References

Beier, G., Niehoff, S., & Xue, B. (2018). More sustainability in industry through industrial internet of things? *Applied Sciences, 8*(2), 219.

Bostrom, R. P., & Heinen, J. S. (1977). MIS problems and failures: A socio-technical perspective. Part I: The causes. *MIS Quarterly, 1*(3), 17–32.

Chakraborty, S., Bhatt, V., & Chakravorty, T. (2019). Impact of IoT adoption on agility and flexibility of healthcare organization. *International Journal of Innovative Technology and Exploring Engineering, 8*(11), 2673–2681.

Hewlett, N. E., & CEA, P. (2006). *The USDA enterprise architecture program.* PMP CEA, Enterprise Architecture Team, USDA-OCIO [Preprint].

Kodali, R. K., Swamy, G., & Lakshmi, B. (2015). An implementation of IoT for healthcare. In *IEEE recent advances in intelligent computational systems (RAICS).* IEEE.

Lee, I., & Lee, K. (2015). The Internet of Things (IoT): Applications, investments, and challenges for enterprises. *Business Horizons, 58*(4), 431–440.

Mahajan, R., & Gupta, P. (2020). Implementation of IoT in healthcare. In *Handbook of research on the internet of things applications in robotics and automation* (pp. 190–212). IGI Global.

Porter, M. E., & Heppelmann, J. E. (2015). How smart, connected products are transforming companies. *Harvard Business Review, 93*(10), 96–114.

Schroeder, A., et al. (2020). Digitally enabled advanced services: A socio-technical perspective on the role of the internet of things (IoT). *International Journal of Operations & Production Management, 40*(7/8), 1243–1268.

Tang, C.-P., Huang, T. C.-K., & Wang, S.-T. (2018). The impact of internet of things implementation on firm performance. *Telematics and Informatics, 35*(7), 2038–2053.

Tesch, J. F., Brillinger, A.-S., & Bilgeri, D. (2017). Internet of things business model innovation and the stage-gate process: An exploratory analysis. *International Journal of Innovation Management, 21*(05), 16.

Tyre, M. J., & Orlikowski, W. J. (1994). Windows of opportunity: Temporal patterns of technological adaptation in organizations. *Organization science, 5*(1), 98–118.

Weber, M., Kipping, G., & vom Brocke, J. (2022). Towards an IoT implementation framework – About a new building project of a hospital in a European Microstate. In *Proceedings of the 17th international conference on design science research in information systems and technology. DESRIST 2022*, St. Petersburg, FL, USA.

Manuel Weber is a PhD student at the University of Liechtenstein (Liechtenstein Business School, Department of Information Systems & Computer Science). His research focuses on the role of change in business process management (BPM) in the context of digitalization and digital transformation.

Gregor Kipping is a research assistant at the European Research Center for Information Systems (ERCIS), University of Münster. In addition, he is a project collaborator and PhD candidate at the University of Liechtenstein. His research revolves around the interdisciplinary field of process science, especially how multiple data sources can be used in business process management.

Jan vom Brocke is the Director of the European Research Center for Information Systems (ERCIS) and a Professor and Chair of Information Systems & Business Process Management at the University of Münster in Germany. He has published in leading journals such as *Management Information Systems Quarterly* (MISQ), *Information Systems Research* (ISR), *Journal of the Association for Information Systems* (JAIS), *Journal of Management Information Systems* (JMIS), *Management Science*, and *MIT Sloan Management Review* (MIT SMR). He is the author and editor of seminal books, including the *International Handbook on Business Process Management, BPM—Driving Innovation in a Digital World, Green Business Process Management*, and the *Business Process Management Cases* volumes 1, 2, and 3. Jan vom Brocke is a Visiting Professor at the University of Liechtenstein and an Academic Research Fellow at Massachusetts Institute of Technology (MIT), Center for Information Systems Research (CISR). He has been named a Fellow of the Association for Information Systems (AIS), a Fellow of the École Supérieure de Commerce de Paris (ESCP) Center for Design Science in Entrepreneurship, a Schoeller Senior Fellow at Friedrich Alexander University (FAU) in Germany, a Distinguished Professor of Process Science at the National University of Ireland, Maynooth University (MU). Professor vom Brocke is an invited speaker and serves as trusted advisor to many companies as well as governmental institutions.

Towards User-Oriented Process Mining: A Collaborative Approach to Minimize Late Payments in Accounts Payable Process

Urszula Jessen, Michal Sroka, and Alessandro Berti

Abstract This paper presents an application of process mining techniques to a real-world accounts payable process within the context of ECE, aiming to minimize late payments.

(a) *Situation faced*: The initial stages of a process-based insight project posed challenges for the process mining team as they were confronted with numerous process variants and comprehensive dashboards that hindered the identification of critical issues within the processes. These complications impeded the understanding and implementation of process analysis for business users, necessitating extensive training and leading to localized optimizations that were inconsistent with the overarching end-to-end process improvement goals.

(b) *Action taken*: To address these challenges, the team initially concentrated on the accounts payable process to demonstrate the practical implementation of process mining techniques. They developed a process analytics pipeline that integrated advanced process mining with machine learning models, generating targeted and actionable insights and recommendations. Furthermore, they leveraged an informal network of experts to address the difficulties of discerning complex patterns in interconnected processes and delivering root cause insights.

(c) *Results achieved*: The process mining team devised a process analysis pipeline comprising the automatic generation of object-centric event logs that were subsequently analyzed using event knowledge graphs. Machine learning models were then employed to uncover root causes, yielding actionable insights that

U. Jessen (✉)
ECE Group Services, Aachen, Germany
e-mail: urszula.jessen@ece.com

M. Sroka
Microsoft, Aachen, Germany
e-mail: misroka@microsoft.com

A. Berti
RWTH Aachen University, Aachen, Germany
e-mail: a.berti@pads.rwth-aachen.de

J. vom Brocke et al. (eds.), *Business Process Management Cases Vol. 3*,
https://doi.org/10.1007/978-3-031-80793-0_9

119

were systematically organized and correlated to facilitate the identification of areas for improvement and the customization of recommendations for various stakeholders.

(d) *Lessons learned*: This project underscored the significance of a clear purpose, a user-centered design, the targeting of the appropriate audience, effective dashboards, an actionable design, and proper data modeling in the process mining and dashboard designs. The findings suggest that a well-constructed framework can offer tailored insight for various process stakeholders and that selecting a suitable data modeling approach is essential to achieving substantial results from process mining initiatives.

1   Introduction

The ECE Group was founded in 1965 and has since grown to become a leading player in the European shopping center industry. ECE's current construction and planning activities amount to €3.2 billion and it manages a portfolio of 200 shopping centers. With €31 billion worth of assets under management and a workforce of 3300 employees, the company has a strong presence in 13 countries. Early in 2020, ECE Group Services started a process mining initiative that aimed to improve its complex and data-intensive processes. The pilot project showed the viability of using process mining tools and methods for process enhancement but also uncovered the need for a structured governance framework and standard operating procedures to conduct effective process analyses. Based on the preliminary results, a dedicated team—*Process Insights*—within ECE began developing new projects to support various business users in optimizing their processes.

The objective of this study is to present a novel approach to process mining analysis that was adopted by ECE and combines the strengths of process mining techniques and machine learning methods. This approach has been applied to a real-world scenario in ECE to demonstrate its efficacy in uncovering complex patterns and root causes in interconnected processes. We describe the design of a process analytics pipeline that integrates recent advancements in object-centric process mining and event knowledge graphs with machine learning models to produce targeted and understandable analyses that lead to actions. The benefits of this approach include enhanced process visibility, the identification of optimization opportunities, and deeper insight into user interactions and behaviors. Our results indicate that this technique has significant potential for improving efficiency and increasing the value of the process mining initiatives.

2   Situation Faced

In the early stages of the process insights project, the team utilized a method based on the standard BPM framework, which included process mining tools and techniques, with the aim of enhancing business processes. The BPM lifecycle model, widely recognized as the standard, encompasses six essential steps: process identification, discovery, analysis, redesign, implementation, and monitoring and control, all of which aim to optimize and streamline processes (vom Brocke & Mendling, 2018; Dumas et al., 2013). The team's approach, in the ECE context, involved defining clear goals and objectives, gathering and preparing data, analyzing processes, identifying improvement opportunities, implementing changes, monitoring progress, continuously reevaluating processes to ensure the desired results were being achieved, and exploring new optimization prospects. However, process analysis projects faced several challenges, including a large number of process variants and standards for different countries and stakeholders. Given the various requirements, the number of KPIs and analyses has been increasing, which made the close monitoring of processes more difficult and time-consuming. The complexity of the processes sometimes makes it challenging for business users to comprehend and utilize process analysis, even with the help of process visualizations.

This resulted in a need for extensive training to boost adoption rates. Working with direct process participants in multiple in-depth workshops sometimes resulted in localized optimizations that were not always aligned with the goal of improving the overall end-to-end process (Cox et al., 2010). Process mining dashboards were also adopted.

Figure 1 shows a simplified and anonymized representation of a typical process mining dashboard for the accounts payable process. Similar dashboards were used by both process participants and management to optimize the process. It highlights how addressing the different needs and requirements of different stakeholders can result in insight that may otherwise be difficult to uncover or put into action.

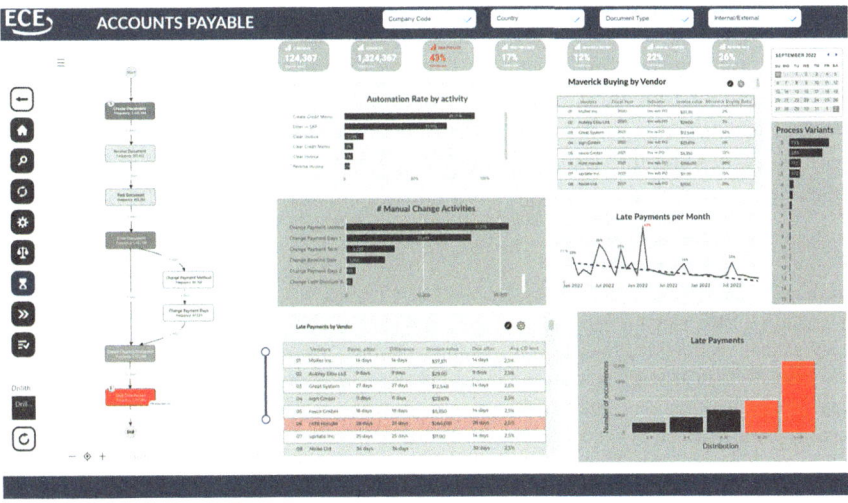

Fig. 1 Simplified representation of a typical process mining dashboard for the accounts payable process

3 Action Taken

To address the described challenges and increase the overall adoption of process mining analysis, we analyzed our objectives and the barriers that prevent business users from utilizing process mining tools. Through a series of informal interviews with our users, we addressed the improvements they desired and what was missing. The biggest issues that we discovered were related to the practical use of dashboards and the abundance of information. Users also pointed out that it takes a lot of effort to uncover the root causes of some problems and it is easy to overlook key points when faced with a large amount of data. The results of the analysis require an in-depth understanding of the underlying structure to find meaningful answers. Additionally, users also mentioned that it can be difficult to communicate the findings with other departments as they often belong to different processes (e.g., procurement and accounting), which makes it challenging to establish common metrics and identify problems at the interface between the different processes.

To formulate the problems and design the improved process mining framework, we adopted the action design research (ADR) method. ADR is a technique for gaining design knowledge through the construction and assessment of IT artifacts in real-world organizational situations. The goal of ADR is to generate prescriptive design knowledge that can be applied to practical issues in the field (Sein et al., 2011).

Given the complexity of the issues, we initially chose to concentrate on a single process and its interactions with other processes. We began with the *accounts payable* process,[1] and after consultations with top management, the research objective established was to reduce the number of overdue payments. This focus allowed us to effectively identify the root causes of the problem and implement targeted solutions while also laying the foundation for future process improvement initiatives. By focusing on a specific process, we aimed to demonstrate the practical application of process mining techniques and the benefits they can bring to the organization. The objective of reducing late payments was selected as it had a direct impact on the financial performance of the organization[2] and could be easily measured. By successfully addressing this issue, we hoped to demonstrate the value of process mining and encourage wider adoption within the organization.

---

[1] Accounts payable is the process of managing and paying a company's bills and invoices from suppliers and vendors. It typically involves the recording, classifying, and paying of bills in a timely and accurate manner, as well as reconciling any discrepancies with suppliers.

[2] Late payments in the accounts payable process can have serious consequences for a company. These consequences go beyond affecting the relationship with suppliers; they can also cause or worsen cash flow problems for suppliers, harm the buyer-supplier relationship, and have the potential to damage the company's reputation. In addition, it can lead to increased costs of borrowing and loss of discounts for prompt payment. Late payments can also negatively impact the company's ability to secure future business as suppliers may be hesitant to do business with a company that has a history of paying late. In some cases, it may even result in legal action against the company, which can lead to significant financial and reputational costs.

3.1   Actionable Dashboards

During the problem formulation stage, we recognized that the primary challenge that needed to be addressed was ensuring the actionability of the process analysis. *Actionability* refers to the ability to act upon a prediction, insight, or label. It is the provision of a recommendation on the easiest way to change an unsatisfactory situation based on a set of rules. It answers the questions "What do I do with this insight?" and "How do I use a model or analysis to act upon an undesirable label?" (Denton & Salleb-Aouissi, 2020). This required us to go beyond simply identifying areas for improvement and provide actionable insights and recommendations that could be easily implemented by business users.

To achieve this, we needed to design a process analytics pipeline that combined advanced process mining techniques with machine learning models to produce targeted and understandable analyses that could be translated into actions. This approach was crucial to ensuring the success of the project and the wider adoption of process mining within the organization. By focusing on actionability, we aimed to demonstrate the practical benefits of process mining and encourage its widespread use in process improvement initiatives.

In the process improvement initiative at ECE, Celonis was used as the primary tool for analyzing and visualizing the behavior of various processes. The Celonis Action Engine, a Web-based application, was employed to turn process analysis insights into actionable recommendations and to provide operational support during the process execution (Badakhshan et al., 2019). However, the effectiveness of the tool was highly dependent on the skill of the process analyst and how they designed the signals extracted from the data model. It failed to address several challenges faced by the ECE team, such as identifying complex patterns in interconnected processes and providing root cause insights based on feature importance calculations. To overcome these limitations, we decided to form an informal network of experts from various fields and work together to find the best solutions for specific challenges.

3.2   Actionable Insight Clusters

To effectively address the challenges posed by the intricate and information-rich processes at ECE, we structured our hypothesis around two key areas. These areas were based on different layers in the process and aimed to answer questions related to process performance, compliance, and quality. The first area focused on answering the question of "what has/would happen?" while the second area focused on answering the question of "why did it happen?" To effectively show the boundaries of different interest clusters, we aimed to illustrate different perspectives from within the organizational hierarchy. It was suspected that people at different levels may have different perspectives on a process and be able to identify different potential actions for improving both isolated and interconnected processes.

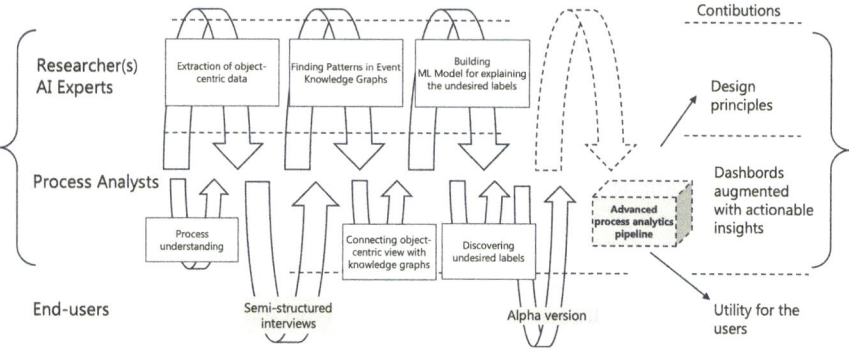

Fig. 2 Cooperation schema adopted during the project, which follows the guidelines reported in (Cox et al., 2010)

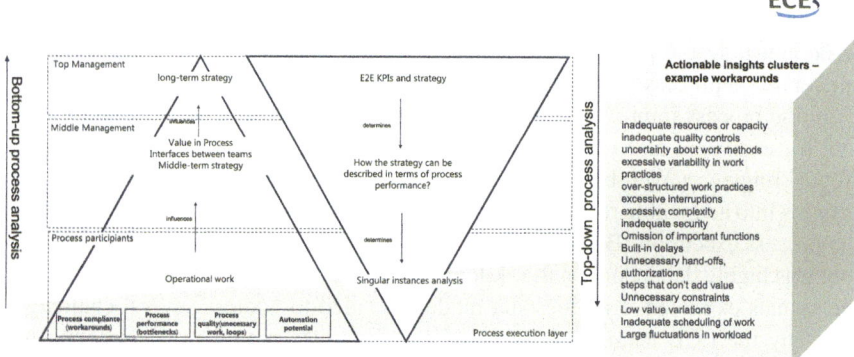

Fig. 3 Example of an actionable insight cluster matrix designed for different process stakeholders

Figure 2 displays the design and testing process of the analytics pipeline. With the support of researchers from the RWTH Aachen University, a generic object-centric model of processes from the SAP system was extracted and some of its features were summarized and analyzed (Berti et al., 2022, 2023). The object-centric approach was particularly useful for questions related to subprocess interfaces and deviations from the standard process. To find broader patterns, especially regarding the overall strategy, we used event knowledge graphs (Fahland, 2022). In contrast to these two approaches, which primarily supported answers to the "what" question, AI experts from Microsoft developed a model for process mining explainability and finding the root causes of undesired process behavior. The methods and findings are discussed in more detail in the following section.

In Fig. 3, we present some of the findings from our analysis of process participants and areas in process analysis that would benefit from dedicated analysis. Our focus during the preliminary stage was to understand the high variability of processes and identify the possible causes. This was done using semi-structured interviews with process participants, where we discussed different instances of deviations from expected process behavior and possible root causes. The results of these interviews, along with literature research on similar problems, are presented in Fig. 3.

In this example, we concentrated on issues that could be explained by process participants using workarounds. The concept of workarounds and how to uncover them has been widely studied in the literature (Alter, 2015). A workaround can be defined as a solution that process participants find to bypass or overcome limitations or obstacles in systems or processes. These solutions are employed when normal procedures are seen as too slow, the necessary information is unavailable, or there are technology malfunctions. The perception of workarounds varies depending on the context of the process or system, ranging from being viewed as necessary to questionable, hazardous, or even illegal (Alter, 2015). Uncovering workarounds created by users can help standardize processes and identify ways to make the process more efficient and effective. After collecting the findings from the interviews and structuring them, we were able to build a cluster of possible root causes that could be addressed with specific actions. For example, problems arising from uncertainty about working methods could be addressed through detailed documentation of the process.

4   Results Achieved

The design of the process analysis pipeline depicted in Fig. 4 was created through collaboration with different parties and developers. The primary source of data was extracted from an ERP System but the plan moving forward is to incorporate data

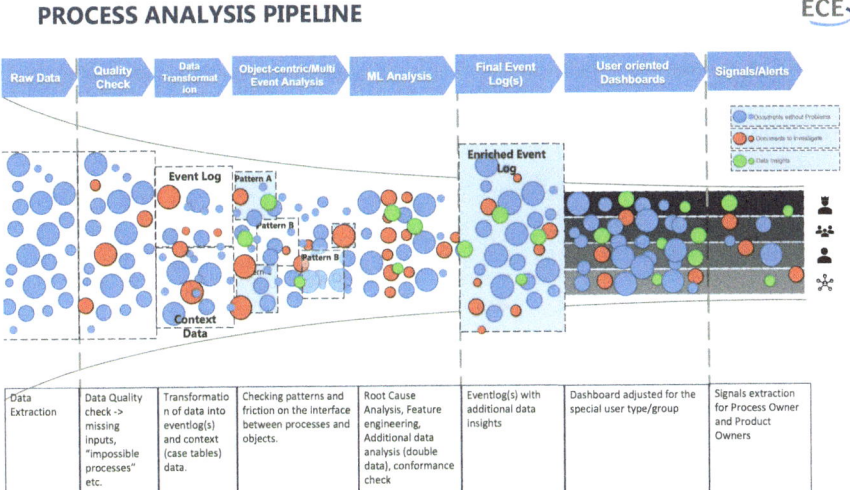

Fig. 4 Data pipeline for process mining adopted in ECE

from other sources such as CRM Systems. The next stage of the pipeline focuses on quality and compliance checks, with plans to add further constraints based on insight from process analysts and end users using user-oriented dashboards. Problems with the data may be identified at this stage. The data is then transformed into flat event logs and enriched with context data and object-centric event logs are also extracted.

4.1 Finding Patterns and Outliers

In addition to the previously mentioned challenges regarding actioning and comprehending the results of process mining analysis, there are also difficulties related to preparing the data to create an event log. Convergence and divergence were two of the most significant problems in this case. *Convergence* refers to the situation where the same activity is carried out in multiple process instances at the same time, resulting in duplicated events and inflated statistics (showing more created orders than actually existed). *Divergence* refers to the observation of multiple executions of the same activity for a single instance that actually belong to different objects, leading to incorrect ordering of activities in the trace (van der Aalst, 2019).

To tackle these issues, we decided to build object-centric event logs and try to look at the processes from different perspectives. In the case of the accounts payable process, we were able to examine all the invoices passing through the system but also all xSuite objects that were loaded and scanned using OCR, as well as the related purchase orders. This multifaceted approach allowed us to gain a deeper understanding of bottlenecks and process issues that had not been feasible when examining the invoice creation, editing, and payment processes alone. An examination of the types of goods ordered, the methods of order release in the process, and the scanning of incoming documents provided insight into patterns across the interrelated processes.

Object-centric process mining was used to uncover the end-to-end process. Figure 5 shows an excerpt from the resulting object-centric Petri net discovered from the SAP system. The process visualizes only one instance of an invoice and the various objects that are interrelated in different processes. The different colors

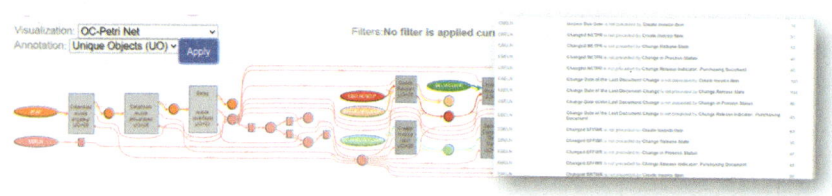

Fig. 5 Representation of an object-centric process model (object-centric Petri net) discovered on an event log extracted for the accounts payable process with deviations from expected behavior

Fig. 6 Event knowledge graph related to the accounts payable process, computed on Neo4J and visualized using Neo4J Bloom

indicate different objects such as an invoice, invoice position, purchase order, or goods receipt. Figure 5 also lists some of the deviations from the expected process behavior found with the OCPM object-centric process mining tool (in particular, using the conformance checking component).

The OCPM tool[3] offers a comprehensive set of features for analyzing and modeling object-centric processes. This example demonstrates various issues that were discovered for the purchase order objects (EBELN).

As object-centric event data can be stored and queried in graph databases quite naturally, the popular Neo4J graph database was used to gain a better understanding of some of the preliminary insights and anomalies, such as maverick buying. Figure 6 shows the resulting example of all the invoices satisfying a required pattern (maverick buying).

4.2 Machine Learning: Finding Root Causes

To provide actionable insight, we needed to uncover the root causes of the problems in the process. Root causes are usually causal links between variables and the outcome. Several root cause analysis methods exist. Most of them include training a machine learning model to predict the value of a selected KPI (e.g., if the payment is going to occur late). The predictions of the machine learning model depend on the values of the attributes of the order and process case and structures learned by the

---

[3] https://www.ocpm.info

Fig. 7 Connection between the numeric values of the features and the target variable of the prediction, discovered using the Shapley method

model. There are many methods for discovering the relationships between the features and the model output.

One of these methods is implemented in the Shapley library (Lundberg et al., 2018). Shapley can provide insight into the decisions of the machine learning model at different levels of abstraction. These include case, cohort, and global level. Such visualization on a case level is shown in Fig. 7. This is also useful for selecting the most important features regarding the target value, for example, whether the payment was on time. The more complex interactions between feature value and their impact on the KPI or model-level structures can be also visualized using dependence plots (Friedman, 2001) and model-level summary plots, respectively. Such analysis can be done on the entire event log or its slices of interest.

4.3 Considering Insight in Relation to Stakeholders

After identifying the problematic patterns and their underlying causes, the next step is to categorize the insights and place them into relevant layers. This enables the systematic organization and correlation of information, which makes it easier to determine which areas would benefit most from specific actions. By attributing the insight to specific clusters, it becomes possible to understand the different perspectives and interests of different process participants and stakeholders and tailor the recommendations accordingly.

The proposed framework provides a structured approach to categorizing and contextualizing insights, making it easier to determine the areas that would benefit most from improvement efforts. In the next stage, the framework should be deployed in a real-world setting and refined based on feedback from stakeholders. This will enable the expansion of actionable insights and the exploration of additional process questions across different processes.

5   Lessons Learned

The key lessons learned from this project on process mining and dashboard design are as follows:

- Clear Purpose: The importance of having a clear purpose and designing objectives that align with business requirements. The dashboard should focus on actionable insights and relevant information for the intended audience.
- User-Centered Design: Placing user requirements at the center of the process mining initiative through repeated prototyping and user testing. Incorporating data from multiple sources for a comprehensive view of the process landscape.
- Targeting the Right Audience: Customizing the design of the process analysis pipeline to meet specific audience needs and requirements. Presenting actionable data that is relevant and useful for the target audience.
- Effective Dashboards: Designing dashboards that are easy to use, visually engaging, and offer a user-friendly experience. Prioritizing key performance indicators and ensuring data integrity for trust in the data.
- Actionable Design: Considering the leverage of each user type and enabling users to easily detect outliers and anomalies. Segmenting and grouping data in a meaningful way and supporting process optimization at all levels of the organization. Avoiding direct correlations to increase trust in the analysis results.
- Data Modelling: The study highlights the importance of proper data modeling in process mining. It was found that traditional event logs often do not appropriately capture the complexities and interdependencies of real-life processes. To address this issue, a variety of approaches have been proposed in academic literature, each with its own strengths and limitations. It is crucial to consider these approaches and to choose the method that is the best fit for the specific process mining problem at hand. In conclusion, this case study has emphasized the potential of data modeling for realizing significant and implementable outcomes from process mining initiatives. The demonstrated use case emphasizes that there is no universal solution for all problems and that a well-designed framework is necessary to providing customized insight for different process stakeholders.

References

Alter, S. (2015). A workaround design system for anticipating, designing, and/or preventing workarounds. In *Enterprise, business-process and information systems modeling: 16th international conference, BPMDS 2015, 20th international conference, EMMSAD 2015, Held at CAiSE 2015, Stockholm, Sweden, June 8–9, 2015, Proceedings* (pp. 489–498). Springer.

Badakhshan, P., Bernhart, G., Geyer-Klingeberg, J., Nakladal, J., Schenk, S., & Vogelgesang, T. (2019). *The action engine–turning process insights into action*. ICPM Demos.

Berti, A., Herforth, J., Qafari, M., & van der Aalst, W. M. (2022). *Graph-based feature extraction on object-centric event logs*. Springer.

Berti, A., Park, G., Rafiei, M., & van der Aalst, W. (2023). *A generic approach to extract object-centric event data from relational databases*. Springer.

Cox, J. F., III, CIRM, C., & Schleier, J. G., Jr. (2010). *Theory of constraints handbook* (pp. 1–217). McGraw-Hill Education.

Denton, S. M., & Salleb-Aouissi, A. (2020). *A weighted solution to svm actionability and interpretability*. arXiv preprint arXiv:2012.03372.

Dumas, M., La Rosa, M., Mendling, J., & Reijers, H. A. (2013). *Fundamentals of business process management*. Springer.

Fahland, D. (2022). Process mining over multiple behavioral dimensions with event knowledge graphs. In W. M. P. van der Aalst & J. Carmona (Eds.), *Process mining handbook* (Lecture notes in business information processing) (Vol. 448, pp. 274–319). Springer.

Friedman, J. H. (2001). Greedy function approximation: A gradient boosting machine. *Annals of Statistics, 29*, 1189–1232.

Lundberg, S. M., Erion, G. G., & Lee, S.-I. (2018). *Consistent individualized feature attribution for tree ensembles*. arXiv preprint arXiv:1802.03888.

Sein, M. K., Henfridsson, O., Purao, S., Rossi, M., & Lindgren, R. (2011). Action design research. *MIS Quarterly, 35*, 37–56.

van der Aalst, W. M. P. (2019). Object-centric process mining: Dealing with divergence and convergence in event data. In P. C. Ölveczky & G. Salaün (Eds.), *Software engineering and formal methods – 17th international conference, SEFM 2019, Oslo, Norway, September 18–20, 2019, proceedings* (Lecture notes in computer science) (Vol. 11724, pp. 3–25). Springer. https://doi.org/10.1007/978-3-030-30446-1_1

vom Brocke, J., & Mendling, J. (2018). Frameworks for business process management: a taxonomy for business process management cases. In *Business process management cases: digital innovation and business transformation in practice* (pp. 1–17). Springer.

Urszula Jessen has over 15 years of experience in process management, process optimization, and process mining. Over the years, she has built robust industrial solutions aimed at improving processes with the support of process mining and machine learning technologies. She is currently working at ECE Group Services, Germany, delivering insights for process improvement. She is also pursuing her PhD at Technology University Eindhoven, where she researches actionable process mining. For the past 2 years, she has been developing solutions to connect large language models (LLMs) to process mining. Her goal is to make process analysis streamlined and understandable, regardless of the user's expertise level.

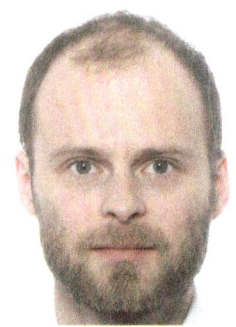

Michal Sroka is an esteemed AI professional with a robust scientific background, holding a PhD in Artificial Intelligence from King's College London and 10-year tenure at Microsoft, where he contributed to the field of process mining, explainable AI (XAI), product recommendation systems, and generative AI. At Microsoft, Michal has been developing sophisticated AI models that not only enhance user experience but also ensure transparency and understandability of AI decision-making processes within business application context. His work in generative AI at Microsoft Copilot Studio involves leading a data science team in creating advanced generative models that serve as a cornerstone for innovative solutions across many business scenarios. Michał is also actively contributing to the growing field of using generative AI in process mining.

Deploying Predictive Models for a Process-Aware Decision Support System

Prerna Agarwal and Renuka Sindhgatta

Abstract

(a) *Situation faced*: In recent years, there has been increasing interest in using machine learning (ML) in industrial applications, such as loan approval process and travel approval process to support decision-making in business processes. This case involved building an ML-based decision support system within the IBM workflow engine that can be used to help knowledge workers make high-quality decisions while executing a business process. The deployment of ML in such systems poses various challenges and concerns.

(b) *Action taken*: There are several requirements for the production of ML systems and significant differences between evaluations in the academic setting and what is required of a real-world system. This includes the ability to cope with dynamic and changing data, model retraining to prevent model decay, low computational costs, and accurate and interpretable models that promote user trust. We present the design considerations for building a process-aware decision support system for business processes and outline the operational decisions of the process-aware feature engineering pipeline, how to choose a machine learning algorithm, and how to carry out end-user model testing. We also present our approach to handle model decay via online training that incorporates user feedback.

(c) *Results achieved*: We successfully deployed the actions in ML-based DSS within the IBM workflow engine by addressing the requirements of various phases of the ML deployment including data preparation, model selection, model verification, and model deployment.

(d) *Lessons learned*: The deployment of an ML-based DSS as a part of a workflow engine presents a distinct set of issues invalidating common assumptions.

P. Agarwal (✉)
IBM Research – AI, New Delhi, New Delhi, India
e-mail: preragar@in.ibm.com

R. Sindhgatta
IBM Research – AI, Bangalore, Karnataka, India
e-mail: renuka.sr@ibm.com

Despite having complex deep learning-based models increasingly developed and benchmarked by the research community, in practice, simpler models with low computational requirements are often chosen. The absence of real-world data with all the necessary characteristics for model verification often requires a synthetic process to generate data representative of the real world that includes drift. User feedback plays an important role in improving the decisions made by ML-based DSSs.

1 Introduction

In any business process application, knowledge workers have to make various decisions as cases progress through the stages of the process. Some of these decisions are governed by predefined rules that the knowledge workers must follow. However, other decisions require the knowledge workers to make optimal decisions based on their experience and knowledge of a process, taking into account various organizational goals and policies. In such circumstances, a machine learning-based decision support (DSS) system can be deployed to help knowledge workers make high-quality decisions based on historical execution data that supports more favorable business outcomes and higher confidence.

Several state-of-the-art machine learning (ML) methods have been used to predict which action to execute next, what other actions need to be executed, the outcome of the execution, and the expected completion time of the partially executed case. These data-driven methods are trained on partial running cases (also called prefixes). Research has evaluated a wide array of traditional machine-learning techniques, such as support vector machines, boosting trees, logistic regression models (Teinemaa et al., 2019), and deep learning (DL) models (Pasquadibisceglie et al., 2021; Rama-Maneiro et al., 2023). The results indicate it is feasible to use such models in a real-world setting for various downstream tasks for business process monitoring. However, there are significant differences between what works in a research setting and what is required of a real-world production system.[1] Furthermore, deploying machine learning models in production systems poses several challenges (Paleyes et al., 2023). As indicated by Sculley et al. (Sculley et al., 2015), only a tiny fraction of the code in many ML systems is devoted to learning or prediction. Additionally, a report surveying 2473 organizations and their experience with ML found high costs, bias in the data, and lack of expertise were the top reasons for deployment failures.[2] Building and deploying ML-based methods for business processes could pose similar challenges.

---

[1] By "real-world production system", we mean a system made available for use by its intended audience.

[2] https://venturebeat.com/2019/07/08/idc-for-1-in-4-companies-half-of-all-ai-projects-fail/

We present an industry case of deploying an ML model within the IBM Business Automation Workflow (BAW[3]) product, which allows users to automate their digital business processes. The goal was to provide decision support for each of the decision tasks in the workflow. Such production ML systems have several requirements over the four main stages of its development cycle (Ashmore et al., 2022):

- *Data management* focuses on preparing the data required to train and build a machine-learning model.
- *Model learning* relates to the training and selection of a suitable model.
- *Model verification* addresses specific functional and performance requirements including the robustness of the model.
- *Model deployment* refers to the integration of the model into the software system and the ongoing maintenance and updating of the model.

In this chapter, we focus on the design decisions that accommodated the requirements and the related challenges in the process of building the ML-based system. While each of these design stages can be broken down into further steps, we have focused primarily on the critical elements that we addressed during the integration of the ML model with the workflow engine.

In the following, Sect. 2 describes the situation faced as a set of requirements for deploying the model as a part of the workflow system. Then Sect. 3 elaborates on the actions taken to address the requirements of the ML-based decision support system. Section 4 presents the model deployed as a part of the workflow engine and, in closing, Sect. 5 outlines the lessons learned.

2   Situation Faced

2.1   Introducing the Context of the Decision Support System

The case study we are presenting here is a subsystem providing ML-based decision support within the IBM Business Automation Workflow product (IBM BAW). An example travel process that was authored in the IBM BAW is shown in Fig. 1. The example process represents a pre-approval and reimbursement for business travel. There are three decision points: (i) Approval of the pre-expense request based on the case details, (ii) approval of the case for travel considering the budget, and (iii) final approval of the case for travel reimbursement. None of these decisions are driven by predefined rules and require the expertise of the knowledge worker. The goal is to provide an ML-based decision support subsystem at each decision point in the business process. As decision support must be provided for every process authored and executed using the product, the approach to the training and use of the predictive models needed to be domain agnostic. At runtime, a prediction API is invoked at the

---

[3] https://www.ibm.com/products/business-automation-workflow

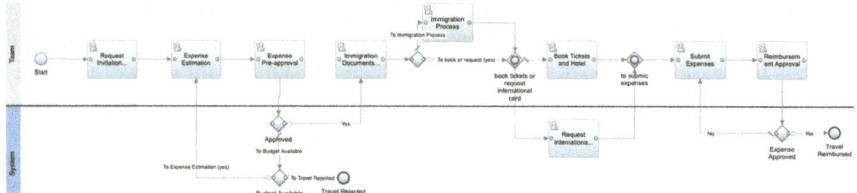

Fig. 1 Example of a business process using ML-based decision support

backend and the predicted decision is provided by the IBM BAW user interface (UI) in order to support the knowledge worker and bolster prediction confidence. A knowledge worker can then take action and has the option to provide feedback on the prediction.

2.2 Requirements for an ML-Based Decision Support System

In this section, we present the essential requirements specific to the industrial deployment of the ML-based decision support system (hereafter referred to as ML-DSS) in our case study.

Data Preparation Data forms an important part of any ML system. The workflow engine emits process logs that are stored in a database accessible to the ML-DSS. At each decision point, our proposed system builds the model using the "legitimate" information available in the system at that particular point in time. It was an important requirement that the system is able to validate that there is no data leakage (Kaufman et al., 2012) and that only *relevant* data is used. As ML-DSS predicts the decisions to be made, another key consideration was to ensure a balance between the number of data samples for each decision class (decision value). Additionally, it was necessary to ensure that the data remains free of *unwanted bias* that could result from the use of predictable features related to, for example, ethnicity, age, or gender. Hence, the information used by the ML-DSS needed to be *relevant, balanced, and free of unwanted bias*. This requirement was addressed during the *data preparation* stage.

Model Selection One of the biggest concerns with model selection is the computational resources required to train the ML model, which impacts the deployment cost of the system. This is especially true when designing an ML system that is part of a product targeting small- and medium-sized enterprise customers. While deep learning models have better performance than ML models, they are resource intensive. Hence, the ML-DSS deployed in our case study needed to have *good performance and relatively modest hardware requirements*. Training and selecting the best-performing model was a part of the *model learning* development stage.

Managing Process Drift Business process executions change in response to seasonal, regulatory, supply, demand, and process reengineering modifications. While some of these changes are planned, others may occur unexpectedly. Most ML algorithms operate under the assumption that the input data distribution is static. However, such process execution drift leads to a shift in the underlying input data distribution. Thus, for example, a change in policy could require changes in what decisions should be made. Hence, the ML-DSS needed to be able to *detect and handle data drift*. This requirement was addressed as a part of the *model verification* stage.

Model Understanding The need to understand and trust ML models led to the development of ML explainers (Lundberg & Lee, 2017) that explain the internal workings of the ML algorithms. However, when deploying the system for non-ML business experts, facilitating understanding requires a "what-if" analysis tool that allows users who are not experts in ML to probe the algorithm using counterfactual analysis to investigate and explore how changes in input affect the predictions for different real-world simulations in order to better understand how the model is behaving. Hence, our case study ML-DSS also needed to provide the option to *perform a what-if analysis* by changing input in a way that facilitates understanding of the ML model's behavior. Understanding of the model is an important requirement addressed as a part of *model deployment*.

User Feedback As knowledge workers play an indispensable role in training the ML-DSS via their feedback, it was *necessary to incorporate user feedback mechanisms*. Hence, the ML-DSS needed to enable users to provide relevant feedback when the model behaves in an undesirable manner. The user feedback then needs to be incorporated into the input to improve model performance. Nonetheless, when designing an online learning system (a system that changes its behavior in response to input) that interacts directly with end-users, the feedback needs to be regulated to avoid biased learning (Wolf et al., 2017).

3   Action Taken

This section details the design decisions related to the requirements of ML-DSSs. The overall architecture of the ML-DSS subsystem detailing the training and testing phase is shown in Fig. 2. An ensemble-based model that addresses the data drift was trained during the training phase. Then the predictions from the models were combined through a weighted majority vote (or sum) to produce the final prediction. During the online/inference phase, we provided a "what-if" analysis to support understanding of the model and incorporate the knowledge worker's feedback for online updates and model training.

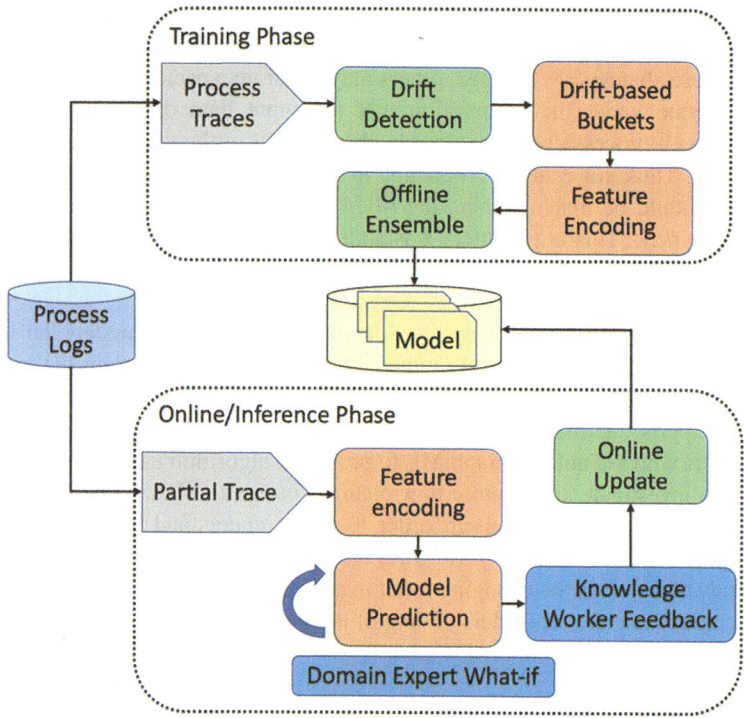

Fig. 2 Training and online phases of ML-DSSs

3.1 Data Processing

The IBM BAW engine emits event data in IBM Business Automation Insights (IBM BAI) that is accessed via the elastic search. The events are stored in various formats[4] that capture the event summaries at various levels, including process summaries, activity summaries, and resource summaries. We used process summaries for our application as it captures the summary of the BPMN process together with the state of the process, based on the most recent aggregated event. The state values include ACTIVE, COMPLETED, TERMINATED, and FAILED. It also captures the business data object that holds the attribute value information for the attribute enabled (also denoted as tracked variables) in the BPMN process. A sample event in the process summary of a BPMN is shown in Fig. 3. As shown in the figure, the "data" field captures the business object containing the business attributes of a BPMN. These process summaries are then parsed to form a regular event log with the *processInstanceId* field mapped to

---

[4] https://www.ibm.com/docs/en/cloud-paks/cp-biz-automation/21.0.3?topic=formats-bpmn-summary-event

trace_id of the event log, the *name* field mapped to *activity_id*, the *timestamp* field being used as-is, the *status* field, and one column for each business data attribute. This ensures that our framework operates on a generic event log structure so that any data source can be integrated into the framework by simply parsing the emitted data to the generic event log structure.

To identify potential sources of leakage and remove unwanted bias due to data attributes, such as ethnicity, age, and gender, that may have been present in the event log, we used the IBM AI-360 toolkit (Bellamy et al., 2018). We also analyzed the distribution of the decision outcomes for each decision point in the business process to check whether the distribution was balanced. In case of an imbalance in the distribution of decision outcomes, we used sampling techniques such as SMOTE (Bowyer et al., 2011) to balance the dataset. Hence, we managed the relevance, balance, and unwanted bias in the event log generated by the workflow engine.

3.2   *ML-Based Model for Lower Computational Costs*

To reduce the cost of the computing resources required for training and runtime execution of the model, we evaluated the existing ML algorithms using different feature encoding techniques as prescribed in the existing literature (Teinemaa et al., 2019). We enhanced the aggregation encoding (Teinemaa et al., 2019) by

```
{
    "_source": {
        "activityId": "d3d81cd6-450d-4d74-9c1a-01efabc42bd6",
        "processInstanceId": "24bee4f0cc0d11e99cb3000000256ad6",
        "state": "Complete",
        "processId": "100bc35f-d900-42db-92c9-3b444409f1e4",
        "name": "Request Invitation Letter",
        "timestamp": "2019-08-27T08:49:16.000-00:00",
        "data": {
            "AutoTrackBODV": {
                "@ids": {
                    "trackingGroupId": "e439610c:978e:4c33:bc7f:2af19284cbaa",
                    "trackingGroupVersionId": "bc8217ae-f454-46fd-a52c-d12ad3506438"
                },
                "BestPaperCandidate.string": "false",
                "ClientInvolved.string": "false",
                "ConferenceLevel.string": "pic top",
                "Cost.integer": 800.77,
                "Duration.integer": 5,
                "EthicalIssue.string": "false",
                "FirstAuthor.string": "false",
                "InvitationType.string": "printed",
                "PresentationType.string": "demo",
                "RegistrationCharges.integer": 867.44,
                "TravelType.string": "international",
                "Visa.string": "true"
            }
        }
    }
}
```

Fig. 3 Sample event emitted as process summary from IBM BAI

extracting additional features from a partial execution trace: (i) *transitions*, counting the occurrence of two successive activity transitions, (ii) *orderings,* counting the occurrence of two non-successive but transitive orderings of activities. Additionally, we used a decision tree-based feature selection approach for dimensionality reduction. Our approach, using logistic regression (LR), provides comparable performance with existing state-of-the-art models including deep learning models.

We experimented with the LR-based model on five widely used real-life event logs from different domains:

1. *BPIC2012*: Loan application processing logs from a Dutch financial institution.
2. *Traffic Fine Management*: Record events related to notifications sent about fines issued by and payments to a local Italian police force.
3. *Hospital Billing*: Execution of billing procedures for medical services from a hospital's ERP system.
4. *Sepsis*: Record of the trajectories of patients with sepsis conditions in a Dutch hospital.
5. *BPIC2017*: An event log from the same financial institution as BPIC2012 containing richer and cleaner traces.

Statistics on these datasets are shown in Table 1. Table 2 presents the results comparing the area under the curve (AUC) as the model performance metric with existing ML and DL state-of-the-art baselines.

Table 1 Statistics on the dataset used

Event log	Traces	Avg. trace length	Activities	Categoric attributes	Numeric attributes
BPIC2012	13,087	20	24	2	2
Traffic fine	150,370	4	11	3	5
Hospital billing	77,627	6	18	5	6
Sepsis	1049	14	16	4	22
BPIC2017	31,509	38	26	8	7

Table 2 Comparing ML-DSS with state-of-the-art **ML** (Teinemaa et al., 2019) and FOX (DL) approaches (Pasquadibisceglie et al., 2021)

Event log	Decision outcome	ML-DSS	ML	FOX (DL)
BPIC 2012	Loan application approval	**0.76**	0.59	0.6
Sepsis	IC admission	**0.86**	0.85	0.73
Hospital billing	Case reopening	**0.75**	0.68	–
Traffic fine	Credit collection decision	0.67	0.67	–
BPIC 2017	Loan application approval	**0.81**	0.72	–

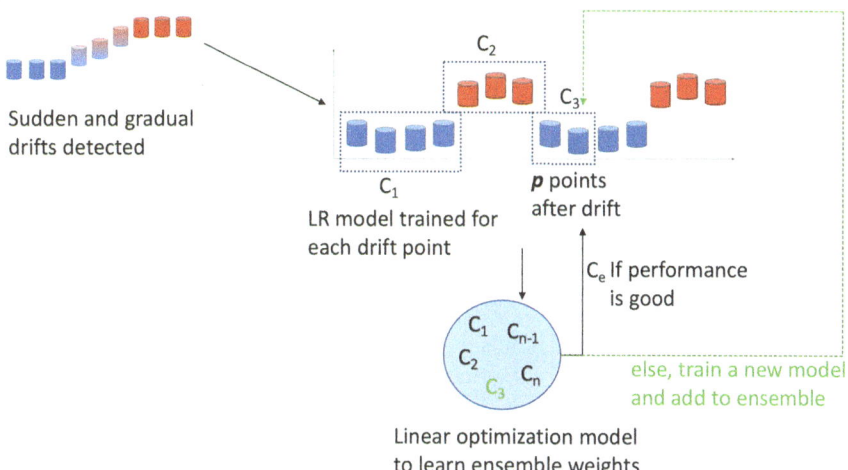

Fig. 4 Handling data drift using ensemble and linear optimization models

3.3   *Managing Data Drift*

Initially, we detected data drift using the detection method proposed by Maaradji et al. (2017). Using a sliding window approach (Maaradji et al., 2017), the method monitors any statistically significant changes in the distribution set of traces. As illustrated in Fig. 4, a logistic regression (LR) model C_i was built for each drift point detected. For each new drift point detected, a new LR model was built using a minimum of p new data points that were collected after the new drift point. To ensure the number of models trained did not keep increasing, we leveraged the knowledge of the current set of trained models (i.e., C_1, C_2,.., C_n as illustrated in Fig. 4) to see whether they could also contribute to providing predictions for these p data points. For this, we formulated a *linear optimization model* to create an ensemble model based on the trained models available for which the ensemble weights have been learned. We used a minimum number of data points, p, with ground truth labels, L, that were provided as human feedback to decide whether this ensemble model would help provide predictions by evaluating the model performance. If the ensemble performance was low, a new model (e.g., C_3) was trained for p points and added to the list of available model ensembles for analyzing subsequent drift points. The use of ensembles helped train models that can handle *seasonal* drifts in the data.

3.4   *What-If Analysis for Model Understanding*

We provided a mechanism to allow a larger set of non-ML experts (e.g., knowledge workers/domain experts) to engage with and understand the ML-DSS by asking questions such as "How would reducing the cost of travel affect the decision?" or

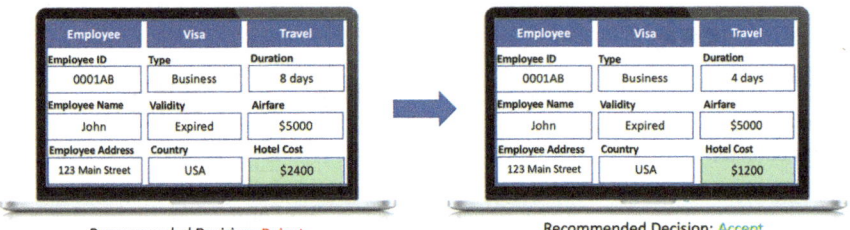

Fig. 5 What-if analysis performed by changing case details in the ML-DSS

"What would need to change in this case for a different decision?" To enable this, we provided a way to visualize the trace and update the attributes shown in Fig. 5. Once the trace and its attributes are updated, the features are extracted, and the new prediction of the ML model is provided. As shown in Fig. 5, when the knowledge worker changes the value of "Hotel Cost" from $2400 to $1200, the model's decision changes. Therefore, the knowledge worker can iteratively update the trace and its attributes to see whether it will change the model's decision. This feature enables a better understanding of the model and may enhance the user's trust in the system. Hence, the final decision can be made by the knowledge worker who can choose the original decision or suggest what changes to make to the case in order to secure a favorable outcome.

3.5 Knowledge Worker Feedback

Knowledge worker (KW) feedback is regulated to ensure that the system does not learn based on erroneous or biased input from one or more workers. Hence, when a KW provides contrary feedback on a prediction made by the ML-DSS, a set of k-nearest traces is extracted and their prediction is evaluated. If the decision for the k-nearest traces is skewed to the prediction made by the ML-DSS, the samples are provided as an explanation to the KW reconsiders the feedback. If the KW continues to give contrary feedback, the input is marked as "to be validated" and flagged for consideration by an expert. If the decision of k neighbors is not skewed (i.e., the model is confused), additional *similar* traces are generated to obtain feedback (decisions) from the KW for training.

Online Training To address scenarios where there is limited training data, we use KW feedback as one of the mechanisms to train the model via online training. Inspired by Wang and Pineau (2016), an AdaBoost-based online learning method is used to train the m LR base models. All data points labeled and used as input for online training were initially assigned an equal weight. The data points are assumed to be sequential based on the start timestamp of the trace. The prediction is then obtained based on the current set of LR models for each data point. If a data point is

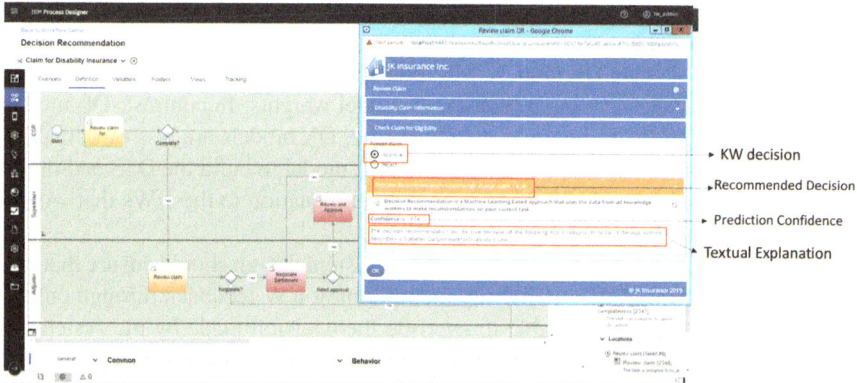

Fig. 6 On-premise integration with the workflow engine

misclassified, then the weight of that data point is increased so that it can be predicted correctly with the next base classifier. Otherwise, it is decreased. The updated weights of the data points are then used to train the next base classifier. Thus, the model ensembles are updated via online training.

4 Results Achieved

The ML-DSS presented here is currently in the alpha stage of deployment for the IBM BAW product. Figure 6 shows the integration into the workflow engine and prediction and model confidence are displayed at each decision point. The proposed system is designed to run on both on-premise and cloud deployments. End users can enable predictions for any decision point and this feature will be enabled for all the KWs working on that decision. As most tasks in a business process are decision or function problems, the overall impact of even a modest improvement in decision time and quality is considerable. ML-based DSS can provide quality predictions that enable the KWs to take timely action, thus scaling the impact.

5 Lessons Learned

The following presents the lessons learned while building this framework and its deployment process:

- *ML vs DL trade-off*: Although deep learning and reinforcement learning are widely popular within the research community, simpler models are often chosen in practice as the cost of training and deploying DL models is often prohibitive. The marginal performance trade-off of a DL model is usually acceptable when handling structured process data. Furthermore, when incorporating user feedback in the runtime systems and updating the model incrementally, ML models are more flexible than DL models. ML models are more readily interpretable and explainable through the interpretation of model weights. In contrast, DL model weights are difficult to interpret, and therefore, DL models are less explainable. For these reasons, our framework used the ML model to build the DSS and interpret its weights in order to provide a textual explanation to the KWs that would build user trust.

- *Decision support with KW supervision*: The system design should ensure that the model learns from KW expertise by incorporating KW feedback through online training. A KW should be able to override the decision made by the system as there are always external or organizational-level factors and attributes that logs are unable to capture. The design ensures decision support for novice KW. Moreover, it should also be ensured that KW feedback is only used to update the model when the feedback is constructive. Otherwise, if the model is updated based on all feedback, it will become highly susceptible to noise. Hence, the design ensures feedback regulation.

- *Building a representative digital twin*: When designing a generic ML-based DSS, it is unlikely that all types of decision scenarios will be available in a real-world dataset(s). Hence, building a robust simulation setup to test the suitability of each system is essential. We simulated approximately 8000 traces for the IBM proprietary travel approval process. Additionally, process variants, data drift, and noise were accounted for. The synthetic data overcame the significant cold-start problem of not having a representative real-world event log.

- *Managing relevant drift in the data*: Managing data drift is a critical requirement when deploying such systems as, in the real world, systems need to adapt to changes in organizational policies and regulations. Therefore, drift detection techniques are usually built by inducing a particular type of drift in the synthetic data and then verifying the accuracy of the ML-DSS's predictions and explanations. There are two particularly common types of drifts observed: (i) process drift, where the control flow, such as addition or deletion of actions, occurs over time and (ii) data drift, where the decisions to be made based on data attributes change over time. However, there may also be other types of data drift that are not predicted, and hence, detecting all possible types of data drift becomes challenging. Therefore, our proposed framework focuses only on drifts that impact the decision. Hence, during the synthetic data simulation, drift in the data was induced so that it impacted the decisions of the KW. Only then was the drift in the decision identified and managed within the described algorithm. Hence, the framework should be capable of validating requirements that may not be pre-identified in the real-world data.

References

Ashmore, R., Calinescu, R., & Paterson, C. (2022). Assuring the machine learning lifecycle: Desiderata, methods, and challenges. *ACM Computing Surveys, 54*(5), 1–111. https://doi.org/10.1145/3453444

Bellamy, R. K. E., Dey, K., Hind, M., Hoffman, S. C., Houde, S., Kannan, K., … Zhang, Y. (2018). AI Fairness 360: An extensible toolkit for detecting, understanding, and mitigating unwanted algorithmic bias. In *Understanding, and mitigating unwanted algorithmic bias.* https://doi.org/10.48550/ARXIV.1810.01943.

Bowyer, K. W., Chawla, N. V., Hall, L. O., & Kegelmeyer, W. P. (2011). SMOTE: Synthetic minority over-sampling technique. CoRR. Retrieved from http://arxiv.org/abs/1106.1813

Kaufman, S., Rosset, S., Perlich, C., & Stitelman, O. (2012). Leakage in data mining: Formulation, detection, and avoidance. *ACM Transactions on Knowledge Discovery from Data, 6*(4), 1–21.

Lundberg, S. M., & Lee, S.-I. (2017). A unified approach to interpreting model predictions. In I. Guyon, U. V. Luxburg, S. Bengio, H. Wallach, R. Fergus, S. Vishwanathan, & R. Garnett (Eds.), *Advances in neural information processing systems* (Vol. 30, pp. 4765–4774).

Maaradji, A., Dumas, M., Rosa, M. L., & Ostovar, A. (2017). Detecting sudden and gradual drifts in business processes from execution traces. *IEEE Transactions on Knowledge and Data Engineering, 29*(10), 2140–2154.

Paleyes, A., Urma, R.-G., & Lawrence, N. D. (2023). Challenges in deploying machine learning: A survey of case studies. *ACM Computing Surveys, 55*(6), 1–29.

Pasquadibisceglie, V., Castellano, G., Appice, A., & Malerba, D. (2021). FOX: A neuro-fuzzy model for process outcome prediction and eXplanation. In *3rd international conference on process mining, ICPM 2021* (pp. 112–119). IEEE.

Rama-Maneiro, E., Vidal, J. C., & Lama, M. (2023). Deep learning for predictive business process monitoring: Review and benchmark. *IEEE Transactions on Services Computing, 16*(1), 739–756. https://doi.org/10.1109/TSC.2021.3139807

Sculley, D., Holt, G., Golovin, D., Davydov, E., Phillips, T., Ebner, D., … Dennison, D. (2015, December 7–12). Hidden technical debt in machine learning systems. In *Advances in neural information processing systems 28: Annual conference on neural information processing systems* (pp. 2503–2511)

Teinemaa, I., Dumas, M., Rosa, M. L., & Maggi, F. M. (2019). Outcome-oriented predictive process monitoring: Review and benchmark. *ACM Transactions on Knowledge Discovery from Data, 13*(2), 1–17. https://doi.org/10.1145/3301300

Wang, B., & Pineau, J. (2016). Online bagging and boosting for imbalanced data streams. *IEEE Transactions on Knowledge and Data Engineering, 28*(12), 3353–3366. https://doi.org/10.1109/TKDE.2016.2609424

Wolf, M. J., Miller, K. W., & Grodzinsky, F. S. (2017). Why we should have seen that coming: Comments on Microsoft's tay "experiment," and wider implications. *Acm Sigcas Computers and Society, 47*(3), 54–64. https://doi.org/10.1145/3144592.3144598

Prerna Agarwal is an advisory research engineer in AI for the Business Process Optimization Group at IBM Research India. Her research interests include machine learning, deep learning, natural language processing, and process optimization. She has a master's in computer science from IIITD India. Her work has been presented at many top conferences such as BPM, KDD, ICASSP, and ICPR and she has several patents in her name. She has served as a program committee member for several prestigious conferences including IJCAI, KDD, AAAI, and ACL. She has also delivered several invited talks and faculty development programs in eminent Indian institutions. She has been a recipient of many awards including the IBM Global Volunteer Excellence Award, Global AI Inclusion Award, Women of Colors STEM Award, IBM Outstanding Technical Achievement Award for her contributions toward building AI capabilities for business processes, and the IBM Academic Ambassador Award.

Renuka Sindhgatta is a research scientist at IBM Research leading research on building predictive and prescriptive solutions that are integral to business process automation. Her research interests include explainable machine learning to augment trust and transparency in automated decision support systems. She has also worked on research initiatives that improved the operational efficiency of software and service delivery teams using machine learning, text mining, and process mining. She has made contributions to mining and analyzing the operational data of conventional information systems and collaborative software platforms. She received her PhD degree from the University of Wollongong, Australia.

Part IV
Democratize: The Scale of BPM

Toward a Process-Centered Organization: The Operational Excellence Journey at Getzner

Magdalena Eggarter, Katharina Keiser, and Sandro Franzoi

Abstract

(a) *Situation faced*: To cope with strong corporate growth and continuously increasing market challenges, Getzner Werkstoffe identified the need to move away from departmental process management toward centralized corporate process management. With this objective in mind, in 2018, Getzner embarked on a journey of developing the whole organization based on principles of operational excellence (OPEX). To this end, several process management initiatives were launched to foster operational excellence and transform Getzner into a process-centered organization.

(b) *Action taken*: Getzner trained several employees to become process method experts (e.g., in lean management, Six Sigma, and business process management) and founded an "Operational Excellence Department" with the objective of strengthening process knowledge throughout the organization. SAP Signavio was adopted to document, model, and integrate the processes. The Getzner House of OPEX was created to be a key artifact that embodied the organizational OPEX strategy and communicated this vision within the company. The Getzner OPEX maturity model was developed to guide the continuous development of Getzner's process maturity. Success stories, process quizzes, and one-pagers for key concepts were introduced and promoted to foster a process culture at Getzner.

(c) *Results achieved*: Implementing the OPEX approach and integrating different process methods allowed Getzner to increase transparency throughout its 500+ documented processes. OPEX is now considered a pivotal part of the overall organizational strategy and is continuing to shape the future development of the company. Developing a process management infrastructure within the organi-

---

M. Eggarter (✉) · K. Keiser
Getzner Werkstoffe GmbH, Bürs, Austria
e-mail: magdalena.eggarter@getzner.com; katharina.keiser@getzner.com

S. Franzoi
University of Münster, Münster, Germany
e-mail: sandro.franzoi@ercis.uni-muenster.de

zation also led to clearly defined responsibilities, higher process affinity among employees, and measurable improvements in key processes.

(d) *Lessons learned*: Reflecting on the OPEX approach used at Getzner, senior management support crystallized as one of the most important success factors. Another key factor in the successful transition toward a process organization is the early development of the necessary capabilities (e.g., through training). Furthermore, choosing suitable tools and technologies that complement and support the overall organizational goals (e.g., scalability) was essential. It also became apparent that while top-down approaches were helpful, building up process knowledge and process thinking from the bottom up (e.g., through continuous engagement with employees) was crucial.

1 Introduction

Getzner Werkstoffe GmbH (henceforth "Getzner") is the market leader for vibration isolation in construction, railway, and industrial applications. Getzner's products and solutions are used to efficiently reduce noise and vibration and extend the life of components. With an annual revenue of 150 million euros and more than 500 employees, Getzner has been an industry leader for over 50 years (Getzner, 2023).

To maintain this position and continuously produce innovative solutions in the future, Getzner is guided by two key operating principles. First, the principle "driven by curiosity" exemplifies Getzner's striving for novel and innovative solutions that allow them to provide excellent products to their customers. However, achieving their strategic goals not only requires having excellent products, it also requires having optimized processes that contribute to success throughout the entire organization. Therefore, Getzner also has a strong focus on their second guiding principle of "continuous improvement" to support one of their key strategic objectives: process excellence.

In recent years, Getzner has experienced rapid organizational growth (e.g., doubling their head count) that has been accompanied by an organizational transformation to accommodate the changing requirements, in particular, with regard to processes. To continue their past success, the company needed to find new ways to grow and keep improving. To support continuing organizational transformation, Getzner started the operational excellence (OPEX) initiative in 2018. The focus of OPEX was the organization-wide integration and optimization of processes on all levels in order to create a foundation for continuous process improvement and organizational growth.

Over the past few years, Getzner has launched several process management initiatives with the goal of fostering operational excellence and becoming a process-centered organization. These initiatives included adapting their organizational structure and governance, developing the Getzner House of OPEX and the Getzner OPEX maturity model, adopting new process management technology, and instilling a culture of process thinking through various cultural measures (e.g., success stories and Christmas quizzes). In this chapter, we shed light on Getzner's OPEX journey to showcase its transformation into a process-centered organization. For this purpose, we rely on established frameworks from the field of BPM, including the six core elements of BPM (Rosemann & vom Brocke, 2015) and the BPM life cycle (Dumas et al., 2018).

The remainder of this chapter is structured as follows. While Sect. 2 outlines the situation Getzner was confronted with, Sect. 3 presents the various process management and OPEX initiatives that were implemented to remedy the existing pain points. Subsequently, Sect. 4 highlights the results achieved and Sect. 5 reflects on the lessons learned from Getzner's OPEX journey.

2 Situation Faced

Since 2012, Getzner has almost doubled in size and transformed from a medium enterprise into an industrial organization. With this growth, structures, roles, and processes had to change within the organization. Processes fit for a small and medium-sized enterprise (SME) were no longer appropriate or able to fulfill the needs of a growing international company. This became especially apparent when looking at interdepartmental processes across the organization. Within and across departmental borders, challenges around roles and responsibilities, the distribution of work, and coordination had accumulated. At this point, Getzner was primarily focused on processes within the individual departments. To cope with the organizational growth, it was necessary to shift the focus from departmental processes toward corporate process management. However, among other things, the existing organizational structure was not overly supportive of overarching corporate-level process management and it became evident that a new governance setup was required.

In addition, when faced with problems or opportunities for improvement, there was a lack of clear guidelines on how these situations should be handled and responsibilities were only vaguely defined. As a result, each problem was being addressed by multiple departments at the same time with almost no coordination between them. Due to this siloed thinking, several projects were initiated by different departments that attempted to solve the same issue, which created even more inconsistencies.

Furthermore, the growing number of employees brought different viewpoints and approaches to the organization, leading to processes being executed differently. This not only led to misalignments and discrepancies, in some cases, it also resulted in inconsistent process outputs. Hence, the need for standardized, coordinated, and more transparent processes and clearly defined roles and boundaries within and across the departments became apparent.

As the organization grew, these challenges became increasingly noticeable. Changing market situations, organizational requirements, and situational and contextual factors (vom Brocke et al., 2016) required a different approach to continuous improvement and process management. After carefully evaluating the situation and identifying the existing pain points, Getzner's senior management devised a plan to take action. In 2018, they decided to focus on OPEX to transform Getzner into a process-centered organization and overcome the problems that troubled them. At Getzner, OPEX is understood as an essential part of the organization that facilitates and enables continuous and sustainable improvement, especially in relation to processes. With this approach, Getzner sought to create a culture of continuous improvement while increasing efficiency and productivity throughout the organization. To achieve these goals and the overall vision, Getzner launched several process management and OPEX initiatives that are outlined in the following section.

3   Action Taken

Facing continuous organizational growth and its concomitant challenges, Getzner decided to develop the organization based on the principles of OPEX in 2018. By combining methodological elements of lean management (Roth & Zur Steege, 2015), Six Sigma (Barone & Lo Franco, 2012), and BPM (Dumas et al., 2018), Getzner's OPEX approach aimed to shape the organization's strategy, increase organizational efficiency, and solve process-related issues. In particular, Getzner implemented a variety of specific actions including establishing an OPEX department, introducing the Getzner House of OPEX, and adopting new technological tools for process management. Generally, the actions and process improvement initiatives at Getzner broadly align with the phases of the BPM life cycle (process identification, discovery, analysis, redesign, implementation, monitoring, and controlling) (Dumas et al., 2018). In the following sections, we present specific actions that were taken to holistically transform Getzner's processes with the OPEX approach. These actions include setting up a process-centered organization, developing strategic artifacts, adopting process management technology, and creating a culture of operational excellence.

3.1   Setting Up a Process-Centered Organization

In 2018, Getzner's management realized that a stronger process orientation was needed to deal with the company's changing circumstances. Continuous process improvement through the integration of sustainable optimization and process efficiency was deemed crucial to achieving one of the main strategic goals: operational excellence.

As their first key action, senior management introduced a new position, the "Head of Operational Excellence", and hired an expert with considerable experience in process management (especially lean, BPM, and Six Sigma methods) to fill this position. In addition, an OPEX steering committee (consisting of C-level executives, the Senior Vice President of Production, and the Head of OPEX) was established to evaluate potential projects in relation to resources required, costs, and benefits and which methods should be used. After an initial evaluation by the new Head of Operational Excellence, the need for a broader process focus and stronger methodological support was identified. In response, an organization-wide training plan was implemented, where appropriate employees from various departments within the organization were selected to receive training in lean management, Six Sigma, and BPM methods. Within this training, employees attended certificate courses, some of which lasted a couple of months (Green Belt), while others lasted over a year (Black Belt). This training was also reflected in the relevant position descriptions of the participating employees (e.g., process manager and Six Sigma Green Belt). At first, the trained employees were exclusively located within the individual departments (e.g., logistics, sales, technology, or production). However, the resource allocation for process initiatives was being hindered by the different departmental priorities of middle management and coordination across departments was still problematic. Therefore, a separate department, the OPEX department, was established to handle and coordinate process improvement initiatives and serve as a center of excellence for process management at Getzner. The new OPEX department consisted of three business process managers, one Six Sigma coordinator, and one lean management coordinator. All other trained employees remained in their departments to implement their process method know-how directly. This organizational setup—a central OPEX department and trained process experts within other departments—allowed Getzner to address the problems that had plagued them in the past, such as difficult coordination and misalignment.

3.2   Developing Strategic Artifacts

In addition to restructuring the organizational departments, Getzner also made an effort to integrate the OPEX approach into the organizational strategy. For this purpose, two strategic artifacts were developed: the Getzner House of OPEX and the Getzner OPEX maturity model. The goals of these artifacts are threefold. First, they are intended to guide the internal alignment of the OPEX strategy with the overall organizational strategy. Second, they place special emphasis on progress and provide measurable goals and guidelines to ensure continuous process improvement. Third, they facilitate the communication of OPEX goals, tasks, and visions throughout the company.

The Getzner House of OPEX, which is illustrated in Fig. 1, summarizes the key objectives, visions, and requirements that surround Getzner's OPEX strategy. It builds on three pillars that translate high-level goals into tangible outcomes and guide day-to-day practices. These pillars encompass the objectives, visions, and requirements for Six Sigma, BPM, and lean management that support Getzner as it strives for quality, consistency, and efficiency throughout its processes. Together, all three pillars contribute to Getzner's overall OPEX strategy. The high-level

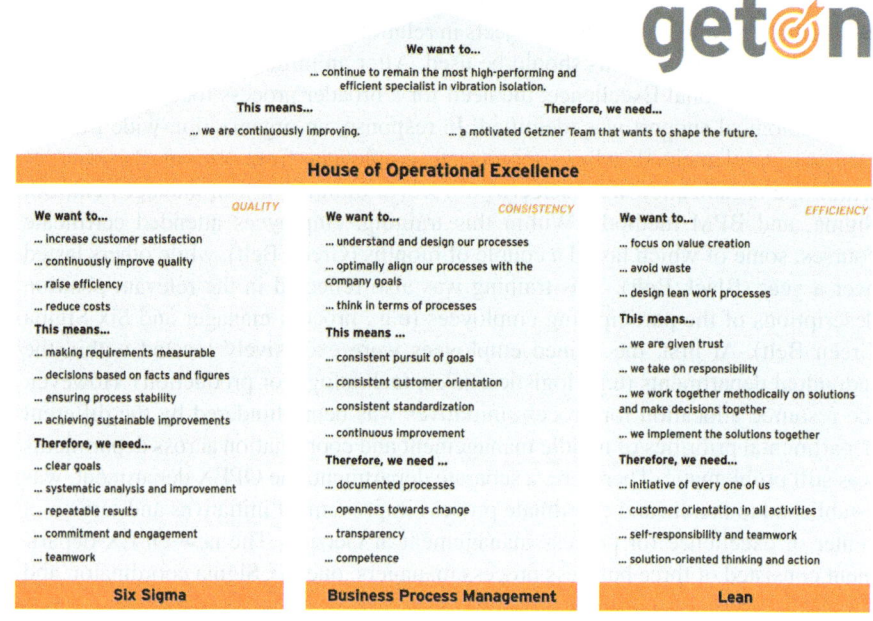

Fig. 1 Getzner House of OPEX

objectives, visions, and requirements are depicted in the "roof" of the House of OPEX at the top of Fig. 1. In addition to operationalizing the OPEX strategy, the House of OPEX also emphasizes the importance of the "Getzner Team" throughout the OPEX journey and is a valuable tool for communicating OPEX goals within the organization.

As a second strategic artifact, the Getzner OPEX maturity model was developed. It builds on the principles of business process maturity models from literature (e.g., van Looy et al., 2011, 2017) and provides a foundation for comparing maturity across several dimensions within the organization. Getzner's maturity model is comprised of five distinct levels that describe the maturity of the respective areas related to operational excellence: (1) unaware/survival, (2) managed, (3) standardized, (4) integrated/predictable, and (5) operational excellence. Maturity level one (unaware/survival) is characterized by a lack of transparency, no documentation, and people working without clear processes in mind. Maturity level two (managed) introduces transparency by documenting the processes and allows for measuring and implementing potential improvement opportunities. Maturity level three (standardized) adds clear and repeatable process guidelines to a managed process that helps create reliable outcomes. For example, the IT incident management process is now already digitalized, standardized, and scalable across all Getzner's locations around the globe. Maturity level four (integrated/predictable) subsumes two categories of processes: first, processes that are integrated into the overall process landscape and connect to several other processes with seamless transitions and interactions, and second, processes that are understood well enough to be able to predict their outcomes and optimize them accordingly. Getzner's goal is to achieve this level of maturity for several key processes. Finally, maturity level five (operational excellence) is an ideal state that suggests that all processes within the organization are perfectly optimized. This ideal state serves as an internal vision for OPEX and is characterized by continuous improvement and innovation.

3.3   Adopting Process Management Technology

Information technology is a central driver for successful process management (Rosemann & vom Brocke, 2015) that facilitates process improvement throughout the entire BPM life cycle (Dumas et al., 2018). Hence, it is crucial to identify suitable tools that support an organization's process goals. Even before starting the OPEX initiative, Getzner used an internal tool to start documenting processes in order to help establish a process landscape. However, the existing tool relied on an internal process modeling language (rather than BPMN 2.0) and did not have the necessary capabilities for a process-centered organization. Therefore, after an extensive market evaluation, Getzner decided to adopt SAP Signavio as its new process management technology. The main reasons for this decision were the BPMN 2.0 support, functionality, ease of use, and its capacity for integrated and holistic process documentation, modeling, analysis, and management. In addition, external factors such as the ongoing transformation of the organization's enterprise resource planning system also played a role because it required comprehensive process documentation. By implementing the new process management technology, Getzner was able to map their processes at different levels of abstraction (from strategic processes to operational processes), which provided the foundation needed to become a process-centered organization. Furthermore, the no-code handling of the tool facilitated easy modeling, maintenance, and information gathering and required less training than the legacy system. Thus, more employees were able to use the technology for process management and it became easier to build up process capabilities within the organization.

3.4   Creating a Culture of Operational Excellence

People and culture are essential core elements of process management in organizations (Rosemann & vom Brocke, 2015). Hence, to successfully achieve operational excellence at Getzner, it was deemed crucial to foster a vibrant process community within the organization. Specifically, that means including all employees in process improvement initiatives, valuing their ideas, improving overall process knowledge, and encouraging process thinking. In this regard, Getzner's main objective is to create a culture of continuous improvement and operational excellence. As part of a long-term communication concept, several initiatives were launched to promote process thinking and strengthen the process community.

First, Getzner proactively promoted and communicated process improvement *success stories* in which employees successfully applied OPEX methods to optimize certain aspects of a process. These success stories were published on the organizational intranet and distributed on flyers throughout the organization's headquarters. In doing so, fruitful projects were given a platform to shine that increased their visibility and highlighted employees' contributions. Emphasizing successful initiatives also increases the motivation to engage in continuous process improvement initiatives driven by OPEX methods.

Second, Getzner introduced an *OPEX Christmas Quiz* that could be accessed through QR codes distributed all over the company's headquarters or over the intranet. In this quiz, employees answered a number of questions (varying in difficulty) related to OPEX key concepts and the organizational OPEX strategy to win prizes. Each question was accompanied by a training video that revealed the answer. Hence, the focus was on holistically spreading knowledge of OPEX and process management. This gamified approach to organization-wide OPEX training was intended to create awareness of process management and strengthen the overall process knowledge on all organizational levels.

Third, Getzner developed and distributed easy-to-understand *one-pagers* that described various key concepts and terms of OPEX and process management (e.g., "What is BPM?"). These one-pagers were intended to help employees understand important process terminology, allow for individual self-learning, and provide easy access to process knowledge and resources. Figure 2 illustrates two example approaches (the Christmas Quiz and BPM one-pager) to creating a culture of process thinking and operational excellence.

Fig. 2 Initiatives to foster a culture of process-based thinking

4   Results Achieved

By implementing this OPEX approach, Getzner strived to achieve the goal of continuous and sustainable growth by focusing on process management. In general, the presented initiatives allowed Getzner to improve overall process awareness, increase productivity, and accelerate its journey to becoming a process-centered organization. More specifically, several factors that facilitated this successful OPEX journey can be highlighted.

First, Getzner was able to solidify process thinking and operational excellence within the organizational culture. While most employees were skeptical of process-oriented improvements before the OPEX initiatives, they now actively use process management methods and reap the benefits in their day-to-day work. Moreover, the initial push of the methods applied has shifted toward a supportive pull from employees and management. This was emphasized by one of Getzner's process managers, who stated, "Now, when departments face challenges, especially, but not only, with interfaces, they actively seek out the OPEX department to collaboratively find the best way to solve their issues based on methodological knowledge and experience from previous projects. This really makes our job worthwhile, since it has become apparent that people not only use but also value the OPEX initiative when addressing their daily challenges."

Displaying success stories of various projects completed and disseminating OPEX knowledge through the Christmas Quiz helped shift employees' thinking about processes and process management. This shift also became visible in the employees' reported use of and familiarity with OPEX methods. Overall, the actions taken and, especially, the successful outputs achieved helped foster an openness toward process management and OPEX methodologies within the organization. These successful outputs include, for example, the optimization of a production process with Six Sigma and lean management methodologies, which resulted in estimated savings of 5 million euros over the next 5 years.

Second, the implementation of SAP Signavio as the main tool for process management drastically simplified and streamlined process documentation and process modeling activities within the organization. Compared to the previous legacy system, the visualization of processes with SAP Signavio (BPMN 2.0) allows for the standardized documentation of processes and provides transparency about roles and responsibilities within and across processes. The comprehensive documentation also helped speed up the onboarding of new employees and reduce the potential for conflict within the organization.

Furthermore, Getzner has established a process landscape with various end-to-end processes. In total, there are more than 500 BPMN process models officially published in Signavio (Level 3 and below) that are established in the organization. Overall, more than 1000 BPMN models have already been created (e.g., support or situational models not yet published) since Getzner adopted SAP Signavio in 2020. The degree of documentation achieved using these BPMN models, especially in relation to the IT systems utilized, is also crucial for several ongoing projects. For example, the established process documentation informed and guided the recent ERP transformation to SAP S/4 HANA and facilitated a much more efficient organizational system for this project. All in all, BPMN models have become an important tool within the organization and are frequently used in daily business.

Third, Getzner built a broad repertoire of process capabilities through various internal training offerings. More specifically, around 10 percent of all employees at headquarters received comprehensive training for lean, Six Sigma, or BPM methodologies, which has given them a strong foundation when applying these approaches in continuous process improvement initiatives. Now, the majority of all employees are proficient in (or familiar with) process methods due to the spillover effects of training on other employees who repeatedly collaborate with process experts. By participating in OPEX initiatives, employees further increase their knowledge of OPEX methodologies, which facilitates a continuous improvement cycle. Applying OPEX methods is the de facto standard for conducting continuous improvement projects at Getzner. In total, over 100 projects have already been initiated using OPEX methods.

Fourth, founding the OPEX department, which consists of three business process managers, one lean management coordinator, and one Six Sigma coordinator, created an important point of contact for employees with process-related questions. For this purpose, bringing in experts with different areas of expertise (lean, Six Sigma, and BPM) together in the OPEX department turned out to be crucial to leveraging the benefits of, for example, the cross-fertilization of process methods. Additionally, this central department and the concomitant change in the organizational structure allowed for easier communication and coordination across departments as well as more clearly defined roles and responsibilities. As one process manager reported, "Becoming part of the Operational Excellence Department has made aligning resources to the most critical projects and improvement initiatives within the overall organization possible by allowing resources to be specifically allocated for such purposes."

Fifth, process management and OPEX methods have not only become an important part of optimization within the organization but have also made their way into the organizational strategy. The corporate strategy has been extended by including OPEX goals as a pivotal part of the overall organizational development. With the help of the Getzner OPEX maturity model, these goals have also become measurable and present a tangible roadmap for the future of Getzner. With process management as a central pillar in the organizational strategy, Getzner has also laid the foundation for continuing its journey of operational excellence. This enables process-centered organizational growth and opens possibilities for future process improvement initiatives and new approaches such as process mining.

5   Lessons Learned

To transform an organization into a process organization, initiatives covering all core elements of BPM (Rosemann & vom Brocke, 2015) are necessary. Reflecting on Getzner's journey of transitioning to a process-centered organization by focusing on operational excellence and applying various process management methods, several aspects crystallized as key factors for success.

First, it became evident that strategic alignment of OPEX goals and continuous backing of senior management is crucial and should be a prerequisite for establishing organization-wide process management approaches. In this regard, it is especially important to allocate the necessary resources (e.g., employees, IT, etc.) to process management initiatives as a lack of resources is the main cause for project delays. One key aspect that facilitated the necessary strategic alignment was the inclusion of the OPEX goals within the overall corporate strategy.

Second, having a suitable organizational setup and governance structures that clearly outline the respective roles and responsibilities turned out to be a key success factor. In particular, establishing a separate, centralized department for OPEX proved valuable when coordinating and implementing initiatives. Through this central department and the trained employees within all other departments, clear responsibilities were defined and communication and coordination across departments were improved.

Third, it is important to develop the necessary process management capabilities as early as possible. This can include hiring process experts to guide the overall process management approach or training employees in process management methods. In regard to training in particular, it became apparent that a combination of theory-oriented education and direct application in practice proved to be the most effective training strategy for fostering knowledge transfer. This helped to ensure widespread process knowledge throughout the organization and allowed for bottom-up process improvement. In order to reach the state of operational excellence, it has become obvious that the entire organization needs to be properly trained in the methods and principles of operational excellence. The extent of this training depends on the roles and responsibilities of the training participants.

Fourth, it proved immensely helpful to leverage process management technology. In this regard, it was important to choose a suitable tool that fit the purpose of the overall organizational goals (e.g., scalability and efficiency). Relying on process management technology helped in the documentation of processes, increased transparency in the process landscape, facilitated the analysis of existing processes, and helped identify process improvement opportunities on all process levels.

Finally, Getzner's OPEX journey showed that process awareness cannot be created through top-down management alone. Instead, continuous, informal leadership (e.g., soft skills, empathy, etc.) on all levels is necessary to communicate the vision of a process organization to employees. Supporting this, a culture of process thinking was fostered with various initiatives such as the Christmas Quiz, sharing success stories, one-pagers on key concepts, and the Getzner House of OPEX. All of these actions helped create a culture that promotes process management, in which every employee can contribute to process improvement. Moreover, by using such tools, Getzner has learned that transparent communication is key to cultural transformation. A thorough, long-term communication strategy helps ensure the ongoing transparency of OPEX methods, improvement initiatives, and results.

References

Barone, S., & Lo Franco, E. (2012). *Statistical and managerial techniques for six sigma methodology*. Wiley.

Dumas, M., La Rosa, M., Mendling, J., & Reijers, H. A. (2018). *Fundamentals of business process management* (2nd ed.). Springer.

Getzner. (2023). *For a quiet future*. https://www.getzner.com/en/about-us

Rosemann, M., & vom Brocke, J. (2015). The six core elements of business process management. In J. vom Brocke & M. Rosemann (Eds.), *Handbook on business process management 1* (Vol. 4, pp. 105–122). Springer.

Roth, N. G., & Zur Steege, C. (2015). *Excellent lean production: the way to business sustainability* (3th ed.). Dt. MTM-Vereinigung.

van Looy, A., de Backer, M., & Poels, G. (2011). Defining business process maturity. A Journey towards excellence. *Total Quality Management & Business Excellence, 22*(11), 1119–1137.

van Looy, A., Poels, G., & Snoeck, M. (2017). Evaluating business process maturity models. *Journal of the Association for Information Systems, 18*(6), 461–486.

vom Brocke, J., Zelt, S., & Schmiedel, T. (2016). On the role of context in business process management. *International Journal of Information Management, 36*(3), 486–495.

Magdalena Eggarter is currently a business process manager at Getzner Werkstoffe GmbH in Austria. She holds a BSc in Business Administration with a major in information management and IT from the University of Liechtenstein, as well as a MSc in Information Systems with a major in data science from the University of Liechtenstein. During her studies, she worked as a student assistant at the Hilti Chair of Business Process Management at the University of Liechtenstein. In 2018, she joined Getzner Werkstoffe GmbH gathering experience in the field of information technology, especially in the areas of IT service management, document management, and IT governance. In 2020, she started working on business process management topics within the IT department, and when the Operational Excellence Department was founded, she joined the business process management team full-time.

Katharina Keiser serves as Head of Operational Excellence at Getzner Werkstoffe GmbH and is responsible for the development and implementation of the company's OPEX initiative. She manages a team of professionals and is tasked with introducing Six Sigma, lean, and BPM methodologies to improve operational efficiency and drive business success. She has been with Getzner Werkstoffe GmbH since 2005 and has held several positions. Prior to her current position, she worked as a business process manager for 2 years, where she was responsible for the continuous development of administrative processes. Her expertise in project management has been instrumental in the successful realization of several optimization projects. Katharina's academic qualifications include a BSc in Business Administration with a major in international management and entrepreneurship from the University of Liechtenstein. She also holds an MA in Business Administration with a major in business process management from the Vorarlberg University of Applied Sciences.

Sandro Franzoi is a PhD student at the University of Liechtenstein and a research assistant at the University of Münster. He completed his Bachelor in Business Administration and a double Master in Information Systems at the University of Liechtenstein and the University of Würzburg. Sandro's research interests include the dynamics of processes and organizational routines (and how they can be studied with digital trace data), process mining, and behavioral aspects of business process management.

Toward the Full Application of BPM: The Case of the Brazilian Coffee Cooperative Cooxupé

Luiz Ricardo Brito Ribeiro, Silvia Inês Dallavalle de Pádua, Emerson de Lima Aredes, and José Roberto Corrêa Ferreira

Abstract

(a) *Situation faced*: The objective was to promote business process management (BPM) as a management approach for Cooxupé, the largest coffee cooperative in the world that exports the production of its cooperative members to over 50 countries. The main challenge was to shift the process management approach (PMA) from documentation to a comprehensive application of the BPM life cycle, particularly in the areas of process diagnosis and end-to-end business process performance measurement.

(b) *Action taken*: On this journey, several methods were applied, including business process architecture and Pain/Gain matrix analysis for process prioritization. Process diagnostic techniques, such as BPMN 2.0, capability analysis, and many others were also utilized to address specific process challenges. Effective project management also played a critical role in enabling agile decision-making, overcoming constraints, and achieving predefined goals.

(c) *Results achieved*: Cooxupé achieved significant improvements in business processes leading to a stronger relationship with stakeholders, an increase in cooperative members, and a higher volume of coffee production, a crucial factor for driving revenue. These improvements were reflected in other areas of business performance, such as increased process productivity and an improved flow rate in technology backlog development.

(d) *Lessons learned*: Cooxupé has learned that promoting BPM can produce shifts in the process management approach (PMA) that greatly enhances business

L. R. B. Ribeiro (✉) · S. I. D. de Pádua · E. de Lima Aredes
FEA-RP USP, Ribeirão Preto, Brazil
e-mail: luizrbr@usp.br; dallavalle@usp.br; emersonaredes@polobpm.com.br

J. R. C. Ferreira
Cooxupé, Guaxupé, Brazil
e-mail: jroberto@cooxupe.com.br

process performance and improves the experience for its cooperative members. This was achieved through a structured initiative that applied best practice in project management in order to overcome the challenges of promoting BPM and implementing a well-prioritized action flow.

1 Introduction

The process management approach (PMA) adopted by organizations varies in format and goals. This case examines a BPM promotion project at Cooxupé, a Brazilian agricultural cooperative of coffee producers with over 13,000 members. Cooxupé exports a production volume of over 5 million bags of coffee per year to over 50 countries worldwide. It recently had to revise its PMA to align with its current strategic objectives. The study highlights crucial aspects of project management (PM) and shares critical practices that contribute to the success of BPM promotion.

The end-to-end business process of Cooxupé involves the following steps: (i) Production, this step is carried out by the cooperative members; (ii) reception, this step involves collecting the coffee from the farms and transporting it to the silos; (iii) classification, at this point, the quality of the coffee is determined; (iv) storage, ensuring coffee of the same quality is stored together; (v) blend composition, this step involves combining different qualities of coffee to achieve the desired taste for consumers; (vi) trading, this is the stage where deals are made with the beverage industry; (vii) shipment, the coffee is transported in bags and containers to the harbor for delivery worldwide (Figs. 1 and 2).

As a world-class organization with a presence in multiple countries, Cooxupé is obliged to adhere to various procedural requirements in order to secure the sale of its coffee. These requirements are derived from both local laws and customer demands and are organized into certifications that necessitate an effective monitoring and control system achieved through audits. Cooxupé has demonstrated competence in managing these certifications, and coupled with its substantial coffee production volume, this skill represents a significant strategic competitive advantage. In order to further enhance its process management, it was determined that Cooxupé could adopt the principles of BPM. These principles include the delivery of strategic objectives through the optimization of operations (Hernaus et al., 2016), the improvement of end-to-end process management (Maddern et al., 2013), and a customer-focused approach (Trkman et al., 2015). By embracing these principles,

Fig. 1 Cooxupé's end-to-end business process

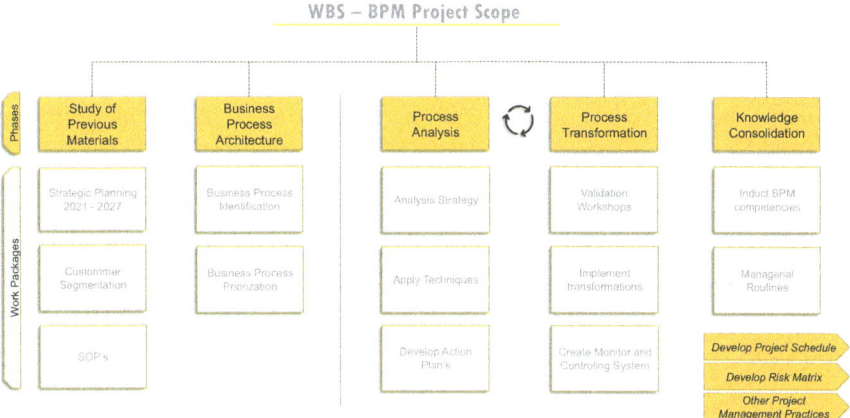

Fig. 2 The scope of Cooxupé's BPM promotion project

Cooxupé can continue to distinguish itself from its competitors and achieve increased success.

Cooxupé has recognized that just managing its certifications was not fully leveraging the potential of BPM. This was evidenced by various challenges in primary processes, such as ensuring the cooperative members' satisfaction with the technical services provided; challenges in support processes, such as enhancing productivity and the flow rate of backlog technology development; and challenges in management processes, including the process management process itself, which was focused primarily on maintaining documentation for certification purposes. These challenges can be further classified and exemplified using Roger Burlton's categorization of business process architecture (BPA) (Burlton, 2015).

The Cooxupé's board made the decision to bring in professional experts in the business process management approach to collaborate with the organization's process analysts and form a "BPM team." The objective of this team was to conduct a comprehensive examination of Cooxupé's processes and identify areas for improvement including the automation of workflows and simplification of processes. Additionally, the team was tasked with finding opportunities to enhance the services Cooxupé provides to its members, such as agricultural technical orientation, crop protection sales, and coffee quality testing. The challenge for the BPM team was to translate these broad goals into a well-defined project scope that was feasible given the time constraints and availability of human resources in addition to the business information available from systems, stakeholders, and in loco observations. Some important questions emerged at the beginning of the project that are addressed in this paper: What are the organization's business processes? Which business process should be improved first? What techniques will be employed? How can the allocation of resources (time, personnel, budget) be optimized to maximize the benefits for business operations and strategy?

2 Situation Faced

The PMA at Cooxupé focused heavily on the administration of standard operational procedures (SOP), that is, on the administration of text-based documents that describe how to proceed with specific tasks (Boet et al., 2019). The concept behind PMA promotes focusing on decisions regarding the selection of methods for diagnosing processes, documentation, professional knowledge, and adequate management of change measurements (Hán et al., 2020). The main purpose of Cooxupé's initial PMA was to obtain certifications. However, they needed to move toward a more comprehensive BPM lifecycle approach that encompasses process improvement initiatives throughout the organization (Bernardo et al., 2017; Morais et al., 2014). This required a shift in the PMA's focus and a broader scope addressing key challenges, such as managing stakeholder expectations and ensuring effective communication.

The PMA's transition posed several challenges including how to overcome the departmental management thinking model within an organization that has 44 branches in various cities. Effective communication and project management strategies were crucial to addressing these challenges and effectively communicating the new PMA to the entire organization. Managing stakeholder expectations and securing buy-in from middle management was also a key consideration. With a workforce of over 2500 employees and a complex organizational structure, many managers had high expectations for immediate solutions and workflow optimization. Therefore, careful attention was paid to leadership development to ensure that middle management was able to maintain a positive attitude toward the new PMA.

A significant part of the daily work performed by employees was heavily documented and subject to audits, leading to a focus on documenting execution errors rather than addressing the underlying causes and improving processes. This mindset hindered the adoption of key BPM principles such as end-to-end process visibility, customer-centricity, and process improvement. To overcome this challenge, the organization needed to shift its focus toward removing barriers that impeded transformation and improving the agility of the service provided to cooperative members. Additionally, fostering innovation within an environment in which a significant portion of the workforce is dedicated to documenting and updating processes is also challenging. To overcome this obstacle, the organization had to find ways to encourage innovation while ensuring that its processes remained efficient, streamlined, and customer-centric.

3 Action Taken

Several actions were taken in order to bring about the desired changes and overcome the barriers to the acceptance of BPM. These included implementing a project management routine that facilitated agile decision-making, developing the business process architecture, prioritizing key business processes, employing appropriate techniques for process improvement, proactively communicating the new PMA based on BPM principles, and training employees in the remodeled processes.

Before choosing BPM as our process management approach, we considered several alternatives. The first option was to create more SOPs and allocate more resources to update documents more efficiently. However, we dismissed this option as we had already obtained the certifications and, thus, fulfilled the desired benefits for the business. The second option was to use the DMAIC cycle and adopt a Lean Six Sigma approach to process improvement, focusing on problem-specific resolutions. While Cooxupé certainly aimed to solve problems, the aim was to conduct comprehensive process analysis to ensure customer success and meet strategic goals. Therefore, we decided to adopt BPM as our primary approach while acknowledging that it may be necessary to combine complementary alternatives, such as total quality or waste reduction, to achieve improvements in specific processes.

The project management approach at Cooxupé followed PMI (Project Management Institute) guidelines and was mainly used to communicate the progress of the project to internal stakeholders. The project schedule was based on a work breakdown structure (WBS) that was divided into work packages and activities with estimable time frames. The project started with 1 month of strategic planning analysis, followed by 1 month for the development of the business process architecture and prioritization of processes. This was followed up with 3-month waves of process diagnosis that led to the definition of an improvement action plan. The project management monitoring and control plan also incorporated agile approaches such as Scrum. This involved weekly reviews of scope and schedule progress, as well as risk monitoring. The PMA changes generated a comprehensive set of improvement action plans that were managed using PMI project management practices including a defined schedule, a defined scope, and responsibilities. All these elements were consolidated into a cohesive project management plan.

After the project management plan was established, the BPM team dedicated their efforts to developing the business process architecture, which sought to answer one of the initial questions regarding the organization's business processes: What are the business processes of this organization? This was achieved by conducting interviews with leaders and observing the execution of business processes on site. Moving forward, the next crucial step was to prioritize the business processes. The allocation of resources and effort was always based on a careful evaluation of priorities. To determine these priorities, we defined criteria that focused on the impact of the process on the cooperative members' experience. The secondary criterion was the potential contribution of the process to the organization's strategic objectives. This prioritization approach was influenced by Roger Burton's Pain/Gain matrix, which provided a clear logic for allocating resources and managing stakeholders' expectations (Burlton, 2018). The process identified as the highest priority for diagnosis was from the Information Technology Development. The aim was to optimize the developers' workflow in order to improve backlog productivity. An agile project management method (Scrum) was used in combination with ITIL, which supported the overall approach.

The successful implementation of the new PMA at Cooxupé required proactive communication with the employees. A crucial moment for this communication occurred during the development of the business process architecture. That was a moment in which business processes were identified and understanding was reached about several elements of the business context (Brocke et al., 2016). This was achieved by engaging representatives from across the organization to identify the life cycle of macro-processes and answer any questions they had about the new PMA. The involvement of external BPM experts reinforced the organization's commitment to the initiative and signaled the significance of the change to internal stakeholders. Hiring specialists also helped to address the challenge of simplifying business processes as they brought fresh and bias-free perspectives to the current organizational culture that helped identify opportunities for improvement. The following table summarizes the opportunities for improvement and the solutions adopted (Table 1).

4 Results Achieved

The implementation of the PMA with a focus on BPM has brought about a significant shift in the organization's approach to problem-solving. Previously, the primary focus was on documentation and audit control. However, by adopting BPM principles, the organization has gained a new perspective on how to address business challenges. The short-term results of the initiative are evident in the process transformations that have been achieved through in-depth diagnostic analysis using various techniques. In the medium and long term, the organization will reap the benefits of a more streamlined and effective BPM approach, which is now better understood and embraced by the Cooxupé team.

Over the course of the project, the focus shifted from solely documenting processes (e.g., through SOPs) to diagnosing and improving them. This change in approach was well received by employees who had experienced both the certification-focused PMA and the BPM approach. The delegation of future changes to the teams responsible for running the processes was seen as a positive development and it was clear that the previous focus on documentation alone was not enough to meet the organization's needs. The shift in approach reflected the organization's move toward a more proactive, solution-focused approach to process improvement.

The implementation of BPM has brought about several short-term benefits for Cooxupé. One of the most notable improvements was the reduction of service lead time for cooperative members. Another benefit was seen in the process of selling agricultural crop protection, which was streamlined from the need to allocate the crop protection to the appropriate means of transport. In addition, changes in the managerial aspects of the technical orientation services process have allowed Cooxupé's management to make better decisions regarding the allocation of agricultural technicians and engineers. The adoption of an agile approach to project

Table 1 Business process improvements: applied techniques and solutions found

End-to-end business process	Opportunities for improvement	Techniques applied	Solutions
From the request for a new system automation to the effective implementation of the functionality	Overload of senior developers Difficulties defining and prioritizing backlog Difficulties determining the expected completion development time	Process mapping BPMN 2.0 Current reality tree—theory of constraints	Agile project management—Scrum—and ITIL Creation of different "rails of development" dedicated to specific topics
From the need for technical support to receiving agronomic guidance	Scheduling technician visits to cooperative members Excessive number of meetings required to monitor the process	Process mapping—BPMN 2.0 RACI matrix OKR—objectives and key results Customer segmentation analysis	Creation of proactive attendance schedule based on customer segmentation Business process intelligence and standardization of managerial meetings
From ordering crop protection to delivering at the farm	Complex and long journey for farmers to buy via Cooxupé's stores Logistic failures in delivering	Capability analysis—lean six sigma Customer journey—design thinking	Elimination of bureaucratic tasks for customers Provide guidance for changes in store infrastructure and shelf positioning
From coffee production by farmers to allocation to the correct silos	Lack of delivery schedule Difficulties arranging enough available truck drivers Excessive bag movement inside storage compartment	Empathy map with truck drivers Logical problem-solving tree	Digitalization of truck driver experience with Cooxupé Complementary analyses to understand opportunities cost for investing in more forklifts or coffee tasters
From new opportunities for process improvement to effective implementation	Functional view of processes Focus on procedure instead of an end-to-end view	Process architecture Process mapping—BPMN 2.0	Creation of a BPM office with new routines based on the BPM life cycle

management also improved the process of technological development. It helped establish guidelines for organizing the team and ensured a smoother flow of high-volume activities. To further enhance the experience of cooperative members, auxiliary measures such as robotic process automation (RPA), self-service, and a knowledge bank were planned to automate the resolution of many calls and free up time for developers to focus on developing new automations.

The long-term impact of the BPM project on the organization can be seen in the development of organizational expertise in process improvement techniques. The training received in methodologies such as BPMN 2.0 modeling, current reality trees, capability analysis, Six Sigma process indicators, empathy maps, customer journey, and logical problem-solving trees has led to new organizational capabilities and inspired the Cooxupé process team to seek out additional training opportunities, such as RPA and design thinking. This demonstrates that the organizational context has become more supportive of BPM initiatives and that the knowledge and skills acquired will continue to benefit the organization even after the departure of the external specialists.

5   Lessons Learned

Cooxupé's experience implementing a business process management (BPM) approach has taught the organization that a shift in process management approach (PMA) can have a valuable impact on business process performance and the experience of its members. This was achieved through a structured initiative that utilized project management best practice to effectively address the challenges of BPM promotion and implement a well-prioritized action flow.

A list of lessons learned in connection with PMA can be summarized as follows:

- Adopting a structured project management approach can help overcome challenges when implementing BPM and ensure a prioritized action flow.
- Organizational context plays a crucial role when implementing BPM and building a favorable environment for its adoption.
- Investing in training and developing skills in process improvement techniques can increase organizational expertise and stimulate further growth in this area.
- Focusing on customer needs and business outcomes can lead to improved process performance and a better experience for cooperative members.

A list of learned lessons connected with project management can be summarized as follows:

- BPM experts make a significant contribution to BPM promotion by guiding the project management planning phase to be more assertive, particularly in relation to scope and scheduling.
- Prioritization is a mandatory action when implementing BPM when there are project constraints related to scope, schedule, and human resources.
- Various areas of project management, such as stakeholder management and communication, make important contributions to understanding expectations and addressing information needs.

References

Bernardo, R., Galina, S. V. R., & From Padua, S. I. D. (2017). The BPM lifecycle: How to incorporate an external view to the organization through dynamic capability. *Business Process Management Journal, 23*(1), 155–175. https://doi.org/10.1108/BPMJ-12-2015-0175

Boet, S., Bould, M. D., Fung, L., Qosa, H., Perrier, L., Tavares, W., & Reeves, S. (2019). Use and implementation of standard operating procedures and checklists in prehospital emergency medicine: A literature review. *International Journal of Emergency Medicine, 12*(1), 1–11. https://doi.org/10.1186/s12245-019-0235-5

Brocke, J. V., Zelt, S., & Schmiedel, T. (2016). On the role of context in business process management. *International Journal of Information Management, 36*(3), 486–495. https://doi.org/10.1016/j.ijinfomgt.2015.10.002

Burlton, R. T. (2015). Delivering business strategy through process management. In *Handbook on business process management 2* (pp. 45–78). Springer.

Burlton, R. (2018). Essentials of business architecture: 'Prioritizing business and process change part 1: A fast-tracked Approach'. Business Process Trends. Retrieved from https://www.bptrends.com/essentials-of-business-architecture-prioritizing-business-and-process-change-part-1-a-fast-tracked-approach/

Hán, J., Petříček, M., & Chalupa, Š. (2020). Business process management approach in the hospitality industry. *Sustainable Hospitality Management*, 145–158. https://doi.org/10.1108/s1877-636120200000024011

Hernaus, T., Bosilj Vuksic, V., & Indihar Štemberger, M. (2016). How to go from strategy to results? Institutionalizing BPM governance within organizations. *Business Process Management Journal, 22*(1), 173–195. https://doi.org/10.1108/BPMJ-03-2015-0031

Maddern, H., Ward, J., & Daniel, E. M. (2013). End-to-end process management: Implications for theory and practice. *Production Planning & Control, 25*(16), 1303–1321. https://doi.org/10.1080/09537287.2013.832821

Morais, R. M. D. E., da Cunha, P. R., & Becker, J. L. (2014). An analysis of BPM lifecycles: From a literature review to a framework proposal. *Business Process Management Journal, 20*(3), 412–432. https://doi.org/10.1108/BPMJ-03-2013-0035

Trkman, P., Mertens, W., Viaene, S., & Gemmel, P. (2015). From business process management to customer process management. *Business Process Management Journal, 21*(2), 250–266. https://doi.org/10.1108/BPMJ-02-2014-0010

Luiz Ricardo Brito Ribeiro Graduated in Business Economics and Controllership from the School of Economics, Business Administration, and Accounting – FEA-RP/USP in Brasil. Holds a Master's degree in Business Process Management (BPM) from the same institution. Specialized in Project Management MBA from FGV and DataScience MBA from Pecege. Certified professional in Project Management (PMP) by PMI, Business Process Management (CBPP) by ABPMP, and Change Management (HCMP) by HUCMI. Works in project development at Polo BPM and Polo Trial for public and private sector organizations, focusing on process transformation using BPM and Lean Six Sigma approaches.

Silvia Inês Dallavalle de Pádua Associate Professor at the School of Economics, Business Administration, and Accounting at Ribeirão Preto, University of São Paulo (FEA-RP/USP). Conducts research in Business Process Management (BPM), project management, sustainability and BPM, and strategic alignment between processes, strategy, customer expectations, and information technology in the graduate program in Organizational Administration at FEA-RP/USP. Holds a postdoctoral degree in Production Engineering from São Paulo State University Júlio de Mesquita (UNESP), in the Department of Production Engineering at the Bauru campus. Earned a Ph.D. in Engineering from the São Carlos School of Engineering, University of São Paulo (EESCUSP, 2004) and a Master's in Production Engineering from the same institution (EESC-USP, 2001). Certified as a Certified Business Process Professional (CBPP) by ABPMP since 2010 and as a Business Process Management professional by BPTrends Associates in 2011. Proud mother of twins, Davi and Gabriel, born in 2006.

Emerson de Lima Aredes Ph.D. and Master's degree holder from FEA-RP/USP (School of Economics, Business Administration, and Accounting at Ribeirão Preto, University of São Paulo), with a Bachelor's degree in Information Systems from the School of Arts, Sciences, and Humanities at the University of São Paulo (EACH-USP). Works as a consultant in Process Management, conducting studies in the fields of Project Management, IT Governance, and Quality. Also holds ITIL v3 certification. Partner and consultant at Polo BPM, a consultancy firm specializing in Process Management, and co-founder of Polo Trial, a platform for managing clinical research centers.

José Roberto Corrêa Ferreira Holds a degree in Business Administration from the Educational Foundation University Center of Guaxupé (2004) and an MBA in Cooperativism with an emphasis on Management and Economics from the Foundation for Research and Development in Business Administration, Accounting, and Economics (FEA-RP/USP). Currently serves as Superintendent of Controllership and Information Technology at the Regional Coffee Growers Cooperative in Guaxupé Ltda. – Cooxupé, and as a faculty member at the Educational Foundation University Center of Guaxupé. Has experience in the fields of Administration, Accounting, Economics, Taxation, Information Technology, and Cooperativism.

Digitization at VBL with Bitkom's Maturity Model Digital Processes 2.0

Martin Appel, Mahmut Arica, Nils Britze, Marc Danneberg, Matthias Möbus, Konrad Schießl, and Ariane Schulze

Abstract

(a) *Situation faced*: The Online Access Act (Onlinezugangsgesetz, OZG) requires public administrations in Germany to provide the majority of their services digitally by the end of 2022. At the same time, VBL, the Pension Institution of the Federal and State Governments, expects the number of pension applications to increase over the next decade. Therefore, they decided to transform their paper-based processes and implement digital solutions.

(b) *Action taken*: VBL identified Bitkom's Maturity model digital processes 2.0 as a suitable and practical evaluation method using it to determine an appropriate degree of digitization for its business processes.

(c) *Results achieved*: The analysis presents the holistic approach that enabled VBL to evaluate its current state of digitization with its new management cockpit. In

M. Appel
Versorgungsanstalt des Bundes und der Länder/VBL, Karlsruhe, Germany
e-mail: martin.appel@vbl.de

M. Arica
FOM University of Applied Sciences, Münster, Germany
e-mail: mahmut.arica@fom.de

N. Britze (✉) · M. Danneberg
Bitkom e. V, Berlin, Germany
e-mail: n.britze@bitkom.org; m.danneberg@bitkom.org

M. Möbus
Fachhochschule Kiel University of Applied Sciences, Kiel, Germany
e-mail: matthias.moebus@fh-kiel.de

K. Schießl
Siemens AG, Amberg, Germany
e-mail: konrad.schiessl@siemens.com

A. Schulze
Software AG, Düsseldorf, Germany
e-mail: ariane.schulze@softwareag.com

addition, VBL was able to take measures to optimize its business processes with regard to their level of digitization.

(d) *Lessons learned*: The Maturity model digital processes 2.0 has enabled VBL to increase its level of digitization and ensure continuous improvement.

1 Introduction

Germany—a digital no-man's land for government services. How can the German administration measure its processes and drive digitization? What do public organizations need in order to be able to implement user-centric digital business processes?

The Act to Improve Online Access to Administrative Services—Online Access Act (Onlinezugangsgesetz, OZG), with user orientation as the top priority in OZG implementation, came into force on August 18, 2017 and obliged the federal and state governments to also offer their administrative services electronically via administrative portals by the end of 2022.[1] Citizens' expectations of public service institutions are high and growing. Currently, citizens—in this case customers—expect digital and automated government services, preferably without media disruption, which means fully digital service. At the end of 2022, not even 100 of the approximately 600 service bundles proposed in Germany had been implemented.[2] Public services often continue to use paper and form-driven processes, for example, health offices were required to report COVID-19 figures by fax.

Given the high data protection requirements, options for administrative services are much more limited than they are in the business world. For example, opportunities for using modern software products, such as public cloud services, and storing and exchanging data via central registers (databases) are often restricted. In addition to the legal and technical challenges, traditional path-dependent administrative processes must be comprehensively transformed to work in the digital age. Individual process steps must be rethought and each process streamlined as a whole. If done right, digital transformation could lead to a reduction in bureaucracy that is visible to customers in the form of digital processes that are easy to use and available at all times. By digitizing and realigning their business processes and specialized procedures, public organizations can achieve gains in effectiveness and efficiency, respond quickly to changing circumstances, and increase their transparency vis-à-vis citizens and companies. The service concept of public organizations is, thus, becoming increasingly important.

A working group made up of various experts from the private sector, public organizations, and academia at Bitkom—Germany's digital intertrade organization—tackled this challenge and asked the question: What does a good digital business

---

[1] https://www.onlinezugangsgesetz.de/Webs/OZG/DE/grundlagen/info-ozg/info-ozg-node.html. 08 Feb 2023.

[2] https://dashboard.ozg-umsetzung.de. 08 Feb2023.

process actually look like? Based on this question, the working group developed a maturity model that is suitable for use in both the private and public sectors. The aim was to make it as easy as possible to start determining the degree of digitization of business processes. In particular, advanced experts within organizations should have the opportunity to identify potential digitization and automation opportunities or to develop internal benchmarking within the organization. The Maturity model digital processes 2.0 was published in 2022.[3] The maturity model itself and the results of its application are presented in the following chapter. In this case study, the model was used to determine the degree of digitization of the pension application process at the Federal and State Government Employees' Retirement Fund (Versorgungsanstalt des Bundes und der Länder, VBL).

2   Situation Faced

As with public administration and the wider economy, digital transformation presents increasing challenges and opportunities for the VBL. The organization is the largest provider of supplementary pensions in Germany. Currently, some 5400 participating employers and about 5 million insured employees use VBL's services. More than 1.4 million pensioners receive a supplementary pension from VBL in addition to their state pension.

2.1   *Digital Strategy, Digital Roadmap, and Level of Digitization*

VBL is digitizing all relevant administrative services and allowing its customers to use modern digital services and processes easily and securely around the clock. By leveraging the potential of digitization, VBL will be able to communicate and collaborate with its customers and partners more efficiently, transparently, and with greater focus on the customer's needs. With its digital customer interface, the company provides a unique customer experience during any interactions between VBL, its customers, and its partners. Expanding processes without media discontinuity and taking IT security and data protection into account, the company identified necessary shifts in processes to improve the experience for customers and partners. Furthermore, in combination with the continuous increase in usage intensity, VBL is improving operational efficiency by reducing process costs. Moreover, the organization is making the most of opportunities for innovation and digital

---

[3] https://www.bitkom.org/Themen/Technologien-Software/Digital-Office/Reifegradmodell-Digitale-Geschaeftsprozesse.html. 02 Feb 2023.

transformation in its internal processes and is, thus, creating secure and modern workplaces that make the company an attractive employer.

VBL has developed a digital strategy to successfully shape the digital transformation. In addition to its goals (including, specifically, "high customer loyalty," "first-class service," and "operational efficiency"), the digital strategy includes focus areas with measures in three digital fields of action:

The digital action area "innovation and digital transformation" includes current and future internal focus areas and measures. The focus is, among other things, on the digitization of internal communication and collaboration, modern administration, and the successful design of digital transformation.

The digital field of action "processes and technology" includes current and future focus topics and measures, such as processes without media discontinuity. The digitization of business processes pursues the strategic goal of "operational efficiency" in particular. This includes increasing productivity, fast process throughput times, improve data quality, and lower process costs. Additional cost-saving potential results from the "digital first" approach and the expansion of digital customer communication.

The "digital customer interface" digital action area includes all current and future focus topics and measures that affect communication and collaboration with VBL's customers.

This triad enable the digitization of processes for customers, from career entry to retirement, as well as the digitization of internal processes for employees. It also sought to introduce processes free from media discontinuity and process automation based on secure and modern IT.

The digital strategy was implemented by, first, planning all strategically important measures in a digital roadmap. In order to achieve the goals of the digital strategy, the digital roadmap, therefore, includes particularly strategically significant measures (e.g., projects such as creating a digital workplace, digital electronic records, digital services, and apps) for the further digitization of core, control, and support processes.

To ensure that the digital transformation could start efficiently, the correct processes had to be identified and the implementation of suitable measures planned for the right time. The progress of milestones and outcomes also had to be continuously monitored. The degree of digitization was used as a key indicator in the identification of processes and prioritization of measures, as well as for measuring the achievement of objectives and "digitization progress." This key performance indicator (KPI) also supports the chief digitization officer (CDO) and digitization management in strategic operational planning and control when implementing the digital strategy. In digitization management, VBL used the Maturity model digital processes 2.0 as a suitable and practical tool for evaluating and determining the degree of digitization of its business processes.

2.2   Bitkom's Maturity Model Digital Processes 2.0

Process analysis can be guided by maturity models that provide orientation when organizations are seeking to improve business processes. There are multiple approaches available, associated with certification standards that can require significant investment. Examples include the capability maturity model integration (CMMI) and the COBIT framework, which is associated with controlling and managing enterprise IT.[4] The Maturity model digital processes 2.0 takes a more general and less standardized approach. It focuses on usability and low-threshold access.[5]

In the Maturity model digital processes 2.0, technology is one among five dimensions and evaluated based on three criteria. The technology basis provides information as to whether the input and output channels are analog, for example, paper-based, or digitized. The process tools evaluate the extent to which software tools are used throughout the process. System integration evaluates the quality with which the technical solutions are connected. The second dimension called "Process Data" evaluates how data generated by processes is handled. Currently, data has also become an important differentiating feature and economic asset for organizations outside the information economy.[6] This is also true for processes that produce the event files that have become the natural resource for process mining.[7] To benefit from these advantages, process data must be collected, made available for analysis, and then used. The dimension "Process Quality" evaluates the process itself and stipulates that if a poor process is simply digitized, the result will be a poor digital process.

Therefore, process quality feeds into the maturity model at this point.[8] In this dimension, the model focuses on whether the process is described, runs without interruption, and ensures legal compliance at each stage. The "Customer" dimension focuses on how customer centric the process is. It also examines the customer benefits and whether participation is possible. The involvement of customers and low-threshold access to the digital service are key success factors in the establishment of digital processes.[9] The fifth dimension "Skills and Culture" includes employee skill sets and organizational culture. Questions evaluate whether employees have the necessary digital skills to carry out the process and whether they are adequately supported during process changes. In addition, it is determined whether managers are setting a good example and whether a digital mindset has been established as the guiding paradigm in the organization.[10]

---

[4] CMMI Institute, 2022; COBIT, 2022.

[5] https://www.bitkom.org/sites/main/files/2022-12/221202LFReifegradmodellDigitale-Gerschaftsprozesse-20.pdf

[6] Porter and Heppelmann (2014)

[7] van der Aalst and Weijters (2004)

[8] Bitkom (2022)

[9] Moormann and Palvolgyi (2013)

[10] Ruschmeier et al. (2021)

Hence, the tool offers the opportunity to continuously measure digitization progress from various perspectives. This makes it particularly suitable for creating agile projects in which teams can independently analyze the progress toward milestones, reprioritize measures, and plan next steps.

3   Action Taken

3.1   *Methodical Embedding in the Fundamentals of Business Process Management*

This case study refers to the business process management cycle as outlined by Dumas et al.[11] The cycle starts with process identification in order to build a process architecture. This is followed by the survey of relevant documentation of the as-is-processes. The information gathered in this stage then forms the basis for the subsequent process analysis. The result of the process analysis is an overview of strengths and weaknesses. Based on this, process improvements can be identified, a to-be-process model designed, and initial steps toward implementing the to-be-process initiated. After the introduction of the to-be-process, process monitoring takes place. Key figure-based monitoring is used to control and monitor the success of the business process. If the key figures frequently deviate from the expectations or targets, it is recommended that the evaluation cycle be repeated ensuring a continuous development process.

One analytical method that can be applied in the process analysis phase is a maturity model. Compared to other recent maturity models, Bitkom's Maturity model digital processes 2.0 considers elements of the Six Core Elements of BPM,[12] such as Strategic Alignment as an enabling factor and Information Technology which, in contrast to the criterion System Integration, focuses on technical interfaces rather than just modelling software. The dimensions People, Culture, and Governance are also considered. Furthermore, the Maturity model digital processes 2.0 incorporates the dimension Process Data, which has become significant given the increasing focus on big data.

In the context of the present case study, the as-is pension application process was already built and the process analysis started immediately. The process analysis was carried out using the Maturity model digital processes 2.0 because the aim was to determine the degree of process digitization.

---

[11] Dumas et al. (2018)

[12] Rosemann and vom Brocke (2014)

3.2 Applying Bitkom's Maturity Model Digital Processes 2.0

VBL integrated the Maturity model digital processes 2.0 as a building block in their digital analysis, a methodical and agile procedure that follows the well-established IDT approach. This approach involves three phases ("Innovate," "Design," and "Transform") and end-to-end process analysis. With a 360-degree view, all process steps, all employees and departments involved in the process, and all software applications and interfaces were considered. The overarching perspective is very important. Without first undergoing process optimization, a poor classical process cannot be transformed into a good digital process. Therefore, the analysis phase at the beginning of the digital analysis is of particular importance (Fig. 1).

The "Innovate" phase analyzes the model's situation and potential. The process assessment and determination of the degree of digitization is carried out with the Maturity model digital processes 2.0. The checklist for the maturity model can be used to perform the process assessment step by step. In the first step, if the process is being evaluated for the first time, important process data is recorded in a process profile. After entering this basic information, the actual evaluation of the five dimensions of the maturity model takes place: Technology, Process Data, Process Quality, Customers, Skills, and Culture. Each dimension has three criteria to be analyzed and evaluated. The evaluation is done by assigning points using a Likert scale, from 1 not digital to 5 fully digital, and is based on facts, expert knowledge, and information. The relevant documentation of the processes (including process models) and supplementary business and technical concepts and IT specifications are important. At VBL, a graphically prepared process model was available for use in the evaluation. If the processes had already been recorded in a BPM tool, the current process case numbers, throughput times, and technical-organizational interfaces were retrieved.

With the Maturity model digital processes 2.0, VBL evaluates both core business processes with medium and high case numbers, such as the pension application process and customer inquiry process, in addition to the control and support processes (Fig. 2).

Using the maturity model and the checklist, the evaluation took place based on the various criteria, from input to the individual process steps and activities, then to the output and communication to the customer. The technical knowledge of the type of data interfaces and the implemented software creates a comprehensible and resilient evaluation result in the form of a score for the degree of digitization. From there, actions and opportunities for improvement can be identified for each

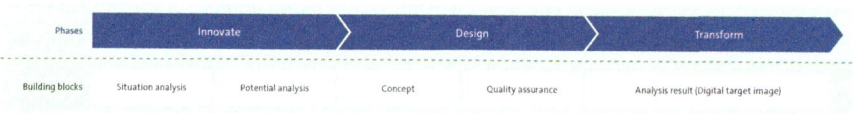

Fig. 1 Process steps of the digital analysis

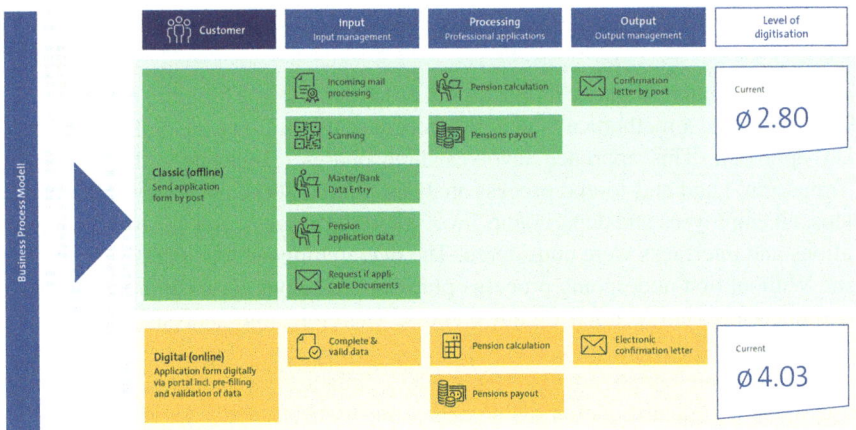

Fig. 2 Example of a process diagram

dimension and criterion. For example, if the degree of digitization for a strategically important core business process is only 3, but the goal of the digital strategy is to achieve at least a 4, then appropriate measures can be designed and implemented (Fig. 3).

The "Design" phase develops concepts and checks the rational feasibility in order to achieve the respective digitization goal, for example, to raise the digitization level of the process to a higher level. In the concept phase, prototypes (mockups or no program functions, etc.) can also be developed to ensure quality. It is important to ensure technical feasibility, positive profitability (quantitative and qualitative factors), and return on investment. In the "Transform" phase of the digital analysis, the results of the digital analysis are presented, including concrete recommendations for action. The comprehensible evaluation and the degree of digitization make digitization measures more comparable and recommendations for action more transparent. Ultimately, individual measures can be prioritized with a low resource expenditure for prompt implementation or several recommended measures can be bundled into a project and included in the strategic planning (digital roadmap).

4 Results Achieved

The Maturity model digital processes 2.0 enabled VBL to efficiently evaluate various core business processes. The new customer dimension and the additional assessment criteria turned out to be significant advantages for VBL. The criteria that are eminently important in practice, such as customer satisfaction and customer centricity, as well as the intensity of the use of digital services, could be taken into account in the assessment. No training was required to use the "assessment tool." Both

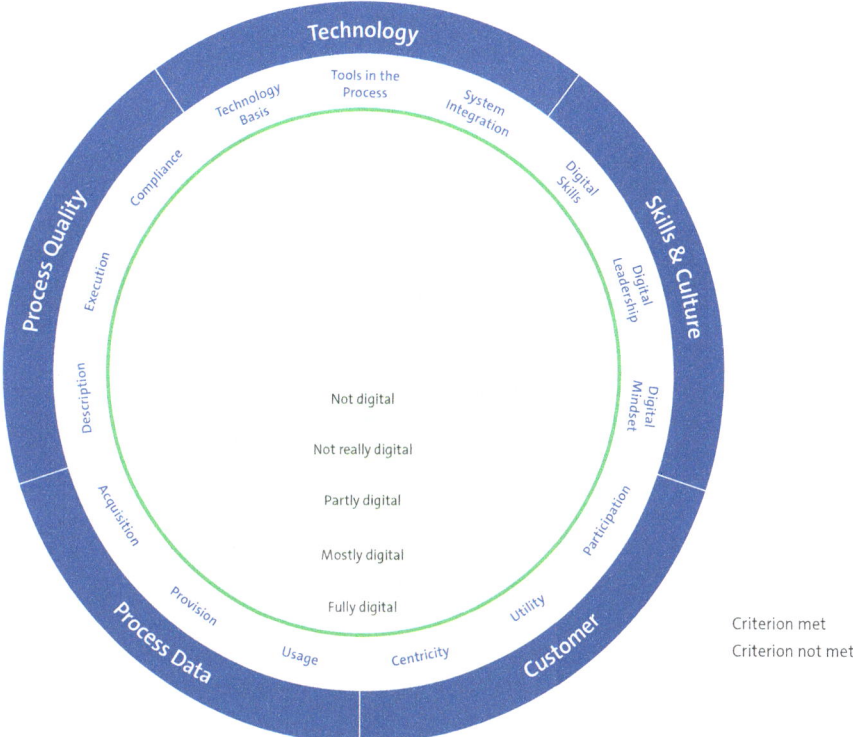

Fig. 3 Results of VBL's Bitkom Maturity model digital processes 2.0

employees from various departments and students carried out the evaluation independently after being given brief instructions. The time required for an evaluation was, on average, about 30 min. The evaluation results only differed in the range of decimal places. Another added value of the maturity model was the development of the management cockpit.

4.1   *Monitoring and Controlling with the Management Cockpit*

The digital management cockpit supplements the previous individual results analysis with a graphically prepared representation of a large number of process evaluations that have been carried out. Primarily, the management cockpit provides a visualization of the current state (e.g., How many and which processes have already been evaluated?). However, the cockpit also enables direct comparison of the different process categories (core, support, and control processes) within the organization. As it is a KPI for controlling and benchmarking, the digital management cockpit shows the degree of digitization, the average value of all process evaluations

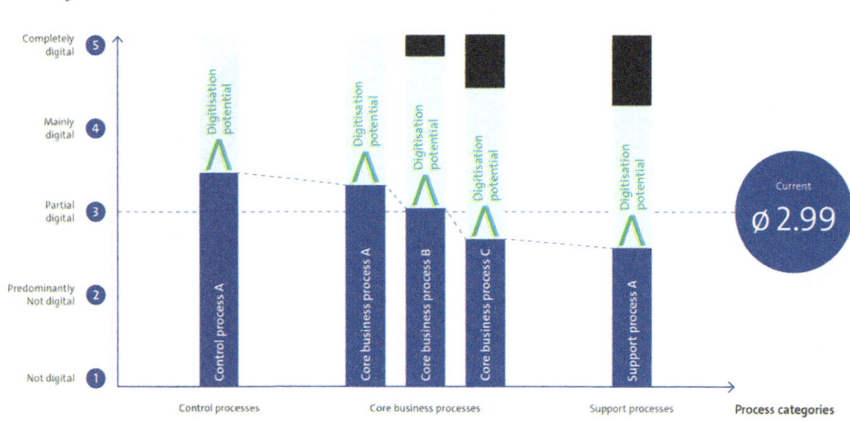

Fig. 4 VBL's management cockpit presenting sample results

carried out. The significance of the KPI increases as more business processes in various process categories are evaluated using the Maturity model digital processes 2.0 (Fig. 4).

The degree of digitization of business processes score and the results of the comparison significantly both support the ongoing control of measures. Together with other KPIs, such as throughput times, process case numbers, customer satisfaction, and return on investment, the result is an almost complete picture of each measure's success. This means that digitization strategies can be implemented successfully and efficiently and, when necessary, updated in a controlled manner.

To ensure the system remains efficient over time, regular repetition of the business process assessment is recommended. The focus of the continuous updating should be the business processes that are essential for implementing a digital strategy. Furthermore, due to the constantly changing framework conditions, the evaluation should take place at specific intervals to ensure more agile development and technological progress. For example, an evaluation of strategically important business processes can be carried out every 12 to 18 months. The degree of digitization can become a particularly exciting kind of benchmark for public administration. In particular, with further dissemination of the Maturity model digital processes 2.0 in public administration and the advancing implementation of the OZG, the degree of digitization of administrative services and authorities can be shown as uniform across Germany.

5   Lessons Learned

The qualitative assessment of business processes using Bitkom's Maturity model digital processes 2.0 is neither complex nor time-consuming. A comprehensible, qualitatively sound, and resilient assessment result was achieved with low resource expenditure. During the application process, it became clear that, with the increasing number of evaluations, it would be possible to undertake cross-process comparisons and both internal and external benchmarking. To facilitate this, the "Management Cockpit" was developed.

More public organizations in Germany could benefit from VBL's experience by embarking on their own digital transformation journey. The maturity model is an analytical tool that can be used to gain an overview of the degree of digitization of various internal processes. Based on this, the organization can determine which steps need to be taken next to achieve progress in digitization and automation. Organizations need to be aware that there is no universal approach to process digitization. In the public sector in particular, the organizational and legal circumstances must always be taken into account when creating an individual transformation agenda. The maturity model helps to make these specific circumstances transparent. This is even more important as it is expected that the implementation pressure in the German public administration will increase further in the coming years. In fact, binding requirements for end-to-end digitization in public organizations are under discussion right now. Therefore, an easy-to-use but comprehensive instrument is needed to support public sector actors in their transformation efforts.[13]

In terms of continuous improvement, the Maturity model digital processes 2.0 should not be applied as a stand-alone; it should be part of a holistic approach to business planning. Such an approach is supported, for example, with the Hoshin Kanri model.[14] Using an appropriate mapping methodology, these improvement projects cannot only be assigned to the digitization strategy; they can also be evaluated in relation to other factors in the company's vision and strategy. Accelerating the progress of digital transformation in industry and public organizations will be one of the most challenging tasks in the next decade. Thus, the objective must be to optimize business processes and gauge the effectiveness of measures in relation to cost and processing time before implementing the automation. In addition, one can use the maturity model to evaluate information, both incoming and outgoing, that is being processed through interactions with the IT architecture. Moreover, looking at clusters of processes, or even value streams, rather than just single processes could lead to more interesting insight into inherent weaknesses. In an additional stage, the maturity model could be expanded to include a "Cost and Value" dimension in order to support facts- and figures-based decision-making for the release of process optimization [ISO 9001]. Finally, it should be noted that Bitkom's Maturity model

---

[13] https://www.onlinezugangsgesetz.de. 06 Feb 2023.

[14] Schießl et al. (2021)

digital processes 2.0 itself must also meet the requirements of digitization and automation.

References

Bitkom. (2022). Reifegradmodell Digitale Prozesse 2.0. https://www.bitkom.org/Themen/Technologien-Software/Digital-Office/Reifegradmodell-Digitale-Geschaeftsprozesse.html. 23 Jan 2023.

Bundesministerium des Innern und für Heimat. (n.d.-a). Dashboard Digitale Verwaltung. https://dashboard.ozg-umsetzung.de. 08 Feb 2023.

Bundesministerium des Innern und für Heimat. (n.d.-b). Onlinezugangsgesetz. https://www.onlinezugangsgesetz.de/Webs/OZG/EN/home/home-node.html. 08 Feb 2023.

Bundesministerium des Innern und für Heimat. (n.d.-c). Onlinezugangsgesetz Grundlagen. https://www.onlinezugangsgesetz.de/Webs/OZG/EN/home/home-node.html. 08 Feb 2023.

CMMI Institute. (2022). https://www.cmmiinstitute.com, 04.02.2023 COBIT. https://www.isaca.org/resources/cobit. 03 Feb 2023.

Dumas, M., La Rosa, M., Mendling, J., & Reijers, & Hajo A. (2018). *Fundamentals of business process management* (2nd ed.). Springer-Verlag. https://doi.org/10.1007/978-3-662-56509-4

Moormann, J., & Palvolgyi, E. Z. (2013). Customer-centric business modeling: Setting a research agenda. In *2013 IEEE 15th conference on business informatics* (pp. 173–179). https://doi.org/10.1109/CBI.2013.33

Porter, M. E., & Heppelmann, J. E. (2014). How smart, connected products are transforming competition. *Harvard Business Review*. https://hbr.org/2014/11/how-smart-connected-products-aretransforming-Competition

Rosemann, M., & vom Brocke, J. (2014). The six core elements of business process management. In *Handbook on business process management 1: Introduction, methods, and information systems* (pp. 105–122). Springer.

Ruschmeier, R., Alt, J., & Hammerschmid, G. (2021). Erfolgreiche Digitalisierung braucht begleitenden Kulturwandel. Kienbaum Consultants, https://me-dia.kienbaum.com/wpcontent/uploads/sites/13/2021/07/Kienbaum_Studie_DigitaleVerwaltung2021.pdf

Schießl, K., Weigert, A., & Beitinger, G. (2021). Integrating Hoshin Kanri into business process management: A holistic approach at Siemens electronic works Amberg. In *Business process management cases Vol. 2: Digital transformation-strategy, processes and execution* (pp. 317–330). Springer.

van der Aalst, W. M. P., & Weijters, A. J. M. M. (2004). Process mining: A research agenda. *Computers in Industry, 53*(3), 231–244. https://doi.org/10.1016/j.compind.2003.10.001

Martin Appel is Head of Digitalization Management at VBL, the largest supplementary pension institution in Germany. As CDO, he developed the digital strategy and manages the digital transformation and implementation of the digital roadmap. With a degree in business administration, he has more than 20 years experience in developing digital processes, implementing online services, and building modern digitization platforms with high usage intensity and customer satisfaction.

Prof. Mahmut Arica, Ph.D. is Professor of Business Administration at the FOM University of Applied Science. He has over 20 years of project and management experience at, for example, IBM, Siemens, Capgemini, and Oracle. Mahmut Arica teaches marketing, strategic management, and digitalization at one of the largest private universities in Europe.

Nils Britze is the Lead of Digital Transformation at Bitkom, where he drives the organization's digital transformation initiatives. His interdisciplinary educational profile includes studies in political science, economics, and sociology at the Technical University Brunswick and the University of Economics in Prague. Recently, he completed an Executive MBA in Business and IT at the School of Management at the Technical University Munich. His passion for digital transformation has led to more than 20 publications with more than 50 different co-authors.

Marc Danneberg is Head of Public Sector at Bitkom—Germany's digital association—and is responsible for all aspects of digital administration and public procurement. Before joining Bitkom, Marc worked for a German software company in the field of scientific innovation and policy consulting. Marc studied public administration and economics in Konstanz, Belfast, and Budapest.

Prof. Matthias Möbus, Ph.D. is Professor of Business Administration at Fachhochschule Kiel University of Applied Sciences. His professional focus is on business process management, digital business and digitization, customer relationship management, and sales management. In addition to his professorship, he advises companies in practice. Matthias has already optimized several hundred business processes.

Konrad Schießl is Business Process Architect at Siemens Electronic Works Amberg, one of the leading digital factories for programmable logic control systems. He holds a German Diplom in Electrical Engineering from the University of Applied Sciences of Regensburg. Konrad has over 25 years of experience in quality management and process management and has conducted numerous projects implementing management systems for quality, EHS, and OHSAS, in both Europe and China.

Ariane Schulze is Strategic Account Executive for Defense and Aviation at Software AG. She was the team leader of the internal control system at BWI GmbH, the IT system house of the German Armed Forces. She holds a German Diplom in European Public Administration from the University of Applied Sciences of Harz as well as a Master of Arts in Peace and Conflict Studies from the Otto-von-Guericke-University Magdeburg. Ariane has over 10 years experience in process management and has conducted numerous projects as a BPM consultant.

Total BPM: What Does a Company That Uses 100% BPMS Look Like?

Sérgio Luís Haas and Nivea Teixeira da Silva Haas

Abstract

(a) *Situation faced*: A Brazilian nonprofit organization had to find a solution that could offer management, governance, and compliance independently of development teams, with low development and maintenance costs, while also offering quality and information security.
(b) *Action taken*: The best solution to meet these requirements was the comprehensive adoption of a BPMS that would be organically and easily adaptable to the desired reality of the company.
(c) *Results achieved*: Today, the organization does not use any other management solution, not even ERP. It only uses BPMS to develop its management solutions.
(d) *Lessons learned*: The large-scale uptake and deployment of BPMS proved to be superior to traditional management systems or ERP and was easier for all the relevant stakeholders to use. The solution can also efficiently be changed when new requirements are emerging.

1 Introduction

The Instituto Espírita Batuíra de Saúde Mental is a nonprofit, medium-sized, philanthropic hospital located in the city of Goiânia in the state of Goiás in Brazil. With 75 years of service provided to people with mental disorders under its belt, it is currently offering support to 133 people. However, continuous financial pressure and limited resources meant the organization urgently needed a management solution to ensure sustainable business operations. In addition, the compliance demands of regulatory agencies is high in this industry in which 90% of the patients treated are suicidal.

S. L. Haas (✉) · N. T. da Silva Haas
Instituto Espírita Batuíra de Saúde Mental, Goiânia, Brazil
e-mail: batuira@batuira.org.br

© The Author(s), under exclusive license to Springer Nature Switzerland AG 2025   187
J. vom Brocke et al. (eds.), *Business Process Management Cases Vol. 3*,
https://doi.org/10.1007/978-3-031-80793-0_14

The institution's executives had to identify and implement an efficient and effective management solution that catered to these many challenges yet still guaranteed dignified and adequate treatment for the people, the patients, and their families, who trust the organization with their personal challenges. So that the institution would not be constrained by a ready-made market solution, which would potentially not have met the needs of the hospital and, thus, ensure that the unique work and engagement practices are truly reflected in the solutions, the decision was made to adopt a business process management system (BPMS). A specific requirement was that the system needed to provide decision-relevant data in real time without relying on multiple data conversions across various systems as used to be the case. The hospital did not have access to any internal expertise in areas such as database or IT infrastructure management.

In light of these circumstances, the organization made the bold move to aim for just *one* BPMS to support their various patient-facing processes, as well as all of their back-office processes including finance and human resources. Placing all of the management systems on the BPMS platform, ensuring scalability and information security in a transparent manner, and maintaining process performance and conformance were of the utmost importance. As the staff were rather time-poor, system training needed to be streamlined. Moreover, it was essential that the system was able to take over mundane work so that staff could focus on their demanding humane work as much as possible. Therefore, changes in the known logic of the hospital's business process needed to be kept to a minimum.

The overall mantra of the organization's transformation was *"trust the process."* The project is an example of hospital process management (HPM), a subset of business process management that is still in its infancy. Though a number of publications have provided valuable insight (Ferrante et al., 2016; Gomes et al., 2018), the very specific focus of a hospital like the one in the case study here meant that even the general models of process lifecycle management from the healthcare sector were often not directly applicable. Indeed, in this case, they required substantial individualization and tailoring to the medical nuances and regional compliance frameworks (Buttigieg et al., 2016; Pufahl et al., 2022). As is common in the healthcare sector, detailed guidelines, procedures, and checklists enforced by system-supported processes were needed to ensure consistency in the services provided (Combie et al., 2017).

2 Situation Faced

The initial scan of available solutions showed that the domain-specific support capability in common ERP solutions was underdeveloped. Furthermore, the cost of configuring and implementing such an off-the-shelf solution was beyond the budget of this nonprofit hospital. Thus, it quickly became clear that the future system backbone of the organization needed to be process-centric and had to facilitate self-service to a large extent (e.g., for reporting purposes). Despite this, advanced robotic process automation (RPA) or the use of API to integrate various systems was out of the question as this level of technical capability is too demanding in terms of the technical expertise required. Nevertheless, embedding scheduling solutions that catered to a mobile workforce through, for example, VOIP and WhatsApp integration, was very much a requirement.

In light of these requirements, the decision was made to select one, and just one, BPMS solution, because a process-based system was considered more organic and easier to adapt to the rather unique requirements of this institution. Furthermore, due to the high degree of risk to hospitalized, suicidal patients, several of the processes directly related to the patients needed to be developed in a way that catered to these unique and uncommonly sensitive process requirements. As an example, Fig. 1 visualizes the hospital's treatment process. The hospital's way of working is also exposed to frequent change, so the ability to facilitate rapid and convenient process changes was important and the assessment was that such changes could be easier facilitated by a BPMS than an ERP system.

3   Action Taken

After several searches for platforms, among the many in Brazil and abroad, the organization opted for a national low-code BPMS system that had a compelling list of clients and came with a price that was within the hospital's budget. The system was cloud-based, supported BPMN 2.0, and the vendor provided capable support and training. It also complied with Brazil's data protection legislation whereas most platforms assessed failed to meet these requirements. An implementation partner was then hired to implement the selected BPMS platform as the hospital did not have any information technology or infrastructure staff. Integration with the hospital's telephone system also needed to be built into the BPMS to ensure patient calls would be traceable. Integrating WhatsApp helped with this and improved the user experience of the largely mobile workforce.

It was less so technical and more so people issues that created roadblocks during the implementation. In fact, creating a "process culture" was the biggest challenge. The work was previously demand-driven and tasks were dealt with on an ad hoc basis as they emerged. Thus, implementing routines as part of defined, prescriptive business processes was a tremendous shift for the hospital staff. This shift was made possible through the gradual and continuous implementation of new processes. At the peak of the project, a new process was developed and put into production every 15 days using a *"minimum viable process"* approach. In 2022 alone, 24 new solutions developed using the BPMS were delivered.

No team received any specific training on processes or on using the solution. This unusual approach was adopted by the president of the hospital intentionally so that the new system could be presented as an organic solution. With each new solution, the teams were informed that a new process was being made available, that it was intuitive, and that, in case of doubt, they should only contact their supervisors.

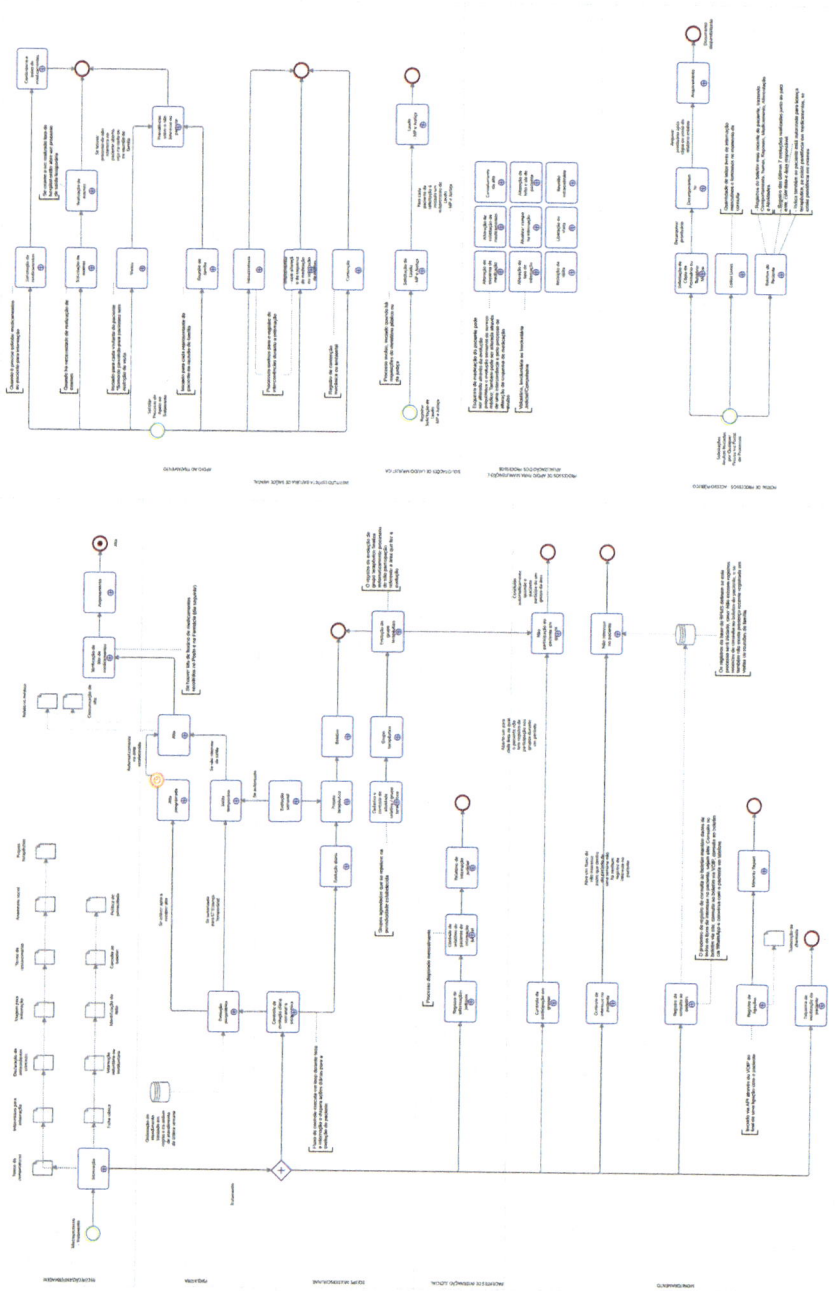

Fig. 1 Treatment macroprocess

The common approach of conducting training before a system's rollout was avoided and the organization emphasized on-the-job training instead. The main reason for this rather unusual decision was that the hospital's staff turnover was very high. This would have greatly increased the cost of training given the ongoing intake of new members. This necessitated a zero-training approach and a strong belief in on-the-job training for all staff.

In terms of overall resourcing, there was a maximum of three people involved in each project, a BPMS low-code developer, a project manager, and an employee who provided the essential domain knowledge for the design of as-is process models (for another example, see Fig. 2).

4 Results Achieved

Reflecting on the results of this BPMS implementation is an important step as the final aim was not "a running new system" but actual transformational change to the organization. Today, at Instituto Espírita Batuíra de Saúde Mental, an average of 1500 process instances are run every day and all internal areas of the hospital work with the BPMS. The hospital's patients are also able to interact with the platform without the need for a separate system. For this, several process roles and services are made available to patients using intuitive Web-based and mobile solutions. No hospital communication occurs outside the platform. Notices, news, and information, among other things, are all linked via processes within the platform.

Furthermore, the hospital's internal business intelligence capability has evolved. Instead of developing several dashboards that need to be assessed, process-embedded KPIs trigger actions automatically. That is, instead of a person needing to analyze several charts, the BPMS itself generates tasks when a certain threshold metric is reached. Thus, logs and changes are traceable and aggregated for all solutions developed with the BPMS platform. Thus, each member of the team knows exactly what they have done and, above all, what is still left to do.

All the legal documentation of the hospitals is also produced by the BPMS platform—from insurance documents to regulatory reports. For this purpose, document control was also built into the BPMS. No paper-based lists of any kind are allowed in the hospital, which also facilitates the protection of confidential and private hospital and patient data.

Finally, all human resource processes are managed within the platform. This includes processes such as recruitment, dismissal, payroll, and leave management, to name a few.

The solutions previously delivered by an ERP are also now delivered by the BPMS. The managers' view allows access from anywhere, at any time, and without any human interference in their intermediation. It is possible to have a complete and total view of all processes, tasks, and activities in a single place and to see what has been done and, mainly, what has not yet been done by members or teams. The

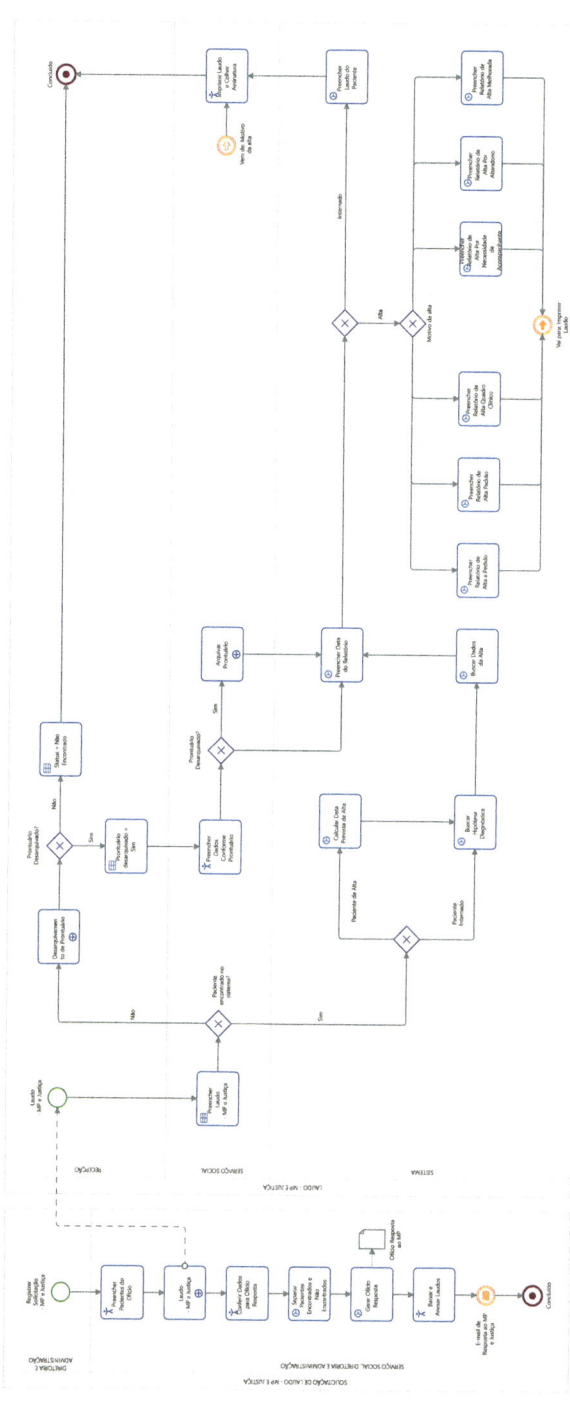

Fig. 2 The to-be judicial process

adaptation of team members from all areas was essential for the progress of tasks and, above all, the treatment given to each patient.

The end-to-end as-is process modeling within the BPMS added significant value for the hospital as it was possible to identify, without error, and without any doubt, how processes in the various areas begin and end. These models facilitated important conversations regarding current shortfalls and a new, process-based operating model was jointly designed, which ensured broad user acceptance before the technical process implementation started. In particular, rework was identified as a significant inefficiency in the language of lean management. Addressing rework, primarily via revised business rules, not only accelerated the processing time, it also significantly reduced the use of subprocesses and the duplications of various forms.

The BPMS was particularly valuable for addressing crucial patient-related risks. One of the major risks for the organization is the abandonment of psychiatric patients by their guardians. To prevent this from happening, several processes were developed and interrelated via messages to ensure organization-wide transparency. These processes generated important, real-time KPIs and created a new dynamic for the experience of the team, the family members, and, in particular, the managers.

The other risk, even more important, is the possibility that the patient may commit suicide inside the hospital. Such cases, beyond the personal tragedy, generate substantial legal and financial difficulties for the organization if any form of non-compliance or negligence is detected. To increase the surveillance of suicidal patients, dedicated processes were developed, such as converting phone calls into text (voice to text) through the hospital's cloud telephony center. Then text mining services identified and showed the team and managers relevant keywords that might indicate suicidal intentions. Follow-up actions are then authorized by those responsible for the patient's hospitalization. These processes are part of an internal project called the Minority Report Against Suicide.

Another interesting capability provided by this BPM project is related to the patient's experience participating in collective therapy activities. It was previously impossible for managers and directors to know which patients had participated in such therapies and the scope of group therapies offered as part of the treatment. Now, in addition to managing all ongoing treatment groups, it is possible to identify their frequency and, above all, which patients do *not* participate in the collective therapies. This example shows how the BPMS rollout has allowed managers to be even more informed of and involved in the day-to-day operations of the organization. This also facilitates improvements in the reformulation of therapeutic groups through continuous management by managers who can now design new therapy guidelines that are more attractive to patients and, consequently, beneficial to their treatment.

The entire process landscape and interplay between organizational areas, processes, embedded tasks, and patients were visualized in interactive and innovative displays (Fig. 3). Each click on a circle expands the view from process to patient. By clicking on the circle representing a patient, the user is directed to the specific outstanding task for that patient. As intended, system training has been minimal as

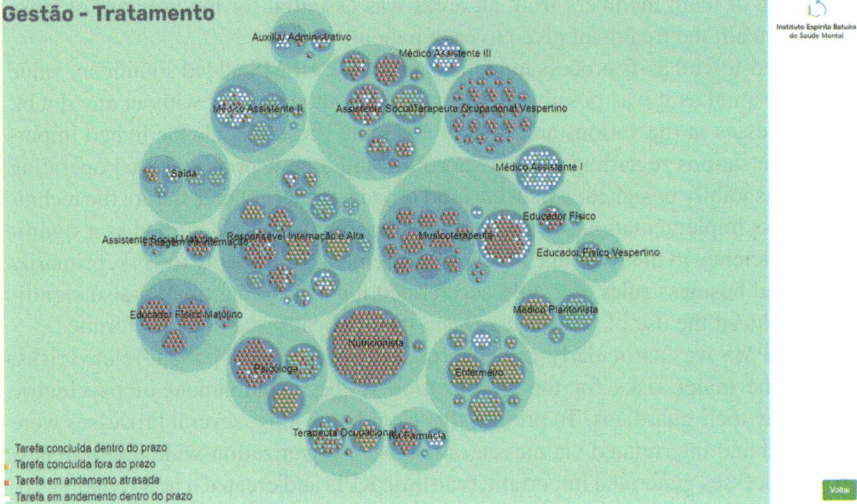

Fig. 3 Process landscape admission and discharge

the intuitive environment and a well-defined role concept facilitated a smooth system adoption.

Today, the new "culture of processes" within the hospital supports the continuing evolution of work and the dissemination of new processes. Such a cultural shift does not happen overnight and team members had to experience the benefits of thinking and working from a business process perspective, personally witnessing the operational gains, before truly adopting the mindset. Managing by processes allowed the president, directors, and team leaders to invert their position in relation to the results of the work done, moving from being passive actors (process observers) to proactive actors (process designers). Without any human interference, they can now obtain the process-based data and information relevant to their roles and can initiate process changes as needed.

The process-centric system rollout made it possible to identify new management processes that could not have been resourced before that are now up and running and completely automated. The implementation of the organization-wide BPMS has resulted in an average decrease of 70% in human tasks. Indeed, in one of the value chains, an impressive 85% reduction in human tasks was achieved.

5   Lessons Learned

In the case of this Brazilian, nonprofit hospital, a BPMS solution proved to be superior in terms of quality and cost compared to a traditional IT or ERP solution. As it is more organic, it allows for greater user participation and incremental process development, from an initial minimum-viable process to a well-tested, operationally efficient process that is accepted by internal and external stakeholders (e.g., patients).

One of the initial difficulties of the project was the overall orchestration of the process landscape, that is, crafting a process architecture facilitating a shared understanding of the interplay between the various processes and a deep understanding of how each of them added value to the business. During the project's progression, occasional employee reluctance to engage with a process-based system and the changes it brought to established working practices was another challenge. It was noticed that an overall lack of familiarity with technology was causing discomfort in some employees and that the time to build the required levels of comfort varied among staff. As a result, some old staff continued but no longer desired changes to the working practices.

It is worth remembering that at no time was there any training explaining how the new process-based applications work. Staff were only instructed to clarify their doubts with the hospital administrator. Despite this, many employees consulted their co-workers, even though the practice was considered inappropriate. One of the outcomes was that many employees simply did not perform the task, even though they knew that all the tasks on their to-do panel screen should be carried out. Management addressed this issue with ongoing communication about the process benefits and staff gradually accepted the system once they began observing the benefits among their colleagues.

The pinnacle of the solution will be when more than 5000 process instances generated in the various automated solutions, in all areas of the hospital, are up and running and covering: hospitalization, treatment, purchases, inventories, scheduling, accounting, finance, budgeting, human resources, and planning, among others, and all of these are being developed using the one BPMS. In the near future, it is envisaged that the hospital will continue to develop a higher level of BPM maturity (Cleven et al., 2014), which will allow it to consider even more advanced BPM solutions, such as AI integration or process mining.

References

Buttigieg, S. C., Dey, P. K., & Gauci, D. (2016). Business process management in health care: Current challenges and future prospects. *Innovation and Entrepreneurship in Health, 3*(1), 1–13.

Cleven, A. K., Winter, R., Wortmann, F., & Mettler, T. (2014). Process management in hospitals: An empirically grounded maturity model. *Business Research, 7*, 191–216.

Combi, C., Pozzi, G., & Veltri, P. (2017). *Process modeling and management for healthcare.* CRC Press.

Ferrante, S., Bonacina, S., Pozzi, G., Pinciroli, F., & Marceglia, S. (2016). A design methodology for medical processes. *Applied Clinical Informatics, 7*(1), 191–210.

Gomes, J., Portela, F., & Santos, M. F. (2018). Introduction to BPM approach in healthcare and case study of end user interaction with HER interface. *Procedia Computer Science, 141*, 519–524.

Pufahl, L., Zerbato, F., Weber, B., & Weber, I. (2022). BPMN in healthcare: Challenges and best practices. *Information Systems, 107*, 102013.

Sérgio Luís Haas is a mathematician and systems analyst in Brazil. He currently works in process management. He is the creator of the theory of metaprocesses in management and its use by companies.

Nívea Teixeira da Silva Haas is a mathematician and hospital administrator with more than 15 years of experience. She currently manages a hospital organization with unprecedented characteristics in Brazil: It is 100% free and has fewer employees than treatment beds.

Part V
Culturalize: The Adoption of BPM

Process Mining in Battery Life Cycle

Riccarda Mark and Ilario Angilletta

Abstract

(a) *Situation faced*: A charged battery for the IoT-enabled bike locks is essential for the bike rental process in the DB Connect bike-sharing system. To ensure the availability of the bikes, the battery must be charged at regular intervals in addition to the classic maintenance processes. If the battery dies, a bike is no longer rentable to the customer. As the rental stations are located outside, the bikes are exposed to external influences such as temperature, humidity, and sunlight, all of which directly impact the charging cycle of the batteries. The project presented provides an initial idea of how we can support decisions in future maintenance processes to achieve an optimal cost-benefit ratio.

(b) *Action taken*: Bike maintenance is a process that can be well represented in discrete, finite events. To analyze the performance of the process, we focused on the voltage curve of the battery data, although the course of this is difficult to predict. Influencing factors here include weather conditions, frequency of use, and the age of the battery. Typical charging cycles were modeled from the data, forming the basis on which we optimized the maintenance process.

(c) *Results achieved*: The analysis gives us transparency on the number and duration of maintenance cycles per bike in terms of battery charge, including external factors including frequency of use and weather-related variations. In addition, knowing the threshold of the critical voltage allows us to predict and prevent bike failure. This was the starting point for an overall optimization of the predictive maintenance processes.

R. Mark (✉)
Deutsche Bahn Connect GmbH, Frankfurt am Main, Germany
e-mail: riccarda.mark@deutschebahn.com

I. Angilletta
DB Systel GmbH, Frankfurt am Main, Germany
e-mail: Ilario.angilletta@deutschebahn.com

© The Author(s), under exclusive license to Springer Nature Switzerland AG 2025
J. vom Brocke et al. (eds.), *Business Process Management Cases Vol. 3*,
https://doi.org/10.1007/978-3-031-80793-0_15

(d) *Lessons learned*: When presenting our project, we primarily focus on the psychological aspects. By using process mining, we were able to discuss processes transparently with the company process owners and did not have to limit ourselves to the subjective perceptions of the experts, as was often confirmed by the visualizations.

1 Introduction

1.1 Organizational Background

Deutsche Bahn Connect GmbH brings travelers and employees to the rails by focusing on connecting mobility. Since it was founded in 1996, the company has not only been active as a central fleet manager in classic vehicle fleets, it is also a pioneer in the bike- and car-sharing markets. The company is also making an active contribution to the mobility revolution by developing apps and Web applications for companies and municipalities. Deutsche Bahn Systel GmbH is a wholly owned subsidiary of DB AG and a digital partner for all group companies. DB Systel develops effective and efficient customer solutions based on innovative technology such as the cloud, big data, the Internet of Things, and artificial intelligence. Based on this strong foundation, DB Systel also offers consulting and development services for process mining tools and their use within the group. Process mining is now a well-established technology at Deutsche Bahn which is being used to analyze many administrative processes.

1.2 Our Use Case

In this chapter, we focus on maintenance processes within the bike-sharing business of DB Connect. Currently, around 13,000 bicycles offer flexible connection mobility and practical additions to public transport in over 80 cities and municipalities. DB Connect's bike-sharing business operates under the "Call a Bike" brand and is one of the oldest bike-sharing services in Germany. The systems offered are largely station-based, but free-floating systems are also provided in a few metropolitan regions. They can be used by our customers throughout Germany, around the clock, regardless of whether it is a business or private trip. All bicycles are of high-quality workmanship and maintain our standard with very good riding comfort. To ensure this, our own bicycle workshops and service teams are on site locally so as to always guarantee a roadworthy riding experience. The success of our maintenance efforts was confirmed in May 2019 by a top test verdict from Stiftung Warentest, a renowned German product testing foundation.

In order to keep our maintenance quality ahead of the competition, we decided to review the suitability of process mining the IoT data from our bikes to seek out

further potential for improvement and establish the basis for predictive maintenance. Maintenance is characterized by two goals, which must be balanced appropriately. The most obvious goal is to meet customer expectations regarding the
availability of bikes in the city. This goal competes with the need to keep the maintenance cost low in favor of affordable rental rates while always ensuring operational safety for the customers.

The bicycle locks used by Call a Bike have a SIM card. They send a stream of
information about their location and status (open, locked, remaining battery voltage) at specific times, for example, upon the start of a rental period. This data stream
is a valuable source for determining the best maintenance strategy. This study shows
how we analyzed this data stream with the help of process mining.

2   Situation Faced

Maintenance fixes damage but can also prevent it. Most damage is mechanical, such
as flat tires or worn brakes. Some damage, if undetected, might pose a serious threat
to safety, while others prevent the usage of the bike. As the battery for the IoT lock
is the central component required to lend the bike to the customer, in the event the
battery fully drains, the bike cannot be lent to a customer until the battery has been
recharged. This has a negative impact on both our image as a reliable service provider and our revenue if the customer decides to use a different means of travel.

2.1   Optimization Goals

The battery's function is to communicate with the booking systems and open and
close the lock at the customer's request. Regularly charging the batteries is, therefore, a prerequisite for renting bikes. It is common to perform such standard maintenance on a regular schedule, with the interval between consecutive maintenance
interventions usually chosen conservatively and uniformly for all bicycles. Some
maintenance can be performed on site at the stations by the mechanics. Other activities involve logistical effort because the bike must be transported to the maintenance
center, as is the case when lock batteries must be charged. Previously, the field service team would attend when locks had a low battery charge; this is displayed in the
dispatch tool on their handhelds. However, predictive maintenance was not taking
place in this case.

If the maintenance must be carried out in the workshop, the bicycles are not
available to customers for a considerable amount of time. Predictive maintenance
promises to optimize service intervals by considering factors of individual bikes
like age and frequency of usage. This would increase the availability of an individual vehicle and keep safety high. However, such optimization is limited due to the
fact that transporting a bicycle from its location to the workshop is expensive.

Picking up several bicycles and bundling them into one transport might be more efficient than exploiting each individual vehicle's optimal maintenance schedule. The presented study provides an initial indication of how we can support decisions about the maintenance process in the future to achieve an optimal cost-benefit balance.

- Which bike station needs to be visited tomorrow?
- Which bikes are to be picked up for maintenance at the station visited?
- What maintenance do the bikes require?
- To which station should the freshly maintained bike be delivered?

One further concern was the concurrent maintenance processes. The next generation of IoT-enabled battery-driven locks is currently being introduced into the standard maintenance process for mechanical parts. This learning process is assumed to cause some loss of efficiency as empirical values on seasonal fluctuations must first be gained.

3   Action Taken

In order to carry out predictions for the maintenance process, two data sets were available:

- Event log of ERP system.

- Maintenance is a process best represented by a series of discrete and finite events. The process starts with a trigger like a damage report or a scheduled task and ends with a freshly maintained bicycle back at the station. Process mining is perfectly suited to analyzing the performance of this process. How often are the tasks performed? How long where the bicycles available for rent?
- IoT data streams from lock batteries.

- The voltage information of the locks' batteries is reported as a stream of data representing signals with a (mostly) steady progression. These signals are hard to predict. User demand depends on many external factors including the weather and public events. The difficulty of predicting a battery's range can be observed in electric cars and cell phones. Temperature and age of the battery have a complex influence on the device. The energy harvesting performed by a small solar panel on the floor of the bicycle's front basket (which may be covered or shaded by trees) has an additional, nearly random influence on the device.

Usually, a list of use cases from different industries (Solterbeck, 2021) and our practice of questioning the capabilities of our tools (Zaimoglu, 2021) help to quickly define a suitable environment for each new project. The number of relevant use cases, which mix IoT data and process mining methods, is still very small and none of the use cases we found felt like a useful reference Bertrand et al, 2022) . All the commercial tools we know of that specialize in process mining lack specific capabilities for processing analog signal streams. We started our work without the assistance of a best practice guideline and our toolchain was an improvised combination of a standard data science tool and a commercial process mining tool. No adverse effects materialized as a result of proceeding without a role model.

In this study, the scope is limited to the voltage curve of the battery extracted from the IoT data stream (Koschmider et al., 2020). Enhancements to this approach are still under development.

3.1 IoT Data Stream

Picture 1 shows typical curves of three individual batteries' charge cycles. The cycle duration varies from 25 days in the cold winter month to several months during the warm summer period. The minimum voltage and the peak voltage are mostly independent of such influences and are in the range of 3.5–4.1 V (Fig. 1).

The data source contains roughly one data point from every day. Unfortunately, the measuring frequency varies. If the bike is placed somewhere with poor cell phone reception, we receive no information until the bike is moved again. Furthermore, we can identify the usual anomalies, like jitters in the analog measurement devices that are used in the transmission technology and occasionally cause an abrupt and undesired change in the signal characteristics. When the voltage has fallen below roughly 3.5 V, the battery is completely drained and stops sending signals. The next signal is not sent until the battery has been charged in the workshop.

Figure 2 shows the most important event types that we want to associate with the discharge curve. A description of each type follows in Table 1.

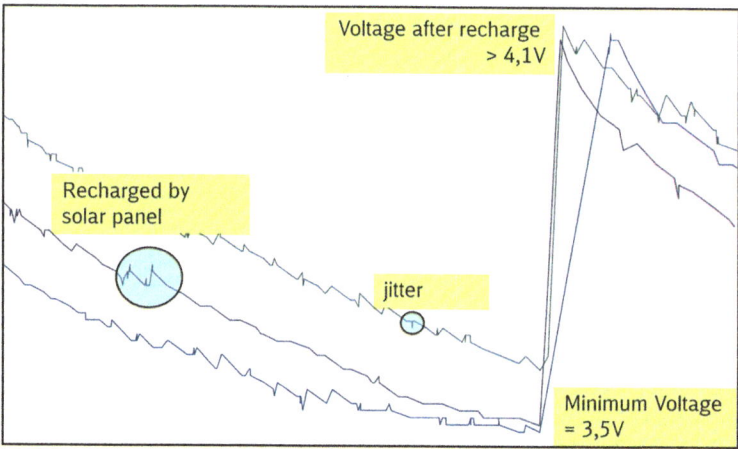

Fig. 1 Typical battery (dis)charge curves

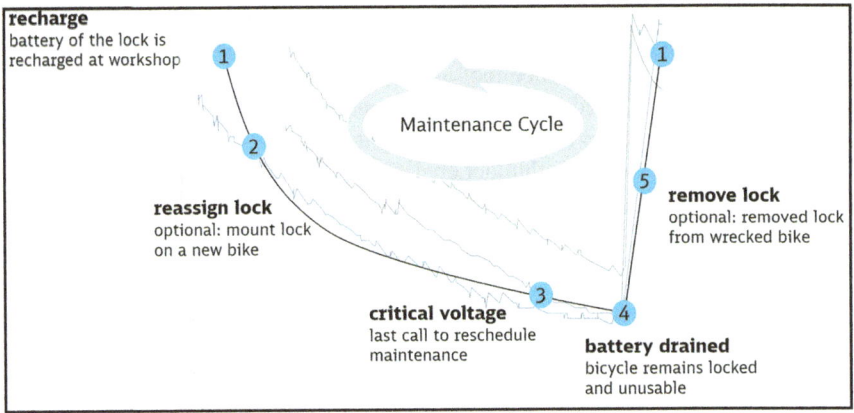

Fig. 2 Map of activities related to raw battery data

Table 1 Event types derived from the batteries' IoT data

Event type	Description
Recharge	Each lock needs to be recharged at some point in time. All other events are optional. therefore, the recharge event is our start event. The battery charge cycle starts with a recharged lock and ends when the lock is recharged again
Battery drained	This event is generated when we receive a signal indicating 3.5 V. In winter, no more signals will follow until recharge is accomplished. in the summer, the sun might have enough energy to bring the battery back to life. However, we cannot ensure that the customer will expose the battery to the sun, such that the power will be sufficient to close the lock when they finish the ride
Critical voltage	To avoid a bike draining on the road, we need some time to organize pickup. These preparation activities have to be decided and performed a certain number of days before the battery will become drained. The critical voltage (3.5 V) is usually reached around the same number of days before the battery is fully drained. therefore, when the critical voltage is reached, we should inform the crew that the bicycle needs attention
Reassign lock and remove lock	The lock keeps track of the bicycle it is assigned to. When the lock is not assigned to a bicycle, we can assume that the lock is waiting to transform a "naked" bike to an operational ensemble. While the lock is charging, the lock is removed from the bike and reattached when it is fully charged. Given delays in the workshop, the lock may have already had some voltage loss before it was reattached. there is no point in tracking the voltage of an unassigned lock

3.1.1   Detection of the Recharge Event

In Picture 3, we show a recharge curve with a long series of peaks and the battery does not really seem to drain any further. Such atypical behavior can occur if the bike is broken several times and the lock is brought back to the workshop often. Another reason could be a broken measuring unit. The most probable reason is that the sun is shining bright enough to fill the batteries cells again and again. Therefore,

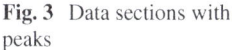

Fig. 3 Data sections with peaks

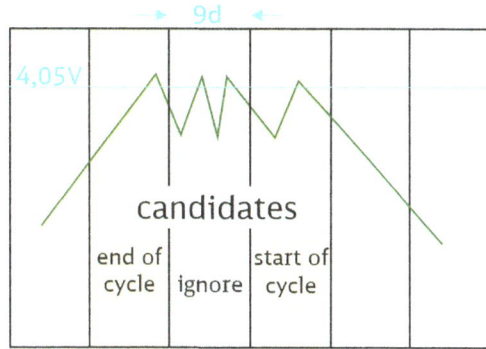

we have to determine whether we should trust the data and make a recommendation based on it or not.

Our approach is to section the data into 9-day periods. A typical 25-day cycle moves through three sections. The first section contains the starting recharge event. The last section contains the trailing recharge event. The middle section does not have peaks of 4 V or higher (as summer data is not considered here). We can then declare each section with one data point higher than 4.05 V a candidate for a recharge event. If the candidate has only two candidate neighbors, then we ignore it. Figure 3 shows a schematic representation of the candidates and the loading cycle derived from them. Either the battery is in good shape and there is nothing to report or the battery is broken and we distrust it completely. We can determine this by examining whether the candidate follows a previous section that also contained low voltages. If so, then its peak is the trailing recharge event from a maintenance cycle. If the candidate precedes a section with low voltages, then its peak is the start recharge event to a new maintenance cycle.

As we set the section size to 9 days, we need up to 18 days of data to determine whether we can consider the data trustworthy. The battery can be drained after 25 days, meaning this leaves us 7 days left to inform the maintenance staff about a necessary intervention.

3.1.2 Critical Voltage and Battery Drained

The most interesting part of the battery data is the prediction about the date when the battery will stop providing power. We do not currently have such a prediction in place. The positive effect of the solar panels, which prolongs the battery's charge cycle, is totally random. In the summer, the effect is more pronounced than in winter. That is until the customer forgets a flyer in the basket or positions the bike under a tree with a dense canopy of leaves. In such circumstances, the battery can only dream of an unobstructed flow of sunshine on a sunny December day.

As we want to communicate that a battery is low before the battery is completely drained, we decided to set a constant threshold of 3.7 V. We might adjust this value when we have a few more seasons of experience. Meanwhile, we have time to learn about battery capacity and expected cycle times from the literature. For example, from ZVEI (2013), we learned to derive life cycle information from data samples and we obtained a physical model for the battery life cycle from Xu et al. (2018):

$$L = 1 - \left(1 - L'\right)e^{f_d}$$

where L is the battery lifetime, L' is the initial lifetime, and f_d is the degradation rate, which depends on the temperature of the cells (not the environment) and the discharge curve (speed and depth). We will continue to apply such insights in subsequent years as we collect enough sample data to fully understand the impact continuous charging through solar panels has on the device.

3.1.3   Data Quality

A typical high-end ERP system includes thousands of tables and attributes and it may be difficult to determine which combination best describes the required process step. Fortunately, once the correct attributes are combined, the solution is deemed valid for all cases in the event log. In the case of the batteries, the data structure is extremely simple—each data point is a tuple of a timestamp, a lock ID, and the voltage. Unfortunately, the resulting curve changes from charge cycle to charge cycle. Figure 4 shows an example of when a battery has probably only been partially charged.

We have several options for handling such data:

1. When we detect this anomaly, we mark it with a special start event ("partial recharge"). This way, the anomaly is converted into a normal event log.
2. When we detect the anomaly, we discard the cycle as outliers are not suited to draw general conclusions.
3. When detected, we ignore the anomaly and accept the random reaction of our algorithms to this situation.

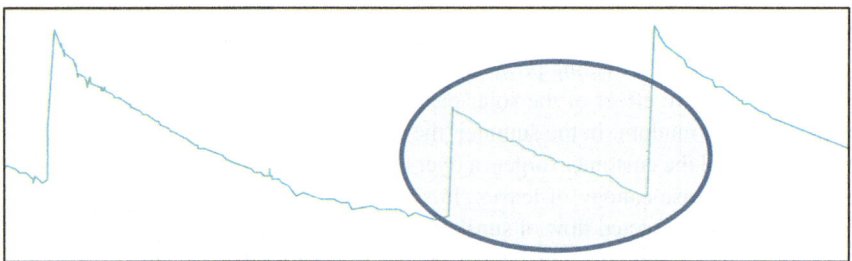

Fig. 4 Readings from a partially charged battery

Only options 1 and 2 are acceptable. Option 1 creates more process variants and increases the effort required of the business analyst. Option 2 becomes a problem if the supposed outlier turns out to be a frequent case. Option 3 would be a catastrophe. If the data is not treated as a (broken) cycle on its own, then it must be part of the subsequent or preceding cycle. Thus, such cycles would be interpreted incorrectly and compromise the overall quality of the event. Unfortunately, option 3 will organically apply for any undetected anomalies. Therefore, anticipating as many anomalies as possible in the data is a prerequisite for building a trustworthy event log.

3.2   Visualization and Enhancements

As shown in Fig. 5, the events resulting from our transformation efforts fit into any process mining tool very well. Typical KPIs, such as lead times, are calculated automatically. Furthermore, many skilled data analysts can build dashboards that can be implemented by interested business analysts without additional training. It is not necessary to understand battery physics to accomplish this work.

This visualization does not yet offer an end-to-end view. We look forward to adding stations, customer bookings, maintenance teams, and workshop locations in the future. The ability to meet our need to include all these objects in the model reflects the usefulness of process mining tools for applying an object-centric perspective.

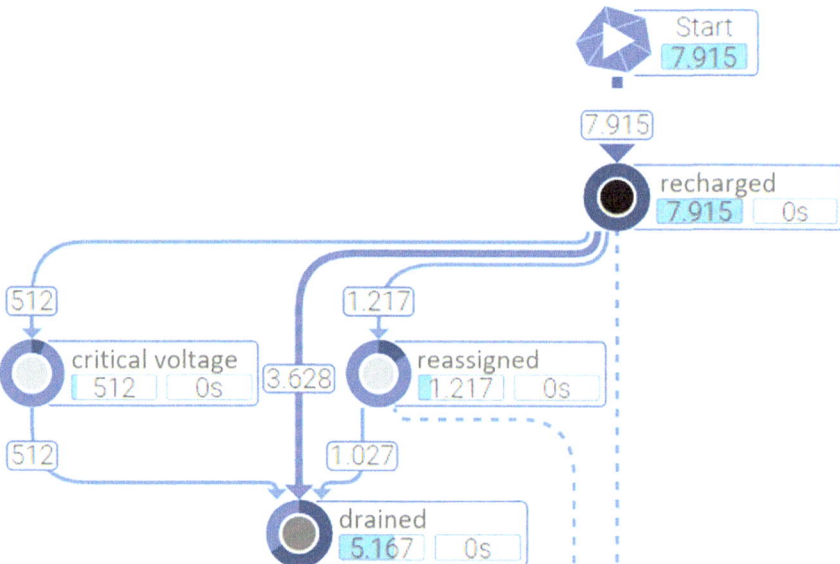

Fig. 5 Visualization of test data in a commercial process mining tool

Our colleagues are excitedly awaiting these additions. They have seen that a business-compatible representation of this very technical topic is finally emerging.

Our future sources for useful insights will be the following:

- Logistical processes

- We can use information about when a bicycle was picked up and brought into the workshop. The battery data just informs us that there was a recharge, all of which are performed in the workshop. However, at present, we do not know whether this was the main reason for the workshop visit. Such information is important for deciding how we can most effectively optimize the maintenance process (Becker & Intoyoad, 2017).

- Sales systems

- The sales system has a record of bookings and each booking is related to a bicycle number, which is then related to a lock number. These relationships allow us to determine a utilization rate that indicates how often a bike has been booked and how long it spent waiting for customers. This utilization rate is useful for estimating the financial benefit of higher bicycle availability.

4   Results Achieved

Process mining has allowed us to retrospectively measure the availability of a battery, the number and duration of maintenance cycles per bicycle, the different ranges reached by the batteries in summer and winter, and the battery's capacity loss over time. We have also gained additional insight into the recharging capabilities of the integrated solar panel. We can now determine the number of batteries that will most probably be fully discharged within the next few days and, thus, we can anticipate the need for maintenance for this failure. This is still far from an overall optimization but the improvements demonstrate the feasibility of the approach.

Thus, at this stage, the greatest effect of our approach has been psychological. Decisions are not just proposed by an algorithm in a black box but can be reproduced by human stakeholders in the context of their well-known process. The process mining visualizations that we have developed have been able to facilitate useful discussions with the process experts and have stimulated their imagination and further process improvement. Quantitative analysis and a process-focused business perspective have been perfectly combined into one picture.

5   Lessons Learned

Deutsche Bahn runs a highly technical business and all our assets (trains, vehicles, tracks) provide mobility services to our customers or are under maintenance. The use case presented in this paper shows how technical data and related management processes can be combined into one dashboard in a way that is relevant to the majority of our value-creating processes. Due to the lack of commercial process mining tools that combine both views, such projects will always feel a little bit like research projects. This does not promote the speed and acceptance of our work.

The compression of IoT data to a meaningful event log is tedious and needs a combination of data science skills and a concept with a manageable level of detail in the process steps (Badakhshan et al. 2022). Such breadth of skills is rarely found in individuals, so success depends heavily on having an interdisciplinary team of process and data experts. In addition, the team needs business domain knowledge in order to deliver substantial value to the business and fulfill its main reason for existing. The willingness to approach each other and to understand the relevant limitations and opportunities are a self-evident prerequisite for successful cooperation. We have limited influence on commercial tool producers. Therefore, we will continue to concentrate on enhancing our skills and building teams and alliances of individual DB employees with a strong focus on identifying what benefits we can draw from the available data in terms of better understanding and improving our processes.

References

Badakhshan, P., Wurm, B., Grisold, T., Geyer-Klingeberg, J., Mendling, J., & vom Brocke, J. (2022). Creating business value with process mining. *The Journal of Strategic Information Systems, 31*(4), 101745.

Becker, T., & Intoyoad, W. (2017). Context aware process mining in logistics. *Procedia CIRP, 63*, 557–562.

Bertrand, Y., De Weerdt, J., & Serral, E. (2022, March). A bridging model for process mining and IoT. In Process mining workshops: ICPM 2021 international workshops, Eindhoven, The Netherlands, October 31–November 4, 2021, Revised Selected Papers (pp. 98–110). Cham: Springer International Publishing.

Koschmider, A., Janssen, D., & Mannhardt, F. (2020, May). Framework for process discovery from sensor data. In EMISA (pp. 32–38).

Solterbeck, R. (2021). Process Mining – Anwendungsfälle und deren Übertragung auf die Deutsche Bahn. Bachelor thesis. Goethe Universität Frankfurt am Main.

Stiftung Warentest. (2019). Alle Testergebnisse für Bikesharing. https://www.test.de/Test-Bikesharing-Anbieter-Zwei-sind-gut-vier-mangelhaft-5460567-0/

Xu, B., Oudalov, A., Ulbig, A., Andersson, G., & Kirschen, D. S. (2018). Modeling of lithium-ion battery degradation for cell life assessment. *IEEE Transactions on Smart Grid, 9*(2), 1131–1140. https://doi.org/10.1109/TSG.2016.2578950

Zaimoglu, G. (2021). Entwurf einer cloudbasierten Process Mining Engine zur Erkennung von Prozessen bei der DB Systel GmbH. Bachelor thesis. Hochschule für Wirtschaft und Recht Berlin.

ZVEI. (2013). Zentralverband Elektrotechnik- und Elektronikindustrie e. V., Fachverband Batterien, Hrsg., Definition verschiedener Lebensdauer-Begriffe für Batterien, ZVEI Merkblatt Nr. 23, Ausgabe August 2013, Frankfurt a. M.

Riccarda Mark is a senior lean business consultant at DB Connect. Riccarda completed her studies at the University of Würzburg with a bachelor's degree in economathematics in 2017. Subsequently, she began to focus more deeply on the data-driven optimization and digitalization of operational processes in the aviation industry. Since 2022, she has been responsible for lean management and process optimization using process mining at DB Connect GmbH.

Ilario Angilletta is the Chief Consultant of the Department of Process Intelligence at DB Systel. Ilario completed his studies at the University of Dortmund with a master's degree in computer science in 1995. He has since gained insight into retail and the automotive industry before continuing his career at DB Systel GmbH in 2007. In 2017, convinced by the RPA, he founded the Process Intelligence Unit together with other process enthusiasts. In 2018, he added the topic of process mining to his portfolio and, since then, has been advising various business units at Deutsche Bahn on data-driven process optimization.

Process Mining as a Driver for Business Process Management: The Case of the Enervie Group

Ralf Plattfaut, Carolin Vollenberg, Peter A. François, Max Aberman, Jannis Nacke, and André Coners

Abstract

(a) *Situation faced*: At the end of an unsuccessful BPM initiative, Enervie had the opposite of a process mindset. Any endeavor in BPM was seen as a waste of resources and business departments were reluctant to discuss their processes. Therefore, Enervie's BPM capabilities were poorly developed and there was no transparency regarding their existing processes. As a result, problems frequently arose during process execution and the source of these issues would remain unknown, allowing them to recur constantly.

(b) *Action taken*: To uncover the issues' root causes, the company decided to implement process mining (PM) in its most critical end-to-end processes. Due to the general aversion to BPM in the organization, they did so without developing any other areas of BPM. The introduction of PM started as a pilot project in the purchase-to-pay process. The further rollout of PM continued in different processes or departments, specifically the meter-to-cash process, the accounts receivable process, and the controlling department.

(c) *Results achieved*: This approach enabled Enervie to restart its BPM initiative and build corresponding capabilities. The PM implementation was perceived as successful and further improvement initiatives were started. This included a permanent center of excellence for PM. During the project, the company rapidly built its BPM capabilities. The involvement of employees from all levels

R. Plattfaut
University of Duisburg-Essen, Essen, Germany
e-mail: Ralf.Plattfaut@icb.uni-due.de

C. Vollenberg (✉) · A. Coners
South Westphalia University of Applied Sciences, Hagen, Germany
e-mail: Vollenberg.Carolin@fh-swf.de; Francois.Peter@fh-swf.de; Coners.Andre@fh-swf.de

P. A. François
South Westphalia University of Applied Sciences, Soest, Germany

M. Aberman · J. Nacke
ENERVIE Gruppe, Hagen, Germany
e-mail: Max.Aberman@enervie-gruppe.de; Jannis.Nacke@enervie-gruppe.de

© The Author(s), under exclusive license to Springer Nature Switzerland AG 2025
J. vom Brocke et al. (eds.), *Business Process Management Cases Vol. 3*,
https://doi.org/10.1007/978-3-031-80793-0_16

211

led to the continuous development of additional ideas for use cases. The concrete data gathered using PM gave the initiative credibility and enabled the PM team to overcome the negative BPM mindset. The project's success has, thereby, motivated staff to acquire further BPM capabilities.

(d) *Lessons learned*: PM on its own can be used to launch BPM initiatives. The objective data and insight into end-to-end processes gathered using PM give credibility to BPM initiatives. Due to this, even small-scale experiments – like the optimization of one end-to-end process – can drive large-scale organizational change. Last, an agile approach drives the organizational culture toward the acceptance of BPM initiatives.

1   Introduction

Business process management (BPM) has been widely researched and adopted by many organizations. As a result, BPM and its goals are well defined, and different approaches (e.g., lean six sigma and total quality management) were designed for specific contexts (e.g., manufacturing) (vom Brocke & Mendling, 2018). Six core factors have been identified for BPM: *strategic alignment, governance, methods, information technology, people, and culture*, which require competencies in several capabilities (Rosemann & de Bruin, 2005). Based on the advancements of capabilities in these areas, the maturity level of an organization regarding BPM can be assessed (Rosemann & vom Brocke, 2015).

Process mining (PM) is a growing technology trend that brings concepts from data mining into BPM, providing fact-based and objective insights (Kipping et al., 2022). PM thereby uncovers possible process variants, accurately reflecting employees' actions while carrying out these processes. PM can also be used to identify patterns, create process models, and measure quantified indicators using real-time data. According to van der Aalst et al. (2012), there are two main drivers for using PM: "On the one hand, more and more events are being recorded, thus, providing detailed information about the history of processes. On the other hand, there is a need to improve and support business processes in competitive and rapidly changing environments" (van der Aalst et al., 2012, p. 170). PM has a wide range of potential applications, such as process discovery, enhancement, and conformance (van der Aalst, 2018). It also provides numerous opportunities for structure and performance transparency in business processes (Scholz & Vrohlings, 1994).

The Enervie Group is an organization consisting of companies formed by Mark-E and the Lüdenscheid public utility company ("Stadtwerke Lüdenscheid"), with a history dating back to 1906. The company's service area covers the city of Hagen and significant portions of the Märkischer Kreis, serving around 450,000 inhabitants. With approximately 1,000 employees, the Enervie Group collaborates with private, commercial, and industrial customers, municipalities, public utilities, and the housing industry. The Enervie Group supplies electricity, gas, heat, and drinking water to its customers as a regional utility. Additionally, the company provides energy-related services and manages the region's electricity grid, with some of the energy produced and procured in-house. In order to reliably ensure the supply of the inhabitants and businesses, the Enervie Group needs optimized and robust processes.

2 Situation Faced

Enervie had previously attempted to start a BPM journey. Processes were set to be optimized and consequently improved using Robotic Process Automation (RPA). The company did not build internal knowledge but let a consultancy firm handle the optimization and the RPA development. However, this project was unsuccessful, as the consultancy firm tried to start automating large, complex processes but could not implement them satisfactorily in the given timeframe. The failure of the RPA project led to employees becoming suspicious and unwilling to participate in further BPM advancements. There was a consensus among employees that "*if everyone would do their job properly, we would have solid processes.*" Further small, uncoordinated attempts to optimize only parts of processes (e.g., only in one department) led to negligible results, intensified by the company's aversion to BPM.

The absence of a process mindset and organizational BPM skills at Enervie led to extensive problems and inefficiencies in business processes. The organization rarely monitored process indicators or quantified process problems. Without accurate data, Enervie relied on intuitive controls for its processes, which often resulted in flawed decision-making. In addition, business experts at Enervie carried out processes based on subjective experience. New employees were then trained based on this knowledge. Therefore, there was no common understanding of processes between different roles and departments. The diversification of labor within the processes increased this effect. Many other mental process models existed in the minds of the process participants. At the same time, the business experts could not differentiate between the actual and target processes. In the few cases where documentation existed, it either did not follow a precise notation or was outdated, leading to a further lack of clarity in Enervie's processes. As a result, the processes at Enervie needed more transparency, standardization, and optimization.

Enervie's lack of transparency in its processes meant that process analysis was only carried out sporadically for specific projects such as software implementation. Even then, there was no structured modeling or central control. This resulted in processes being performed case by case without standardized or optimized procedures, which created inefficiencies and waste. Weaknesses in cross-departmental processes were usually not identified, and dependencies were widely unknown. For example, in the purchasing department, many invoices were issued without purchase requisitions or individual purchase orders, despite the existence of framework agreements. The faults in these processes frequently created confusion and service delays, which could have been avoided if the processes had been more transparent and standardized. Additionally, the lack of data made it difficult to quantify the problems, and specific starting points for improvement were needed. As a result, problems were tackled with unconvincing motivation, leading to suboptimal outcomes. Enervie needed to establish a more data-driven approach to its processes to identify inefficiencies and improve its processes.

Enervie relied on harmonized software solutions to achieve some degree of standardization in its processes. Since the privatization of the energy market, the German energy sector has been subject to strict regulations imposed by the federal network agency ("Bundesnetzagentur"). Although these regulations allow the use of existing solutions within the market, such as specific templates for SAP ISU, they are not always the best fit for the necessary processes, requiring constant refinement and adaptation. Unfortunately, Enervie's process analysis was often limited to processes within a single department, which hindered the identification of cross-departmental issues and inefficiencies. The lack of a holistic approach to process optimization meant that Enervie's technical and software infrastructure was not optimally aligned with its processes, leading to disruptions and inefficiencies that were often difficult to explain. Enervie, therefore, had a low level of BPM maturity, with many opportunities for optimization and standardization left untapped.

To improve BPM maturity, Enervie needed a more comprehensive approach to process analysis, including cross-departmental perspectives and a focus on aligning technical and software infrastructure within processes. By adopting a more strategic and data-driven approach to BPM, Enervie was able to improve its BPM maturity level, streamline its processes, and create a more efficient and effective business operation. To address the identified challenges, the company made a strategic decision to launch a PM initiative that aimed to find practical solutions.

3   Action Taken

Enervie adopted the commercial PM platform Celonis, handling the implementation by a diverse team of experts. This team comprised external consultants specializing in Celonis and two professors acting as academic consultants regarding PM for the pilot project. In addition, two newly hired employees with expertise in business informatics and agile methods were hired to steer the initiative from the company's perspective. The organization chose this strategy because of the experience of the previous failed BPM project. They sought to build long-term knowledge within the company and retain control over the project. In addition, as the project progressed, domain experts and management of the involved departments were involved in the implementation. The PM initiative was divided into three phases: 1) Piloting PM in Purchase-to-Pay, 2) Rollout of PM in Meter-to-Cash, Accounts Receivable and Controlling, and 3) Setting Up Organizational Capabilities for Process Management and Mining.

3.1 Piloting Process Mining in Purchase-to-Pay

Enervie initially focused on the cross-departmental purchase-to-pay (P2P) process as it had been identified as having a high business impact as well as a high potential for improvement. The P2P process was to be optimized to improve the customer experience and break down the existing departmental barriers for BPM. Several departments (procurement, technical service, meter reading, internal audit) are all stakeholders in this process and would frequently blame other departments for any issues that arose. PM was leveraged to provide transparency, ensuring process knowledge, reliability, and compliance. The pilot project for the introduction of PM took five months to enable full process discovery.

The implementation and development of PM use cases for the P2P process followed an agile approach overseen by the newly hired employees. This approach was designed to meet the requirements of the project's character and the cultural situation in the conservative working environment of the energy supplier. It included sprints to develop use cases, with each iteration operationalizing the vision by formulating achievable goals. This approach was chosen because the PM implementation only had a vision rather than clearly defined goals. Key performance indicators were defined and – using PM – automatically collected and updated in real – time. The calculated Key Performance Indicators (KPIs) and PM results enabled more efficient process planning, analysis, and monitoring and, in addition, gave Enervie insights into the causes and effects of process weaknesses and deviations. Enervie decided to use the PM tool as a management tool and involved both operational and strategic departments.

The initial test users were drawn from the operational procurement department and pilot users were trained. Additional users were later included to familiarize all operational staff with PM, its applications, and benefits for their daily work. In total, since the completion of the pilot, 20 employees have been making direct use of the PM tool within the P2P process. Employees in the procurement department were nominated as the process owners. An open training initiative allowed all interested employees to develop new requirements and analysis ideas, which were then prioritized, built, and integrated into the central PM dashboard using an agile approach. Simultaneously, further investigations were conducted at the management level to identify significant process problems and define additional efforts.

3.2 Rollout of Process Mining in Meter-to-Cash, Accounts Receivable and Controlling

Based on the results and successes of the PM pilot project, it became clear that introducing PM in additional processes would offer extensive benefits for Enervie. The success of the pilot project was repeatedly brought up in various hierarchical levels of the company (including by the board of directors, divisional, and operational managers). The core elements, advantages, and future visions for PM at Enervie were also explained to a wide range of employees, including operational staff. As a result, an increasing number of departments began to recognize the advantages and potential use cases for PM in their areas. Process transparency and key performance indicators were crucial selling arguments for many departments. The possible automation improvements based on the clean and extensive PM dataset further drove departments to request the introduction of PM to their processes. Consequently, within 11 months, PM was rolled out in several projects for various business areas in the second phase.

For strategic reasons, the next process analyzed with PM was the meter-to-cash process in the power grid unit. It included activities ranging from the preparation of meter readings at the customers' location to clearing invoices from the energy supplier. The process is owned by employees in the power grid and the meter reading department. However, this process is very complex due to the various stakeholders involved – physical assets at a customer's location must be read, invoiced, and booked correctly by different departments. The parties involved are the power grid, meter reading, internal auditing departments, Enervie Service GmbH, and an external service provider.

"Things can go wrong at three different stages: Meter reading, invoicing, and posting," explains the external implementation consultant. *"We wanted to start there and find out where things might go wrong."* A typical error scenario would run as follows: A customer's meter is read correctly but a valid bill cannot be generated, which triggers a long chain of faulty processes that must be manually resolved. For Enervie, this meant high financial losses. If a meter could not be billed in one year, the billing process would also fail in the following years. Within this process, PM was primarily introduced to create transparency and to maintain and ensure compliance with the frequently changing regulations and prevent such faulty process executions.

At first, data inconsistencies and the need for many clarification cases led to prioritizing error correction over holistic processual analysis with PM. The PM analysis identified several causes for these inconsistencies which triggered both process optimization and automation. Since the implementation period, 35 users have been utilizing the PM tool in the meter-to-cash process.

Later on, PM was implemented in the accounts receivable processes and the controlling departments as there was a high level of interest in PM in these areas. In accounts receivable, the receivables management, sales management, meter reading, and internal auditing departments were involved. Due to legal changes, the pandemic increased the demand for information on open receivables within accounts receivable. For example, customer contracts could not be terminated even if bills were not paid during a Corona-induced lockdown. Therefore, PM was chosen to reduce highly repetitive reporting tasks and provide a basis for further analyses, operational support, and business process improvement for the energy vendor unit and its 20 included users. The aim was to monitor receivables across different SAP clients in real time.

In the controlling department, PM was chosen to simplify financial controlling tasks for noncontrollers within the company. Stakeholders like the controlling, technical service, meter reading, and the internal auditing departments are relevant here. Six employees are now using the implemented PM.

A culture of continuous improvement based on regularly automated KPI reporting and regular analysis meetings has been established in almost all departments based on the developed PM solutions, which generated a positive attitude toward PM (and BPM, respectively). The company, therefore, decided to continue to expand the initiative by building capabilities.

3.3   Setting Up Organizational Capabilities for Process Management and Mining

Using PM within Enervie has helped build organizational capabilities for BPM and PM. During the PM implementation, there was a shift toward using the PM tool as a holistic solution for different aspects of process management including process analytics, automation (e.g., email notifications including automatic extraction of required data), preparation of readings from other systems, automatic data enrichment and linking, process optimizations, key performance indicator reporting, and monitoring.

Based on the success of the PM implementation and the establishment of organizational capabilities for process management, Enervie decided to establish a Centre of Excellence (CoE). This CoE is entirely self-sufficient and managed by the two employees who joined the company at the beginning of the PM journey. The CoE is usually allowed a quota of consulting hours to be used in areas that are lacking capacities. This strategy has proven to be efficient for Enervie. At the start of the CoE, only two processes were actively managed by the CoE although the plan was to eventually oversee all PM processes. Going further, the CoE received additional support in the form of two additional employees formally employed in other business departments but effectively controlled by the CoE. Recently, the CoE expanded again and now has eight internal developers managed directly by the CoE. Currently, there are a total of 83 active users, and the trend is still increasing.

Moreover, PM experts have been identified within different business departments who are solely responsible for that department. Five employees are currently operating in the three departments outside the CoE, building up department knowledge and transferring that into further PM improvements for the individual department. This scenario takes the pressure off the CoE and allows it to concentrate on further PM rollouts across the company, creating a network of experience and knowledge transfer.

Further PM projects are planned for additional departments and processes. The CoE intends to introduce a group-wide PM roundtable to exchange PM knowledge and further discuss use cases within the energy supplier. The company plans to promote discussion across departments and advance process capabilities (especially BPM knowledge and process attitudes). Further, this is intended to offer interested employees the opportunity to learn about the added value of PM and increase process management sensitivity.

4   Results Achieved

Our case study shows how Enervie, an organization with underdeveloped capabilities in BPM, was able to achieve a higher level of BPM maturity as an unforeseen windfall within one and a half years of implementing PM. The company considers the implementation a success and is working on improving other processes using PM while, simultaneously, continuing to improve its BPM capabilities.

Results Achieved in the Case Study Processes
Regarding the optimization of the different processes, Enervie achieved several results. We present the main operative results in the following Table 1.

In the *P2P process*, Enervie started using PM as a pilot project and achieved significant results. Enervie's procurement department observed significant benefits. Not only did PM improve compliance checks and transparency, it also increased cross-departmental process knowledge. Moreover, they identified process activities that require significant manual rework using quantification rather than trusting subjective statements. Before implementing PM, "*in purchasing, people were spending 40 percent of their time on processes where something is wrong,*" according to the former head of procurement. They were able to reduce this effort using PM. Overall, PM enabled Enervie's process thinking by allowing the employees to identify, discover, analyze, redesign, and monitor the P2P process (Dumas et al., 2018).

Within the *meter-to-cash process*, Enervie was able to cure several reoccurring issues. PM was used for the analysis and modification, which was tied to eliminating the root cause instead of manually mitigating the symptoms. Based on the

Table 1 Results achieved in the processes under study

Process	Operative result
P2P	Effort and error reduction Development of process thinking
Meter-to-cash	Root cause analysis and optimization Quality improvement First automation pilots
Accounts receivable	Real-time and standardized process monitoring Effort reduction
Controlling	Holistic process transparency Simplification of the target process

problems and derived requirements of the involved domain experts responsible for clarifying the problematic cases, dashboards were created within the PM environment to analyze, prioritize, and efficiently explain the problem cases.

The improvements to the meter-to-cash process and other components of the BPM initiative in the power grid department resulted in an overall reduction of 76% in the number of clarification cases within one year. In addition, the number of missing settlements decreased by 60% over the same period. This immensely improved process quality and freed up working capital for the company.

PM assisted also process automation in the power grid department. When combined with automation technologies, PM can be an essential tool for providing ongoing support within a company. Action-oriented PM expands on this idea by introducing a method that adds a constraint monitor and an action engine to enable the continual management of operational processes and the automatic execution of actions to enhance the process. At Enervie, simple processes were automated first, such as the automatic email generation for specific automatically detected scenarios, previously a very mundane and time-consuming task. Later, more complex automation was conducted using PM, involving several process steps and interfaces between tools. Such automation enabled further time-savings and reduced rework in error-prone tasks.

Accounts receivable achieved real-time receivables monitoring across two SAP instances instead of a once-a-month update allowing managers to react to issues quickly. In addition, the monthly manual effort of 6 hours creating the receivables monitor was eliminated. The dataset created also provides a basis for building operational apps in receivables management and will bring many more improvements in the medium to long term.

The *controlling* department aimed to simplify operations associated with budget reporting for business unit experts by generating it in Celonis instead of SAP. With this, it was possible to create further value-adding results, for example, combining different views into one standardized view of the process, a better commitment presentation to provide a more accurate picture for the business experts, and a pilot for replacing the investment report. Additional reports required by the federal network agency can now be implemented quickly and easily.

Enervie exceeded the expected benefits of the PM implementation. For example, one employee stated that *"I expected to understand the business processes [...] better, and the result is even better than just understanding."* Furthermore, they *"[...] expected that the technology would show which process parts create the greatest inefficiencies to know where to start the improvement [...], but it did not only this."* The head of the network management at Enervie also drew a positive conclusion: *"We have created the right combination of experts [...], very experienced colleagues from the specialist departments, and the competence center, which coordinates and communicates the interfaces. But, in the end, the system only works well if everyone involved also trusts the results of the analysis."* Overall, the expectations regarding the implementation success of PM were exceeded.

Organizational Results Achieved

While the PM initiative focused on improving processes with the process clarity and understanding gained, the company had to build the required BPM knowledge to realize the improvements rapidly. The progress achieved in the P2P process during the project (mainly lesser process disruption and higher customer satisfaction) led to the acceptance of BPM and the employees' willingness to develop BPM capabilities. The skills acquired in this way initially served the PM project; they have also enabled BPM capabilities more generally.

After the project presented here, further initiatives regarding PM and BPM were initiated and are ongoing. In addition, continuous development in terms of PM and especially in BPM capabilities has been planned and created. As a result, what began as a technological project now delivers additional value across the business. *"It's quite unique for a medium-sized energy company to have such a unit that drives digital transformation,"* agrees one implementation consultant specializing in PM. *"You can see what successes can be achieved when digitalization is really taken seriously."*

Even though PM is primarily associated with the capability factor of "information technology," the introduction and use of PM helped Enervie develop capabilities in all the six core capability areas in BPM (Rosemann & de Bruin, 2005). Figure 1 shows the improvement achieved in the different BPM capability areas. Identifying as-is processes and checking the conformances and weaknesses of processes provide the basis for enhancements. In addition, redesigning processes supports the strengthening of BPM capabilities. Thus, it has been observed that a "comprehensive BPM approach requires alignment to corporate objectives, adequate governance, and an employees' customer focus and involves, besides a cross-functional viewpoint, strategy, operations, techniques and people" (Rosemann & de Bruin, 2005). While working with Enervie as it adopted PM, we found that their

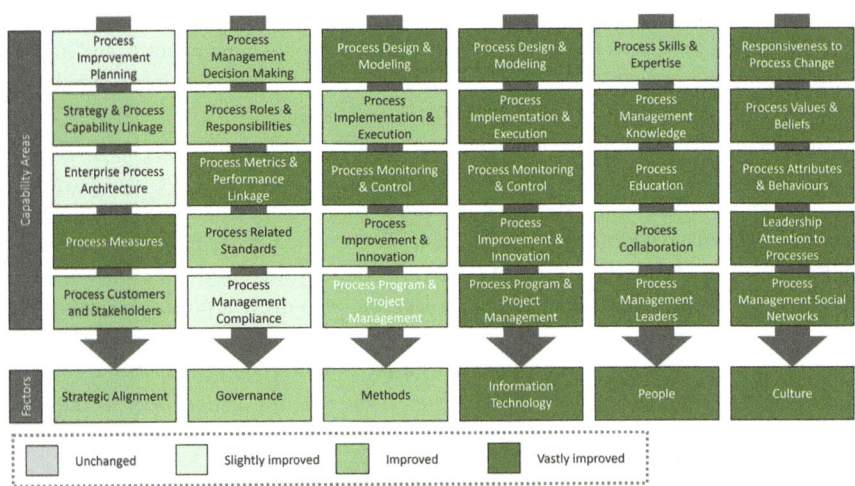

Fig. 1 Summarizing improvements on the level of BPM

requirements have changed and their capabilities have vastly improved in the process.

Enervie started its BPM journey with an initial maturity level of one, according to Roseman and de Bruin (2005). The organizational capabilities structured along the six core factors had not yet been built. Processes were managed sporadically and performed on a case-to-case basis. Enervie had few BPM skills (e.g., rarely monitoring or process modeling within only a few existing processes, usually with disappointing results). Problems were often managed by "firefighting" rather than using structured or holistic process improvement approaches.

Regarding BPM, the company did not follow the typical steps by sequentially reaching the maturity levels as defined by Roseman and Bruin (2005). Instead, they leapfrogged several stages of the BPM maturity model. They implemented PM right away while a successfully implemented PM is somewhere on level five ("optimized") in the maturity model of BPM (Rosemann & de Bruin, 2005). The typical procedure for achieving BPM maturity includes planning, strategic alignment, process modeling, analysis, design, implementing the processes, monitoring, refinement, or process performance measurement. In contrast, Enervie immediately started implementing advanced BPM technologies without first establishing the more essential components associated with earlier maturity levels.

The project's success and the credibility given to the project by the traceable and verifiable key indicators have led to a rapid acceptance of the project and a broad desire to participate, which was different from the previous RPA initiative.

5 Lessons Learned

While accompanying the project as it introduced PM in the company, we made four main observations. First, PM can be used to kick-start BPM initiatives. Second, PM and objective data can give credibility to BPM initiatives. Next, small-scale experiments can drive large-scale organizational change, and finally, an agile approach drives the acceptance of BPM initiatives.

Process mining can be used to kick-start BPM initiatives. While PM is a technology that can empower existing BPM initiatives, starting a PM initiative can also kick-start BPM in a company. PM has been described as being used at higher maturity levels. However, Enervie has managed to use PM without developing any other meaningful BPM capabilities first. Instead, the PM implementation has started a BPM initiative, including the establishment of BPM capabilities and a process mindset. Moreover, other capabilities were gained as a windfall during the project (see Fig. 1). PM can therefore enable an organization to leapfrog from almost no BPM maturity to higher maturity levels.

Process mining and objective data give credibility to BPM initiatives. The measures of processes and possible issues in processes provided by PM help BPM teams determine which processes and tasks need to be improved urgently in an objective and verifiable manner. Being able to prove the existence of these errors—and possibly even show their origin—enables fast improvement, clear and easy communication, and acceptance and, thus, improved change management. By providing clear and reliable metrics, PM gave the BPM initiative credibility, leading to decreased stakeholder resistance. The measured benefits can be used for promoting the initiative among employees with a negative mindset. The metrics collected also led to a feeling of accomplishment after a successful optimization, which facilitated verbal endorsements of the project across the company (e.g., *"we managed to increase measure x by y percent"*). Furthermore, the continuous improvement since has inspired the departments strive to increase their measures further, thus increasing openness to the additional activities of the BPM initiative.

Small-scale experiments can drive large-scale organizational change. The use of proof-of-concept projects has proven effective. Performing an initial trial based on "easy" use cases has allowed the company to build trust and interest to facilitate further advances in PM and BPM. The cascading of success led to an organizational-wide acceptance of PM and caused a mindset change among employees. By actually understanding and solving the problems domain experts faced in their daily business, an innate drive regarding process optimization was created. By simultaneously providing access to the necessary toolset and training, the company was able to scale the initiative significantly. Small proof-of-concept-driven PM initiatives can serve as an example for the entire company and can be used to initialize a company-wide BPM initiative. In this case, a trial project managed by two new employees led to the implementation of an entire BPM department and wide-ranging cultural and methodological changes. By including employees right from the beginning and nominating direct contact persons in the operative processes, the change management within the process optimization was included automatically.

The agile approach drives a thriving organizational culture toward the acceptance of BPM initiatives. The agile process of getting to know the organizational unit, implementation, validation, value creation, and continuous improvement strengthens the intrinsic motivation to accept BPM initiatives. Transparency is essential for change management. The transparency and openness with which Enervie carried out the PM initiative contributed significantly to the acceptance and use of the calculated data. As several departments are involved in most processes, a lot of communication is usually necessary to capture the entire as-is process. Also, constant training and change management are essential to both ensure that domain experts accept PM and enable them to use it in an increasing number of processes. Iterative development with high stakeholder involvement allows the company to organically grow the project, consider new insights, and adjust the project's goals accordingly. Fast incremental development of solutions and especially solving the problems and pain points in operational processes creates goodwill among domain experts, thereby playing an essential role in change management.

References

Dumas, M., La Rosa, M., Mendling, J., & Reijers, H. A. (2018). *Fundamentals of business process management* (2nd ed.). Springer.

Kipping, G., Djurica, D., Franzoi, S., Grisold, T., Marcus, L., Schmid, S., vom Brocke, J., Mendling, J., & Röglinger, M. (2022). How to leverage process mining in organizations – Towards process mining capabilities. In C. Di Ciccio, R. Dijkman, O. A. Del Río, & S. Rinderle-Ma (Eds.), *Business process management* (Vol. 13420, pp. 40–46). Springer International Publishing.

Rosemann, M., & de Bruin, T. (2005). Towards a business process management maturity model. ECIS 2005 proceedings.

Rosemann, M., & vom Brocke, J. (2015). The six core elements of business process management. In J. vom Brocke & M. Rosemann (Eds.), *Handbook on business process management 1* (2nd ed.). Springer.

Scholz, R., & Vrohlings, A. (1994). Prozeß-Leistungs-Transparenz. In M. Gaitanides, R. Scholz, A. Vrohlings, & M. Raster (Eds.), *Prozeßmanagement: Konzepte, Umsetzungen und Erfahrungen des Reengineering* (pp. 57–98). Hanser.

van der Aalst, W. M. P. (2018). *Process mining: Data science in action* (2nd ed.). Springer.

van der Aalst, W. M. P., Adriansyah, A., et al. (2012). Process mining manifesto. In F. Daniel, K. Barkaoui, & S. Dustdar (Eds.), *Business process management workshops: BPM 2011* (pp. 169–194). Springer.

vom Brocke, J., & Mendling, J. (2018). Frameworks for business process management: A taxonomy for business process management cases. In J. vom Brocke & J. Mendling (Eds.), *Business process management cases* (pp. 1–17). Springer International Publishing.

Ralf Plattfaut is professor for Information Systems and Transformation Management at the University of Duisburg-Essen, Germany, where he is the founder and head of the Process Innovation and Automation Lab. Prior to this, he worked as a professor at the South Westphalia University of Applied Sciences and as a management consultant in the field of digital transformation at McKinsey and Company. He studied Information Systems in Germany, Liechtenstein, and Australia and holds a PhD from the University of Münster, Germany. He has published multiple articles in various journals (e.g., EJIS, MISQE, BISE, BPMJ) and presented his work at international conferences (e.g., ICIS, ECIS, BPM). According to Wirtschaftswoche 2024, he is among the 20 strongest German-speaking management researchers under 40.

Carolin Vollenberg, M.Sc. is a research assistant and doctoral student at the Department of Technical Business Administration at the South Westphalia University of Applied Sciences, Hagen, Germany. There, she is part of the Laboratory for Experimental Process and ERP Research. Her research focuses on business process management and process automation as well as the adoption and use of digital innovations in the health sector. In the BPM-field she is certified as a Lean Six Sigma Black Belt.

Peter A. François, M.Sc. is a research assistant and doctoral student at the Department of Electrical Engineering at the Soest campus of South Westphalia University of Applied Sciences, where he is part of the Process Innovation and Automation Lab. His research interests include business process management, digital transformation, lightweight IT, and the reuse of information systems artifacts.

Max Aberman, B.Sc. is a data science manager in the Commercial Business Unit of Enervie – Südwestfalen Energie und Wasser AG in Hagen, Germany, and a master's student in informatics and business and in industrial engineering in the Department of Technical Business Administration at the South Westphalia University of Applied Sciences in Hagen. His research focuses on business process management in the energy sector with a special focus on the practical application of process mining.

Jannis Nacke, B.A. is a data science manager in the Commercial Business Unit of Enervie – Südwestfalen Energie und Wasser AG in Hagen, Germany, with more than 2 years of relevant working experience in the field of data analytics specializing in the usage of Celonis process mining. He focuses on digital transformation through data-driven change management.

André Coners is professor for Business Process Management (BPM) and Management Accounting with focus on Management Information Systems. He is a member of the European Research Center for Information Systems and directs the Laboratory for Experimental Process and ERP Research at the South Westphalia University of Applied Sciences, Hagen, Germany. In the BPM-field he is certified as a Lean Six Sigma Master Black Belt.

On the Development of the BPM Governance Matrix: The Case of Endress+Hauser

Jan vom Brocke, Manuel Weber, Christian Stefan Baumgartner, Alexander Röettcher, and Stefan Segerlund

Abstract

(a) *Situation faced*: We are reporting on a large BPM redesign project at Endress+Hauser (E+H), a globally operating company in the measurement and automation industry. E+H aimed to reallocate roles and responsibilities of their business process management (BPM) within the existing organization but lacked a tool or framework to guide them in this endeavor.

(b) *Action taken*: As part of this design science research (DSR) collaboration, we co-developed the *BPM Governance Matrix*, which enables practitioners to integrate and institutionalize BPM within their existing units and the broader management of the entire organization.

(c) *Results achieved*: The main achievement is the development and evaluation of the *BPM Governance Matrix*, which is based on three activity groups (strategy, structure, process) and four responsibility dimensions, adapted from the RACI method (responsible, accountable, consult, inform).

(d) *Lessons learned*: The matrix demonstrates its usefulness by promoting awareness of the process stakeholder's roles and responsibilities. Moreover, practitio-

---

Endress+Hauser (E+H), headquartered in Switzerland, is a global leader in the measurement and automation industry specializing in process and laboratory applications. They employ more than 14,000 people and run production facilities on four continents.

J. vom Brocke
European Research Center for Information Systems (ERCIS), University of Münster, Münster, Germany
e-mail: jan.vom.brocke@uni-muenster.de

M. Weber (✉)
Liechtenstein Business School, Department of Information Systems and Computer Science, University of Liechtenstein, Vaduz, Principality of Liechtenstein
e-mail: manuel.weber@uni.li

C. S. Baumgartner · A. Röettcher · S. Segerlund
Endress+Hauser Group Services AG, Reinach, Switzerland
e-mail: c.baumgartner@sap.com; christian.baumgartner@endress.com;
alexander.roettcher@endress.com; stefan.segerlund@endress.com

ners can utilize and extend the matrix based on their contextual requirements from a bottom-up perspective. Finally, the matrix can be used to promote communication and collaboration within the existing organization. As such, it creates transparency and supports the discourse among process stakeholders, leading to increased acceptance.

1 Introduction

Business process management (BPM) has developed into an integrative management discipline for systematically analyzing, designing, visualizing, implementing, monitoring, and continuously improving processes of organizations (vom Brocke & Rosemann, 2015; Dumas et al., 2018). BPM, as a management program itself, should successfully support the implementation of an organization's strategy and goals rather than being an end in itself (Dumas et al., 2018). Hence, BPM should contribute to and support value generation within organizations and deliver the organization's goals. Therefore, the design and implementation of business processes are key drivers of corporate success and performance. For many organizations, this is a significant concern, so they appoint a chief process officer (CPO) to the senior management level. Due to their authority, such CPOs often have far-reaching decision-making power. They can also serve as change agents or influencers in important BPM transformation projects (Kratzer et al., 2018).

Within this chapter, we report on a case at Endress+Hauser (E+H), a globally operating company active in the measurement and automation industry. They are currently undergoing a major BPM modernization process and, therefore, intend to adapt this management discipline to the new challenges of a rapidly changing world. As part of this endeavor, they aim to reallocate roles and responsibilities within the existing organization. Associated with this large-scale initiative at E+H are topics such as decision-making and the new roles and responsibilities established during the transition from a functional to a traditional process organization.

E+H is aware that there are several success factors within BPM, such as culture, people, methods, strategic alignment, and information technology (IT) (Rosemann & vom Brocke, 2010), which they need to consider simultaneously. In their BPM project, E+H first decided to reorganize the responsibilities. For this, they needed a common understanding and a model for implementing this project in a structured and systematic way. In doing so, they asked themselves where exactly BPM and the associated responsibilities should be allocated and institutionalized within the existing organizational structure.

In addition, E+H is transforming into a process organization and must also take functional interests and decisions into account. This transition is a challenging undertaking, which is why clear roles and assigned responsibilities should support this process. Governance in BPM is an important dimension necessary for achieving sustainable organizational performance. In small initiatives and large-scale projects, a successful BPM requires broad cross-functional collaboration and communication (Spanyi et al., 2015).

To tackle these challenges and provide support during this transformation process, we co-developed a framework dedicated to the holistic and contextualized implementation of governance within their existing organizational setup. Our approach is echoed in the realm of contemporary BPM research studies, calling for the taking of a holistic approach (vom Brocke et al., 2021a, b; Rosemann & vom Brocke, 2010) and consideration of the organization's context (vom Brocke et al., 2016, 2021a, b; Rosemann et al., 2006) when it comes to managing processes in general.

2   Situation Faced

In this chapter, we report on a large-scale BPM initiative at a globally operating company, Endress+Hauser (E+H), headquartered in Switzerland. The case company is a global leader and expert in the measurement and automation industry, specializing in process and laboratory applications. As part of their large BPM project, they aim to reallocate the roles and responsibilities for their BPM within the existing organization. However, they currently lack a management tool or framework to guide them in this endeavor. E+H can also be considered a technology service provider, developing laboratory and industrial solutions for temperature and pressure measurement, analysis, and digital communication. The company runs production units on four continents and owns sales units in more than 50 countries worldwide. Moreover, they cooperate with representatives in another 70 countries. The company is family owned and was founded in 1953.

E+H aims to reorganize its BPM approach by integrating process work within its existing roles and responsibilities. To this end, they launched a project investigating where to allocate BPM within the existing organization. Hence, E+H is facing the question of where to institutionalize and assign responsibilities in BPM within their existing organization. Within this project, their primary focus is on enhancing the customer experience along specific processes. To ensure that BPM activities are carried out efficiently and effectively, specific process stakeholders and actors must be held accountable (responsible). According to E+H, people are key drivers in initiating and implementing any activity utilizing information technologies, different methodologies, and existing strategy specifications. Hence, E+H aims to allocate and embed BPM within the existing organization. Accordingly, BPM should not be a department isolated from the organization and its peculiarities. Based on this goal and demand, the following questions emerged: Who will be responsible for BPM within the organization after the completion of the project? Where to allocate BPM in terms of resources and decisive power?

The following problem has also arisen for E+H: The existing body of literature rarely provides frameworks and reference models to guide them in implementing adequate power and control mechanisms. Hence, contemporary literature inspires but does not solve the problem of how E+H should embed existing process roles within their organization. These models and frameworks fall short in considering the organization's specific context, goals, needs, and requirements for such a large-scale project.

E+H did not want to take all the dimensions into account simultaneously preferring to, first, allocate responsibilities for processes and process areas. In the course of this, there had to be consideration of where and how BPM should be effectively institutionalized. Central to these considerations is the demand for new roles and responsibilities, which will clarify all other issues regarding information technologies (e.g., tools for modeling processes), methods (e.g., different kinds of process visualizations), and people (e.g., their skills and capabilities). Process-oriented collaboration teams make cross-functional decisions. This means that process roles have priority over functional roles. Starting as a traditional functional organization, E+H is striving to move and transform its organization into a process-oriented organizational structure. Currently, employees hold both functional and process roles. During this change and transformation project, they made the following three decisions: (i) New or adapted process roles and responsibilities must first be established before methods for modeling processes or using specific IT are discussed. (i) Strategic process owners are installed with hierarchical decision-making authority for each process or process area. They report directly to the Chief Organizational Officer (COO). (iii) In the matrix of the organization that still exists today, the process role takes precedence over the functional role.

E+H has identified processes in the following subject areas: enterprise development, innovation, market and customer development, fulfillment, value optimization, people management, quality management, IT management, and legal compliance. Inclusion of the finance area has not yet been completely approved internally. E+H has described and visualized processes on four levels. Each level represents varying degrees of detail. While processes on level 4 are visualized using BPMN 2.0, i.e., the most detailed representation, processes on level 0 are end-to-end representations. Each of the level 0 processes was assigned a strategic process owner and strategic process manager in a job-sharing approach. Each of them was assigned at the process level across several entities and, thus, had several responsibilities at the same time.

The main problems and challenges at E+H can be summarized as follows: First and foremost, there were no clear responsibilities at the corporate group level. Furthermore, responsibilities were traditionally organized functionally and not process-oriented. Accordingly, there were no uniform end-to-end views of processes—only in individual units and departments. Essential to E+H's business success is an increased understanding of its customers' needs and requirements.

3   Action Taken

Design science research (DSR) is a systematic and practice-oriented approach dedicated to solving real-world problems by building and evaluating innovative design artifacts. The realm of DSR is in providing practical utility by building means-end relationships. At the core of such a DSR project is the development of an artifact that can be designed at different levels of abstraction (Gregor & Hevner, 2013), such as a process, a method, or a model (framework). However, each design artifact should provide benefits for its target group, such as support to process users (Offermann et al., 2010). Our design artifact in the present case is the *BPM Governance Matrix,* which we explain in this section in more detail. Based on the information provided, we hypothesized that *the development and application of a bottom-up governance framework (model) will empower the organization and positively support communication and collaboration among process stakeholders in the organizational context and at the organizational level.*

In addition to developing such a framework (model), its evaluation in the real-world setting is a decisive step as it proves the artifact's utility (Venable et al., 2016). One can use different methods to evaluate the designed artifacts, such as observations, experiments, prototypes, or analytics. In the case at hand, we aimed for a qualitative evaluation. By utilizing a practitioner's project workshop conducted by BPM stakeholders of E+H, we sought to assess our artifact's usefulness and appropriateness. Our evaluation goal was to foster the discourse on implementing BPM governance within the existing organization and increase communication and collaboration between process stakeholders responsible for the project. Moreover, we aimed to empower the organization by creating "their own framework," which paved the way for a successful implementation of their BPM governance.

Although we did not want to apply established models in the sense of a cookbook approach, we also did not want to have to completely reinvent the wheel, so we began by examining what models already exist. We found that BPM can be institutionalized and organized in many different ways, such as by using (1) a decentralized model, (2) a centralized model, or (3) an integrated structure.

1. *Decentralized: Additional (Process) Roles.* In addition to a traditional functional organization, organizations can set up a parallel process structure. This is reflected in the enactment of (new) process roles such as process owners, managers, or experts, each with different responsibilities. Depending on the company's degree of internationalization, they can stipulate further specializations based on different geographic levels.
2. *Centralized: BPM Center of Excellence.* In contrast to a decentralized model, companies can also establish a centralized BPM unit. Such shared service units can be a powerful institution for supporting BPM across the organization. Within such a unit, an organization can pull together expertise and knowledge that can provide continuous or ad hoc services to other departments within an organization (Rosemann, 2015).

3. *Integration of BPM in an Existing Functional Department.* BPM services and tasks can also be accomplished by employees associated with and working in existing functional departments such as IT, quality control, or business development. Such integrated setups promote synergies and utilize existing knowledge and resources.

In the course of several face-to-face and online exchanges with E+H, we reflected on these existing concepts and evaluated them using practical examples from the practitioners' experience within the organization. All three models and variants have strengths, weaknesses, and limitations. Also, here, there is no one-size-fits-all solution. In particular, the contextual requirements of the organization and its processes need to be considered. We discussed these existing concepts (1–3) with the practitioners and concluded that these models only provide inspiration and do not solve the challenges faced. Effective governance models are usually a smart combination of existing models considering both the strategic orientation and objectives while catering to the organization's specific context (vom Brocke et al., 2021a, b).

We also found similar approaches dedicated to the implementation of BPM governance at the organizational level. The *BPM Governance Framework* by Khusidman (2010) most closely resembled our idea. This framework describes the development of a comprehensive framework and definition of requirements that can be used as a reference for tools, methods, and artifacts to implement BPM successfully.

To support our approach, we refer to two principles that have been established within the BPM community to guide practitioners in designing an efficient and successful BPM within the organizational context. *First*, according to the "principle of context-awareness," BPM at E+H should fit into their organizational context and not follow a one-size-fits-all or cookbook approach (vom Brocke et al., 2014). Therefore, we argue that for the BPM initiative at E+H, it is essential to understand the organization's context, its corporate goals, and the needs of process managers and owners. Only then can the BPM governance endeavor be successfully planned and scaled (vom Brocke et al., 2021a, b). *Second*, the "principle of institutionalization" refers to the idea that BPM, as a process-oriented management discipline, should be embedded within the organization's structure. Therefore, the roles and responsibilities of E+H's process stakeholders should not be isolated from their existing organizational structures and separated from other operational or strategic organizational activities.

Based on (i) the need to integrate effective governance within the organizational structure and activities of E+H and (ii) the shortcomings identified within existing research, we co-developed the *BPM Governance Matrix*. We approached the practitioners in one of their project workshops at the company headquarters. In doing so, we provided the matrix and asked the project members to fill out the essential information, such as the functional designations or names of employees. In addition, we offered them the freedom to adjust or extend the activity groups according to their contextual requirements.

The involvement of the practitioners allowed us to take into account the contextual specialties of E+H, such as the strategic orientation of their business model and

Activity Groups	RACI			
	Responsible	Accountable	Consult	Inform
Organizational Strategy				
...	...	...	...	...
...	...	...	...	...
Organizational Processes				
...	...	...	...	...
...	...	...	...	...
Organizational Structure				
...	...	...	...	...
...	...	...	...	...

Source: vom Brocke et al. (2022).

Fig. 1 BPM governance matrix. (Source: vom Brocke et al., 2022)

the already established process organization in the matrix. Therefore, we used the notion of "activity groups" to address an organization's general activities and description of its existence. For this, we referred to organizational strategy ("yellow"), organizational processes ("green"), and organizational structure ("blue"), as adapted and inspired by Miles et al. (1978). These activity groups formed the horizontal rows of our matrix. Next, to describe governance activities broadly, we used the RACI method and adapted its dimensions: responsible, accountable, consult, and inform (e.g., Costello, 2012). The *BPM Governance Matrix* (see Fig. 1) serves as a guideline and tool to empower and support organizations in implementing governance in organizations in a process-oriented way. In doing so, we did not intend to prescribe standards from the literature but rather to consider the organizational context and provide the users of this matrix with the opportunity to include their ideas, priorities, and insights. Therefore, we advocated that BPM and its established managers should not be placed in an isolated unit but should consciously take into account and utilize the peculiarities of the respective organization. Finally, the BPM Governance Matrix consists of three horizontal rows (activity groups) and four vertical columns (governance activities).

4   Results Achieved

Practitioners at E+H used the matrix at the beginning of their BPM project. The idea of this matrix was that the management could assign specific staff members or insert role designations. We argued that the BPM Governance Matrix supports practitioners in deriving BPM-related tasks on the organizational and process levels. Based on the idea that corporate governance should not follow a cookbook and standardized approach, we saw the benefit of this matrix to account for the peculiarities and specialties of any organization to perform process work successfully. One of the essential features is that users can list various tasks and activities in a bottom-up approach. Any process manager can utilize the three activity groups (strategy, structure, process) as a general guideline and even extend or further specify them according to their needs. As such, it's possible to integrate and combine traditional BPM activities and corporate development initiatives. Moreover, process stakeholders can use it as a socially constructed model to share ideas, facts, and opinions about BPM governance in their respective organizations. Such a shared mental model can also be used to continuously foster coordination and communication among process stakeholders or in ad hoc projects or initiatives.

E+H positively perceived the possibility of adjusting the horizontal dimensions and hence accounted for their experience of the company's BPM and organizational peculiarities and priorities. The opportunity to develop "their own framework" was perceived as a benefit. Further, the co-development of this matrix led to a greater acceptance of applying it in practice. Being involved in the design and evaluation process was key in using this matrix for the BPM project at E+H, which is in contrast to the standardized and traditional models suggested by the handbooks.

The practitioners refined and further specified the row "Organizational Strategy" by "develop a customer-oriented strategy" and "link process goals to strategy," as shown in Fig. 2. For confidentiality reasons, we have not shown the individual role designations, instead providing the key results of E+H below the individual activity groups. For E+H, it was also important that the objectives of each process were linked to the organization's strategy. In the row denoted as "Organizational Processes," E+H mentioned the assurance of communication and collaboration within the organization. They also mentioned that customer experience management should be ensured throughout specific processes. This element is reflected in the row "Organizational Strategy." Regarding the "Organizational Structure," E+H mentions the coordination mechanisms and structural performance evaluation.

	RACI			
Activity Groups	**Responsible**	**Accountable**	**Consult**	**Inform**
Organizational Strategy				
Develop customer-oriented strategy	* * *		* * *	* * *
Link process goals to strategy		* * *		
...				
Organizational Processes				
Ensure communication and collaboration	* * *	* * *	* * *	
Enable customer experience management				* * *
...				
Organizational Structure				
Coordinate mechanisms			* * *	
Evaluate structural performance	* * *	* * *		* * *
...				

Source: vom Brocke et al. (2022).

Fig. 2 Using the BPM governance matrix. (Source: vom Brocke et al., 2022)

When using the matrix, the practitioners added more details that reflect the specifics of the organization. E+H could, thus, assign specific process roles and tasks to these organization-wide tasks and activities. Regarding the RACI method, a range of governance-related tasks can be presented. The inserted process owners and roles can also be considered as a proposal for the time being. However, the matrix allows for collective agreements and provides a basis for final decisions. For example, when using the matrix, E+H also identified overlaps and blind spots. E+H reported that the matrix has provided essential help and support as they plan how to re-implement BPM. The practitioners perceived the matrix as "refreshingly simple" but at the same time "brutally honest." It has helped to unite responsibilities in the organization and within BPM, to present them transparently, and even put them up for discussion. According to E+H, the matrix has helped increase awareness of roles and responsibilities. For E+H, the matrix is a "living document" that provides a basis for discussion and a platform for joint and critical exchange about organizational responsibilities. It promotes communication and conversation between process stakeholders and should do so on an ongoing basis. For the Operations Excellence Office, the matrix has been a helpful tool and one of the department's managers reported that *"For us staff and managers in the Operations Excellence Office, the BPM Governance Matrix helped to create a clear picture. Who is doing what and who is involved."*

The *BPM Governance Matrix* offers several significant advantages to an organization when institutionalizing BPM:

- *Explicitness*: The matrix describes what needs to be done to deliver objectives associated with BPM.
- *Reference*: The matrix is based on both research and practice, and it provides an initial list of key tasks to be covered in an organization to deliver BPM objectives.
- *Fit*: The matrix facilitates consideration of the needs of an organization and, hence, provides a basis for customizing a context-aware governance approach.
- *Adaptability*: The matrix can be adjusted to incorporate organizational change as the organization learns to work with the matrix.
- *Negotiability*: The matrix facilitates conversation on BPM-related tasks, which is probably one of the most important contributions to a successful BPM initiative.

5   Lessons Learned

Organizations regularly face the challenge of implementing BPM governance repeatedly, as more than a one-off project. Ambitions are often high and teams can have several ideas about how to set up an isolated BPM department with activities decoupled from the organization's management and development. From this case study, we learned that it is important to start these discussions early so as to avoid BPM being perceived as an isolated organizational unit and function. BPM should align with the organization and its strategy, processes, and structure to achieve the greatest possible benefit. Otherwise, there can be a lot of resistance on an organizational or personal level.

The *BPM Governance Matrix* can be used as a tool and common ground for the organization to increase its awareness of process and governance realized activities (and tasks). It enables stakeholders to increase their awareness of associated process roles and responsibilities and can improve organization-wide communication in process work. This can provide a valuable stimulus for generating shared understanding in BPM.

While the bottom-up approach ensures that process stakeholders can participate in large BPM projects such as this, by contributing their experience, the matrix provides increased transparency and acceptance of the resulting decisions. In this way, the matrix enables the development of a tailor-made solution for implementing effective and efficient governance mechanisms and structures.

Throughout this chapter, we have urged companies to seek out a tailor-made approach for implementing BPM within their existing organizational units. We used a design-science-oriented approach to develop the *BPM Governance Matrix*, which organizations can use as a communication and collaboration tool for setting the roles and responsibilities within their organizational structure, strategy, and processes.

References

Costello, T. (2012). RACI – Getting projects unstuck. *IT Professional, 14*(2), 64–63.

Dumas, M., La Rosa, M., Mendling, J., & Reijers, H. A. (2018). *Fundamentals of business process management*. Springer.

Gregor, S., & Hevner, A. R. (2013). Positioning and presenting design science research for maximum impact. *MIS Quarterly, 37*(2), 337–355.

Khusidman, V. (2010). BPM governance framework. *BP Trends*.

Kratzer, S., Lohmann, P., Roeglinger, M., Rupprecht, L., & zur Muehlen, M. (2018). The role of the chief process officer in organizations. *Business Process Management Journal, 25*, 688.

Miles, R. E., Snow, C. C., Meyer, A. D., & Coleman, H. J., Jr. (1978). Organizational strategy, structure, and process. *Academy of Management Review, 3*(3), 546–562.

Offermann, P., Blom, S., Schönherr, M., & Bub, U. (2010). Artifact types in information systems design science – A literature review. In R. Winter, J. L. Zhao, & S. Aier (Eds.), *Global perspectives on design science research* (pp. 77–92). Springer.

Rosemann, M. (2015). The service portfolio of a BPM center of excellence,' international handbooks on information systems. In J. vom Brocke & M. Rosemann (Eds.), *Handbook on business process management 2* (2nd ed., pp. 381–398). Springer.

Rosemann, M., & vom Brocke, J. (2010). The six core elements of business process management. In J. vom Brocke & M. Rosemann (Eds.), *Handbook on business process management 1* (pp. 107–122). Springer.

Rosemann, M., Recker, J., Flender, C., & Ansell, P.-D. (2006). Understanding context-awareness in business process design. In *Proceedings of the 17th Australasian conference on information systems* (pp. 1–10).

Spanyi, A., vom Brocke, J., & Rosemann, M. (2015). The governance of business process management. In *Handbook on business process management 2* (2nd ed., pp. 333–349). Springer.

Venable, J., Pries-Heje, J., & Baskerville, R. (2016). FEDS: A framework for evaluation in design science research. *European Journal of Information Systems, 25*(1), 77–89.

vom Brocke, J., & Rosemann, M. (2015). Business process management. In C. L. Cooper (Ed.), *Wiley encyclopedia of management* (Vol. 7, pp. 1–9). Chichester, Wiley.

vom Brocke, J., Schmiedel, T., Recker, J., Trkman, P., Mertens, W., & Viaene, S. (2014). Ten principles of good business process management. *Business Process Management Journal, 20*(4), 530–548.

vom Brocke, J., Zelt, S., & Schmiedel, T. (2016). On the role of context in business process management. *International Journal of Information Management, 36*(3), 486–495.

vom Brocke, J., Baier, M.-S., Schmiedel, T., Stelzl, K., Röglinger, M., & Wehking, C. (2021a). Context-aware business process management. *Business & Information Systems Engineering, 63*(5), 533–550.

vom Brocke, J., Mendling, J., & Rosemann, M. (2021b). Planning and scoping business process management with the BPM Billboard. In J. vom Brocke, J. Mendling, & M. Rosemann (Eds.), *Business process management cases – Digital transformation – Strategy, processes and execution* (Vol. 2). Springer.

vom Brocke, J., Weber, M., Baumgartner, C., Roettcher, A., & Segerlund, S. (2022). *Where to allocate business process management (BPM) in an organization? Developing the BPM Governance Matrix at Endress Hauser*. In Presented at the 20th international business process management conference, Münster, Germany.

**Jan vom Brocke** is the Director of the European Research Center for Information Systems (ERCIS) and a Professor and Chair of Information Systems & Business Process Management at the University of Münster in Germany. He has published in leading journals such as *Management Information Systems Quarterly* (MISQ), *Information Systems Research* (ISR), *Journal of the Association for Information Systems* (JAIS), *Journal of Management Information Systems* (JMIS), *Management Science, and MIT Sloan Management Review* (MIT SMR). He is the author and editor of seminal books, including the *International Handbook on Business Process Management, BPM—Driving Innovation in a Digital World, Green Business Process Management*, and the Business Process Management Cases volumes 1, 2, and 3. Jan vom Brocke is a Visiting Professor at the University of Liechtenstein and an Academic Research Fellow at Massachusetts Institute of Technology (MIT), Center for Information Systems Research (CISR). He has been named a Fellow of the Association for Information Systems (AIS), a Fellow of the École Supérieure de Commerce de Paris (ESCP), Center for Design Science in Entrepreneurship, a Schoeller Senior Fellow at Friedrich Alexander University (FAU) in Germany, a Distinguished Professor of Process Science at the National University of Ireland, Maynooth University (MU). Professor vom Brocke is an invited speaker and serves as trusted advisor to many companies as well as governmental institutions.

Manuel Weber is a PhD student at the University of Liechtenstein (Liechtenstein Business School, Department of Information Systems & Computer Science). His research focuses on the role of change in business process management (BPM) in the context of digitalization and digital transformation.

Christian S. Baumgartner (Customer Success Partner) has several years of experience in operational excellence, customer experience management, and business process management. He is a PhD student at the University of Muenster. His research focuses on business process management in the context of organizational setups and digital transformation.

Alexander Röettcher (Director Global Excellence), has several years of experience in operational excellence and business process management (BPM).

Stefan Segerlund (Customer Success Partner) has several years of experience in operational excellence, customer experience management, and business process management. He is a PhD student at the University of Muenster. His research focuses on business process management in the context of organizational setups and digital transformation.

The manufacturer's authorised representative in the EU is Springer
Nature Customer Service Centre GmbH, Europaplatz 3, 69115 Heidelberg,
Germany. If you have any concerns regarding our products, please
contact ProductSafety@springernature.com

Printed and bound by CPI Group (UK) Ltd, Croydon, CR0 4YY
24/04/2026
02096316-0006